Media Freedom

Media Freedom

The Contradictions of Communication in the Age of Modernity

Richard Barbrook

Pluto Press

LONDON · BOULDER, COLORADO

First published 1995 by Pluto Press
345 Archway Road, London N6 5AA
and 5500 Central Avenue
Boulder, Colorado 80301, USA

British Library Cataloguing in Publication Data
A catalogue record for this book is available from the
British Library

ISBN 0 7453 0944 5 hardback

Library of Congress Cataloging in Publication Data

Barbrook, Richard.
    Media freedom: the contradictions of communication in the
age of modernity / Richard Barbrook.
    230 p.   22 cm.
    Includes bibliographical references and index.
    ISBN 0 7453 0944 5 hbk.
    1. Freedom of the press. 2. Mass media— Social aspects.
3. Mass media— Political aspects.   I. Title.
    PN4736.B37   1995   95–1908
    323.445— dc20   CIP

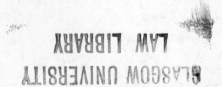
Designed and produced for Pluto Press by
Chase Production Services, Chipping Norton, OX7 5QR
Typeset from disk by Stanford DTP Services, Milton Keynes
Printed in the EC by WSOY, Finland

Contents

Acknowledgements

Respect due: the Centre for Communication and Information Studies and the Centre for the Study of Democracy, University of Westminster; the Cultural Section of the French Embassy in London; the staff of the British Library; everyone at Pluto Press; Jerôme Bourdon; Jean-Claude Burgelman; Annick Cojean; James Curran; Roland Fornari; Pierre Hivernat; John Keane; Raymond Kuhn; Warwick Metcalfe; Rhiannon Patterson; Véronique Petit; Anne Pichon; Vincent Porter; Simon Schaffer; and the workers who built my Amstrad and PC computers.

Acronyms

AFP	Agence France-Presse
ALO	Association pour la Libération des Ondes
APL	Agence-Press Libération
BBC	British Broadcasting Corporation
CGP	Commisariat Général du Plan
CLT	Compagnie Luxembourgeoise de Télédiffusion
CNCL	Commission Nationale de la Communication et des Libertés
CNN	Cable News Network
CSA	Conseil Supérieur de l'Audiovisuel
EC	European Community
ENA	École Nationale d'Administration
FCC	Federal Communications Commission
FM	frequency modulation
FNRL	Fédération Nationale des Radios Libres
FR3	France Régions 3
G-7	Group of Seven (industrial powers)
IBA	Independent Broadcasting Authority
INA	Institut National de l'Audiovisuel
ISA	ideological state apparatus
LCA	Lorraine Coeur d'Acier
NATO	North Atlantic Treaty Organization
NRJ	Energy (radio station)
ORTF	Office de Radiodiffusion-Télévision Française
PAFE	Programme d'Action pour la Filière Electronique
PPF	Parti Populaire Française
PTT	Poste, Télégraphie et Téléphone
RTF	Radiodiffusion-Télévision Française
SFIO	Section Française de l'Internationale Ouvrière
SFP	Société Française de Production et de Création Audiovisuelles
SI	Situationist International
SLEC	Société Locale d'Exploitation Commerciale
SLII	Service de Laisons Interministérielles pour l'Information

SNEP	Société Nationale des Entreprises de Presse
SOFIRAD	Société Financière de Radio-diffusion
SPD	Sozialedemokratische Partei Deutschlands
TDF	Télédiffusion de France
TF1	Télévision Française 1
tsf	télégraphie sans fil (wireless telegraphy)
UNESCO	United Nations Educational Scientific and Cultural Organization
USSR	Union of Soviet Socialist Republics
VCR	video cassette recorder

Chronology

1789	French Revolution begins. Collapse of royal censorship laws. Proclamation of the Declaration of the Rights of Man and the Citizen, including guarantees of the freedom of publication.
1792	Declaration of the French Republic.
1793	Proclamation of a new Declaration of the Rights of Man and the Citizen.
1793–4	Jacobin government reimposes censorship and subsidises republican newspapers as wartime emergency measure.
1794	Overthrow of the Jacobin government. Establishment of the Directory.
1796	Failure of Babeuf's Conspiracy of Equals.
1799	Napoléon Bonaparte overthrows the Directory in a military coup.
1814	Defeat of Napoléon Bonaparte. Restoration of the monarchy.
1848	Overthrow of the monarchy. Declaration of the Second Republic. End of censorship. Suppression of June uprising. Restoration of censorship.
1851	Louis-Napoléon seizes power in a military coup.
1870–1	Franco-Prussian war leads to abdication of Louis-Napoléon. Declaration of the Third Republic. Relaxation of censorship.
1871	Crushing of the Paris Commune.
1872	Introduction of mechanical presses in French newspaper publishing.
1874	Reintroduction of censorship by right-wing government.
1879	Republicans win general elections.
1881	End of censorship. The law of 29 July guarantees press freedom.
1898	Outbreak of Dreyfus affair.
1905	Foundation of the SFIO.
1914	Start of First World War. Censorship imposed as a wartime emergency measure.

1917 Bolshevik Revolution in Russia.
1918 End of First World War. Freedom of publication in France restored.
1920 Foundation of the French Communist Party.
1921 Licences are granted to broadcaster-engineers.
1922 The CSF-SFR company starts Radio Radiola, the first commercial radio station in France.
1923 The PTT establishes the first state-owned radio station in France.
1926 The decree-law of 28 December recognises the duopoly of state and commercial radio stations.
1931 Foundation of Radio Luxembourg.
1933 Nazis seize power in Germany.
1935 Elections to management boards of the PTT radio stations.
1936 Election victory of Popular Front. Léon Blum becomes prime minister. Failure of bill to reform the press. Reorganisation of the PTT radio stations.
1937 Fall of Blum's government.
1938 Failure of strike against austerity measures. Purge of left-wingers from the PTT radio stations.
1939 Start of Second World War. Reimposition of press censorship. Take-over of news services of commercial radio stations. Centralisation of control over the PTT radio stations.
1940 Defeat of France by Nazi Germany. Formation of Vichy regime. Establishment of Radio Vichy and introduction of subsidies for collaborationist newspapers and radio stations.
1944–5 Liberation of France from Nazi occupation. Formation of Resistance coalition government. Purge of fascist newspaper and radio-station owners. Ordonnance of 23 March nationalises all radio stations. Formation of AFP and SNEP.
1945 Declaration of the Fourth Republic. Proclamation of a new Declaration of the Rights of Citizens. Creation of the RTF.
1947 Outbreak of the cold war. Communists leave Resistance coalition government and are also excluded from RTF programmes.
1949 Formation of NATO military alliance. Gaullists are excluded from RTF programmes.

1953	Law of 31 December 1953 gives a monopoly over television broadcasting to the RTF.
1954	Beginning of war of independence in Algeria.
1956	Imposition of censorship over reporting the Algerian war.
1957	France is a founder member of the European Community.
1958	Declaration of the Fifth Republic. General Charles de Gaulle becomes president. Ordonnance of 4 February imposes Gaullist control over RTF.
1961	Army revolt in Algeria collapses after radio broadcast by de Gaulle.
1962	Independence of Algeria. End of press censorship.
1964	Law of 27 June turns RTF into the ORTF.
1968	May Revolution. Strike at the ORTF. Emergency radio and television service run by Gaullist loyalists. End of the general strike. Victory of Gaullists in the June elections. Introduction of advertising at the ORTF.
1969	Resignation of de Gaulle. Georges Pompidou becomes president. Prime Minister Jacques Chaban-Delmas introduces political pluralism at the ORTF with the adoption of the 'rule of three-thirds' for news and current affairs programmes, dividing airtime between the government, the ruling parties and the opposition.
1971	Foundation of APL press agency, the forerunner of *Libération*.
1972	Chaban-Delmas is sacked as prime minister. Law of 3 July reimposes Gaullist control over the ORTF.
1974	Valery Giscard d'Estaing becomes president. Law of 7 August divides the ORTF into seven independent companies. Legal recognition of the 'rule of three-thirds' for news and current affairs programmes.
1977	Radio Verte pioneers illegal free radio broadcasting. Radio Fil Bleu is France's first commercial pirate radio station.
1978	Formation of FNRL.
1979	François Mitterrand, leader of the Socialist party, is arrested for pirate radio broadcasting.
1981	Socialists win general elections. Mitterrand becomes president. Break-down of laws against illegal radio broadcasting. Law of 9 November grants licences to the free radio stations. Formation of NRJ. Launch of Minitel.

1982   Canal Plus is France's first commercial television station. Law of 29 July creates the Haute Autorité as broadcasting regulatory body.

1984   Law of 1 August allows independent radio stations to be owned by commercial companies and to sell advertising.

1986   Granting of licences for fifth and sixth television channels to commercial operators. Victory of parties of the Right in legislative elections.

1986–7   Law of 30 September creates the CNCL. Reallocation of licences for fifth and sixth television channels. Privatisation of TF1. Relicensing of local radio stations.

1988   Victory of Socialists in presidential and legislative elections.

1989   Law of 17 January creates the CSA. Signing of European Convention on Transfrontier Television Broadcasting. Special bicentenary parade in Paris is watched by 800 million television viewers at home and abroad.

1992   Bankruptcy of fifth television channel. State-owned Arte cultural channel receives the vacant frequency.

1993   Socialists are defeated in legislative elections. Edouard Balladur becomes prime minister.

Prologue: The Bicentenary

'Paris was the Centre of the World'

On 14 July 1989 two Bastille day parades took place in Paris. For decades, the fall of the Bastille had been celebrated by a military procession down the Champs-Elysées. But in 1989 Bastille day was the high point of a whole series of events marking the 200th anniversary of the beginning of the 1789–99 Revolution. In a surprise move, the organisers of the bicentenary chose Jean-Paul Goude to organise an additional commemorative procession. As he was best known for directing the videos and designing the costumes of Grace Jones, the Jamaican pop star, Goude's version of the Bastille day parade was radically different from the traditional military procession.

Shrouded in darkness, Goude's parade was opened by over 1,000 drummers carrying French tricolours and lit up by torchbearers. They were followed by a Chinese float commemorating the recent Tiananmen Square massacre. Surrounded by cyclists, a silent drummer beat out a funeral march under a banner proclaiming 'We will continue [the struggle]'. The next float symbolised the African continent by having black drummers and singers performing on a mobile pyramid while white people in colonial uniforms walked by their side carrying torches in honour of the struggle for independence. When this float had passed, the Champs-Elysées was filled by swirling couples joined together in a single dervish costume. This symbol of the Arab world was followed by the Florida Marching Band playing a medley of James Brown songs while doing an imitation of Michael Jackson's 'moonwalk'. Next came drummers from the Soviet Red Army and dancers in constructivist costumes representing the revolutionary hopes of October 1917. At the rear of the march, with a fleet of London buses, a group of British firemen sprayed water over ballet and night-club dancers sheltering under umbrellas. Once the parade had finished, the international theme of Goude's parade was underlined by the concluding moments of the 1989 Bastille day celebrations. Dressed in a French tricolour, Jessye Norman, the African-American opera singer, sang an orchestral version of the Marseillaise against the backdrop of an enormous fireworks display. Finally, with the parade over, both Parisians and tourists were allowed onto the Champs-Elysées to conclude the celebrations. '[T]he most famous street in the world had become a tower of Babel. All the races and all the nations of the world were side by side that evening, Paris was really the centre of the world' (*Paris Match* 1989: 25–35, 36).

During the nineteenth century, the anniversary of the fall of the Bastille was only commemorated by the parties of the Left. But once the republican form of government was established, 14 July slowly became the main national public holiday. Every year, the French people joined together to celebrate the victory of the democratic republic over its monarchist and clerical enemies (Jeanneney 1988: 27–8). The annual Bastille day festivities were inspired by the parades and public events which took place during the 1789–99 Revolution. For example, in 1792 a Festival of Liberty was held in honour of a group of Swiss soldiers who had been imprisoned for mutinying against reactionary officers. Like the 1989 bicentenary event, these celebrations were also centred around a dramatic parade. The first few floats displayed large stone tablets inscribed with the Declaration of the Rights of Man and the Citizen, busts of revolutionary thinkers and ceremonial tombs. At the centre of the procession marched the 40 survivors of the mutiny, accompanied by young women carrying their prison chains. These living martyrs were followed by more floats bearing a statute of the goddess of Liberty, paintings by David and a joker mocking the monarchist critics of the revolution (Ozouf 1988: 67–9).

In many ways, Goude's version of the Bastille day procession imitated the style of this revolutionary festival. While the 1792 parade had a float containing stone tablets inscribed with the Declaration of Rights, the whole 1989 bicentenary procession was designed to symbolise the international spread of these democratic principles. According to the French president, people from all political parties were now united in a common belief in the basic human rights championed by the 1789–99 Revolution (Dupin 1989). Although his different national tableaux were more comic than didactic, Goude's Bastille day parade did successfully symbolise this chosen theme. For instance, while traditionally she is portrayed as a Caucasian peasant women, Marianne, the symbol of France, was represented in Goude's parade by an African-American opera singer.

Citizens or Spectators?

Before the parade took place, the Bastille celebrations were criticised on all sides. For the parties of the Right, Goude's parade was another example of Mitterrand's 'megalomania' (Colombani 1989). For the radical Left, the bicentenary celebrations were an insult to the revolutionary legacy of the past. Above all, left-wing critics attacked the coincidence of the Bastille day parade with the annual G-7 summit of the richest nations of the world. For them, the splendour of the bicentenary celebrations laid on for the 'masters of the world' contrasted strongly with the suffering of the hungry and unemployed in France and other countries. In their view, the people had yet to storm the Bastille of 'economic imperialism'. A few days earlier, these protestors had organised an alternative celebration to commemorate the bicentenary, beginning with a demonstration against the G-7 summit and ending with a concert by Mano Negra, les Negresses Vertes and other sympathetic musicians (Colombani 1989).

In this radical bicentenary celebration, the crowd participated in the event by marching in the demonstration and attending the live concert. Because of this popular involvement, the alternative celebration was closer to the spirit of the 1792 Festival of Liberty than Goude's Bastille day parade was. Back in 1792, 400,000 people did not just watch the revolutionary festival, they also participated in the procession through the streets of Paris. According to one observer, 'everybody wanted to take part in the festival of liberty' (Ozouf 1988: 67–8). By contrast, in Goude's 14 July parade the crowd was only allowed onto the Champs-Elysées after all the floats had passed. Crucially, unlike the alternative bicentenary celebration, the Goude parade was only partly designed to be seen in person. Although 1 million lined the route along the Champs-Elysées, more than 800 million watched all or part of the event on television as French television stations broadcast the celebrations live to viewers in France and 112 other countries (*Paris Match* 1989: 22). With this large audience, the official bicentenary parade could never have been a participatory festival. It had to be a media event.

Although Goude's procession symbolically affirmed the values of the French republic, it also exposed the fundamental contradiction at the heart of the bicentenary celebrations: how to reconcile popular participation with mass democracy. According to the parties of both Left and Right, the events of 1789 should have been commemorated as the advent of basic human rights, such as universal suffrage, equality before the law and media freedom. In the late eighteenth century, the revolutionaries had advocated the protection of these fundamental rights in order to create the conditions that would allow the active participation of individual citizens in political affairs. Above all, media freedom allowed citizens to exercise the right of free speech in print. In the same way as the crowd joined in the 1792 Festival of Liberty, citizens could actively engage in political debates through the printed word.

Nearly two centuries later, Goude's Bastille day parade reflected a fundamental transformation in the interpretation of the rights of citizens, especially media freedom. Although large numbers of people were involved in its organisation, there was little popular participation in the commemorative procession. Although almost all political parties claim to support media freedom, no French government has been able to implement the original version of this basic right of citizens. Instead of the active participation in the media of most citizens, they have redefined the freedom of communications as the passive consumption of newspapers, radio or television programmes made by others. Not surprisingly, the Goude parade reflected this consensus between the major political parties. Although they were celebrating the achievement of the democratic rights of all citizens on 14 July 1989, most of the French population celebrated their right to participate in political affairs by passively consuming the television coverage of the representations of these rights in the bicentenary procession.

The Models of Media Freedom

Within contemporary analyses of the media, this lack of participation by the audience is rarely questioned. Instead, there has been an interminable argument over whether or not the media are a tool of ideological domination. While one side blames the problems of the world on the media's dissemination of the lies of politicians and advertisers, the other side asserts that most people are able to filter out any attempts to mislead them in newspaper articles or radio and television programmes. Yet, despite the intensity of the intellectual debate, both forms of analysis have converged on a common programme: the education of the audience in the skills of media literacy. Whether they are being trained as committed activists or discerning consumers, people need to be able to deconstruct the messages and symbols contained within the output of different types of media. The highest achievement of both contemporary forms of media analysis has been the creation of politically correct couch potatoes.

In contrast, this book shifts the terms of the debate to an examination of the contradiction between participation and democracy within the media. This is achieved through an analysis of the history of the media in a single country: France. As with other social questions, the problem of reconciling participation and democracy within the media can only be understood through the comprehension of practical attempts to realise media freedom over time. Because it was one of the first modern nations, France has played a leading role in developing these successive forms of media freedom, which have later been adopted by other countries. Above all, France is the place where the archetypical revolution of the modern world took place. Across the globe, new nations have constructed their own democratic republics in the image of the French original. The international theme of Goude's Bastille day parade reflected the universal significance of this decisive moment in the birth of modernity. Following the 1789–99 Revolution, 'the vanguard of humanity virtually attained the limit and the aim, that is the *end*, of Man's historical evolution. What has happened since then was but an extension in space of the universal revolutionary force actualised in France' (Kojève 1969: 160).

Despite the optimism of philosophers, the contradictions of modern society could not be transcended in the immediate aftermath of the revolution, especially within the media. For over 200 years, successive generations have developed their own practical interpretations of the abstract right of media freedom proclaimed in the 1789 Revolution. Following the collapse of the absolute monarchy, individuals were allowed to produce their own newspapers and books without state censorship. However, in practice this involvement in media production was limited to a few journalists and printers living mainly in Paris. The price of the democratisation of the media was the ending of any individual involvement in their production. Instead, citizens could only indirectly influence the media through their political representatives. During the past few decades, both left-wing and right-wing activists have tried to create more participatory forms of media freedom. But because these attempts ended in failure, the latest version of media freedom once again accepts the passivity of most of the audience. Yet, as in the past, the present interpretation of this basic human right is only a temporary resolution of the contradiction between participation and democracy within the media.

Despite the compromises and complexities of human existence, the history of this contradiction can be symbolised by a series of models of media freedom. Although they are necessarily ahistorical and abstract, these models crystallise and emphasise different stages in the evolution of the right of media freedom. By constructing a series of mental maps, this book illustrates the ahistorical abstractions underlying the different versions of media freedom. By presenting a political and economic history of the French media, this volume demonstrates the difficulties of implementing these models in practice. Above all, the mental maps symbolise the different practical and theoretical attempts to resolve the contradiction between participation and democracy over time.

Over the 200 years since the revolution, there has been no stable interpretation of media freedom within France. Instead, the abstract principles of this basic right have been implemented through very different media systems. Therefore, in its conclusion, this book examines the continued relevance of the right of media freedom in the contemporary world. Despite the mutability of its meaning, the abstract principles of this right still provide the basis on which to judge specific methods of organising the mass media. With the arrival of a new wave of information technologies, the current consensus between the major political parties is already being disrupted by renewed attempts to implement more participatory forms of media freedom. Faced with similar problems, the rest of the world can once again learn from the French experience of turning the ideal of media freedom into reality.

1

The Liberty of the Individual

The Freedom of the Press

In its first article, the 1881 press law in France promised that all 'printing and book-selling are free' (Ferry 1881: 4,201). With these words, the new republican government finally ended decades of censorship and suppression of radical newspapers and books in France. The new law abolished the need for newspapers to obtain authorisation for publication from the state and to deposit caution money with the courts: the two main methods of control used by previous authoritarian regimes. From 1881 onwards, many different newspapers competed for readers outside of any direct controls by the state.

However, the remaining clauses of the 1881 press law consisted of various restrictions on the absolute freedom of publication promised in its opening words. Despite the abolition of direct censorship, the new law still laid down a series of political offences for which newspaper or book publishers could be punished, such as encouraging mutiny within the armed forces or insulting the reputation of officials of the republic. Similarly, the legal process was protected by restrictions on the coverage of court cases. At the same time, the 1881 law also placed certain restraints on media freedom in the interests of individual citizens. No newspaper or book was allowed to publish any unproven accusations against the 'honour' of any person or organisation. These specific restrictions on the freedom of publication were supplemented by two catch-all clauses. First, a newspaper owner or book-seller could be treated as an 'accomplice' if any 'horrible action' was inspired by their writings. Second, no one could publish anything which was an 'outrage to good morals'. Thus, under the 1881 press law, the absolute freedom of publication was circumscribed in the interests of both state and individual citizens (Ferry 1881: 4,202–3).

However, unlike the censorship imposed by previous authoritarian governments, the new law codified the limits on the liberty of the press within a juridical framework. For instance, the legislation limited the state's use of arbitrary repressive methods against publishers, such as bans on newspapers, fines for editors and the imprisonment of journalists. Similarly, the use of libel writs by individuals to prevent the publication of critical comments was restricted through the introduction of a 'right of reply', which allowed the correction of any libels or defamations by inserting an article in a subsequent issue of a newspaper. Although the enforcement of the right of reply could embarrass the editor of a newspaper, this form of punishment avoided the imposition of imprisonment or heavy fines in most cases of press misdemeanours.

The most effective check on the use of legal restraints against newspapers or book-sellers was the right to trial by jury. By making the successful prosecution of a publisher dependent on a guilty verdict from a jury, the potentially repressive parts of the 1881 law were made largely unenforceable in practice. For example, the refusal of most juries to convict publishers of pornographic material severely limited the application of the powers of moral censorship granted in the new law (Zeldin 1979: 312). Even if a jury did convict an errant publisher, the publicity surrounding an open trial could harm the prosecution more than the defendant. For instance, although while Zola was found guilty of libelling a military officer in a newspaper article during the Dreyfus affair, the scandal caused by the trial eventually led to the victory of the Dreyfusards (Mayeur and Rebérioux 1987: 182–5). Although all controls over newspapers and book-sellers had not been removed, the political censorship of the press became far more difficult after the introduction of the 1881 law.

When a newspaper or book-seller committed an infraction of this law, only one individual was charged with the offence. Each newspaper or book-seller had to nominate a single person as the 'manager' of the enterprise, who became legally responsible for the content of everything published. Although a newspaper or book was created by many people, only one was made responsible for infractions of the law. This provision was not introduced simply for judicial convenience. The responsibility of one individual for the content of a publication was directly derived from the republicans' interpretation of media freedom. Under the press law, freedom of publication could only be exercised by someone who was 'French, an adult, enjoying civil rights and not deprived of his civil rights by any court decision' (Ferry 1881: 4,201). The republican government had replaced arbitrary state censorship with a framework of legal restrictions to create the conditions for the expression of individual opinions in print. Because freedom of publication was derived from the rights of individual citizens, no limited company or other organisation could be directly responsible for the content of a newspaper or book. Under the 1881 law, media freedom was clearly defined as the right of every individual French citizen to publish their own newspapers or books within the framework of the law.

The Republican Settlement

The 1881 press law was a central part of the creation of a democratic republic in France. From 1879 onwards, republican governments introduced legislation that not only established the freedom of the press, but also guaranteed universal male suffrage, protection of civil rights and the establishment of an independent legal system. These laws were designed to end the constitutional instability caused by the collapse of the Second Empire in 1870. When Louis-Napoléon was defeated in the Franco-Prussian war, a temporary republican regime was established to run the country. But after the Paris Commune of 1871, most conservative politicians supported the restoration of some form of monarchy as a bulwark against a social revolution. According to the Commune's supporters, the democratic republic would 'serve as a lever for uprooting the economical foundations upon which rests the existence of classes and therefore class rule' (Marx 1933: 43).

However, the monarchist politicians were unable to agree among themselves over who was to be king. As a consequence, in 1879 the republicans finally defeated their conservative opponents in a general election. But, for the republicans, the end of authoritarian rule was not the prelude to a social revolution. On the contrary, the new government believed that only a republic could assure 'order and stability'. Gambetta, the leader of the republicans, blamed the lack of democracy under earlier monarchies for causing 'revolution, disorder, instability' in France. He believed that universal male suffrage and democratic rights would provide 'a means to resolve peacefully all conflicts' between citizens. In the view of Gambetta and other republicans, granting the political demands of the Commune was the only way to prevent the implementation of its social programme (Barral 1968: 161, 187).

The creation of a legal framework to protect the freedom of publication was an integral part of the new constitutional settlement. During their long struggle for political democracy, the republicans' primary method of winning support among the wider French population had been the sale of their publications. Gambetta and many other republican militants had earned their living by working for newspapers (Zeldin 1980: 154–5). Therefore, the passing of the 1881 press law was a symbol of the triumph of the republican movement over its monarchist enemies. After the 1879 election victory, the party symbols of republicanism were transformed into icons of the state through the introduction of the public celebration of 14 July, the adoption of the Marseillaise as the national anthem and the installation of statues of Marianne in town halls and village squares (Agulhon 1981). These popular displays of republican fervour demonstrated the widespread support for the new constitutional settlement. With the passing of the new press law, the republicans ensured that the creation of media freedom would become inextricably linked with the triumph of the democratic republic in France.

The 1789 and 1793 Declarations of Rights

Under the 1881 press law, media freedom was defined as the right of individuals to publish their own newspapers or books within legal restrictions protecting the interests of other citizens and the institutions of the republic. As with other aspects of the Third Republic, this definition of media freedom was derived from the experience of the 1789–99 French Revolution. After their victory in the elections of 1879 the republicans saw their primary task as implementing the democratic principles proclaimed during the first years of that revolution. Even after the constitutional settlement was consolidated, most republicans continued to believe that the central political conflict within France was over the legacy of the events of 1789–99. In 1891, the left-wing deputy Georges Clemenceau could still claim that: 'this admirable Revolution ... isn't finished, ... we are ... the same men who find themselves fighting with the same enemies' (Barral 1968: 115).

According to the republicans, the democratic principles of the French Revolution had been codified in the 1789 and 1793 Declarations of the Rights of Man and the Citizen. Therefore, after their election victory, they introduced a series of laws to translate the libertarian promises of these two declarations into a precise legal framework. For instance, the 1881 press law was designed to implement the right of media freedom guaranteed by the 1789 and 1793 Declarations (Amann 1975: 118). In article 11 of the 1789 Declaration, media freedom was defined as the extension into publishing of the free speech enjoyed by every individual citizen:

> The unrestrained communication of thoughts and opinions being one of the most precious rights of man, every citizen may speak, write, and publish freely, provided he is responsible for the abuse of this liberty in cases determined by the law. (Jaume 1989: 15)

Because it originated in the early stages of the French Revolution, this definition is called the *Girondin model of media freedom*. Even after the fall of the Girondins, the subsequent Jacobin government formally supported this model of media freedom. In his more radical 1793 version of the Declaration of the Rights of Man and the Citizen, Maximilien Robespierre, the leader of the Jacobins, excluded any justification for political censorship from the abstract principles of the Bill of Rights. Without a specific provision for the legal regulation of publishing, the only justification for limiting of the unqualified freedom of the press was the protection of other rights promised in the 1793 Declaration. Therefore, under article 7 of this Declaration, every French citizen possessed the right to publish newspapers or books without any censorship by the state. 'The right to express his thought and his opinions, either by means of the press, or any other manner ... cannot be forbidden' (Jaume 1989: 300).

The main aim of the 1789 and 1793 Declarations was to win the support of society as a whole for the revolutionary cause. By issuing Declarations of Rights, the revolutionaries hoped to demonstrate that a constitutional government would be dedicated to the protection of the rights of individual citizens. According to the revolutionaries, the lack of clear rules regulating the relationship between individuals and the state had led to the inefficient administration of France by the absolute monarchy. For example, in the introduction to the 1789 Declaration, they claimed that the 'ignorance, neglect, or contempt of human rights ... are the sole causes of public misfortunes and the corruptions of Government' (Jaume 1989: 11–12). Although they did not have the juridical significance of the US Bill of Rights, the 1789 and 1793 Declarations of the Rights of Man and the Citizen symbolised the repudiation of the arbitrary powers exercised by the absolute monarchy. For instance, because the crown had interned political opponents by decree, three articles of the 1789 Declaration promised a fair trial for every citizen accused of any imprisonable offence (Jaume 1989: 11–16). In the same way, the guarantee of media freedom in both Declarations was a response to the repressive policies of the absolute monarchy against newspaper- and book-publishers.

From the time printing in France began, strict controls over the publishing of newspapers and books were imposed by both royal and ecclesiastical authorities. Under the absolute monarchy, around two-fifths of all political prisoners were incarcerated for breaking these censorship laws (Chartier 1990: 82–3). Yet, despite these repressive measures, the state and church were increasingly unable to prevent the sale of unauthorised texts. According to one estimate, in 1764 two-thirds of the books in circulation in France had been printed abroad and smuggled into the country (Chartier 1990: 91–3). In effect, the censorship laws of the absolute monarchy were simultaneously too repressive and too liberal. While state and church censorship outraged the opponents of absolutism, the importation of forbidden publications was increasingly tolerated by the royal authorities. Crucially, these clandestine publications popularised

among the French reading public the criticisms of the absolute
monarchy made by the Enlightenment philosophers (Chartier
1990: 69; Febvre and Martin 1984: 246–7).

Because of this close link between clandestine publishing and
critical ideas, the revolutionaries were determined to abolish all
censorship of newspapers or books by either state or ecclesiastical
authorities. They saw the removal of censorship as only the first
step towards the active participation of individual citizens in
publishing. For these radicals, the freedom of publication was one
of a number of positive rights enjoyed by all French citizens. In
their view, the purpose of the two Declarations was to define the
extent and scope of the inalienable rights of individuals. These rights
were derived from the theories of natural law, which had been
formulated by the Enlightenment philosophers to repudiate the
claims to divine authority made by the absolute monarchy and the
Catholic church.

In their works, the Enlightenment philosophers stated that
human beings were naturally atomised, egotistical and hedonistic
individuals. Therefore both civil society and state were created by
the mutual self-interest of individuals. According to the philosophers, these autonomous individuals were initially only connected
by the reciprocal relationships of trade and commerce. From these
exchanges, a civil society was created by the mutual consent of independent individuals. By deriving the origins of civil society from a
voluntary agreement between atomised individuals, the philosophers
could repudiate the hierarchy of feudal privileges protected by the
absolute monarchy. Instead, according to their theories, every
individual enjoyed the same fundamental natural rights as every
other member of civil society. In turn, the actions of each individual
were only limited by the rights enjoyed by every other member of
civil society. Under the 1789 Declaration of the Rights of Man and
the Citizen, all individuals were granted 'the power of doing
whatever does not injure another' (Jaume 1989: 13).

The Girondin model of media freedom was based on these
natural law theories. Under the absolute monarchy, the taking of
political decisions had been the private affair of the king. Because
royal power was divinely ordained, there could be no public
discussion of the king's policies by his subjects. By contrast, the
philosophers believed that the suppression of political discussion
violated the natural rights of individuals. As freedom of speech existed
before the creation of civil society, no constitutional government
could restrict the exercise of the right of free speech, including by
means of print (Paine 1984: 90). With the right of freedom of speech
protected, individuals would be able to carry out reasoned discussions
of their collective problems and to come to a rational consensus
over the actions needed to be taken. Because the written text

overcame the physical limitations of face-to-face discussions, the extension of the freedom of speech into printing was necessary to allow the participation of the whole country in political discussions. Some philosophers reconciled this limited version of the Girondin model with the continued existence of the hereditary monarchy. By taking advice from concerned individuals, the king could rule in accordance with the principles of natural law. Alongside the three feudal orders, the newspapers and book-sellers would become the 'fourth estate' of the kingdom (Raynaud 1988: 143; Baker 1990: 193–6).

But most revolutionaries supported a more radical version of the Girondin model. In the 1789 and 1793 Declarations, they promised to respect not only the rights of men, but also those of citizens. For the revolutionaries, the natural rights of individuals could only be effectively protected by the exercise of political rights within a constitutional state that emerged as a 'social contract' between autonomous individuals (Sièyes 1982: 85). Inspired by the example of the Greek city-states and Swiss villages, the philosophers believed that individuals would not only enjoy their selfish interests as men in civil society, but also act as moral citizens fulfilling their duties to the state. For the revolutionaries, this 'social contract' demonstrated how the protection of individual selfishness created public harmony (Rousseau 1968: 59–62, 76–7, 99–100).

According to the Enlightenment philosophers, individuals could only overcome their mutual isolation within civil society by directly participating in political decision-making. Before 1789, critics of the absolute monarchy had created their own meeting places for public discussions of political issues, such as cafés, freemasons' lodges and salons. Rejecting the hierarchical world of the court, individuals debated as democratic equals within these institutions (Chartier 1990: 188–204). In contemporary Swiss villages and New England towns, similar public meetings were already being used to make all major political decisions. Inspired by these examples, Rousseau claimed that all citizens had to debate and enact the laws of the republic in person. As in the ancient Greek city-states, the 'general will' of the individual members of civil society would be created through the agora – a public meeting of all citizens (Rousseau 1968: 69).

But after the fall of the absolute monarchy, this utopian vision of participatory democracy was unrealisable in practice. As France was a large nation, political decisions could not be taken at public meetings of all citizens. As a consequence, most revolutionaries came to accept that the 'general will' of a large country could only be created by the representatives of local particular interests discovering their common interests in parliamentary debates. Instead of personally attending the agora, individual members of civil society would influence political decision-making by electing representatives to express their views in the National Assembly (Sièyes 1982: 64–7). With the establishment of representative democracy, the Girondin model of media freedom had to be extended beyond the abolition of censorship. Because they could not personally take part in the discussions of the legislature in Paris, citizens relied on publishing their own newspapers and books to communicate their opinions to their representatives. Thus, although the holding of a national agora was physically impossible, two-way communications could be created between citizens by using the printed word. As a right of citizens, media freedom became an integral part of the formation of the 'general will' of the French nation. In this developed version of the Girondin model, newspapers and book-sellers were at the centre of the 'republic of letters' (Chartier 1990: 39–40, 47; Raynaud 1988: 143).

During the 1789–99 Revolution, the Girondin model of media freedom was temporarily realised. Almost as soon as the king agreed to the summoning of parliament, royal censorship collapsed. Within a few months, 184 new journals had appeared in Paris and 34 in the provinces (Bellenger et al. 1969: 436). From Mirabeau to Desmoulins, almost every prominent revolutionary was involved in writing and publishing their own pamphlets or newspapers. Using hand-operated wooden presses, a single person could produce a daily paper with a print run of around 3,000 copies. Although these publications were only available in Paris and the major cities, the high prices paid for radical newspapers meant these one-man businesses could be very profitable even with a small circulation. For example, Jean-Paul Marat, a leader of the radical Jacobins, easily made a living by selling a few thousand copies of his newspaper within the Paris region. Every day he not only wrote most of *L'Ami du peuple*, but also printed the newspaper on his own printing press (Bellenger et al. 1969: 435–40, 454–5). Not surprisingly, the deputies of the National Assembly had a personal interest in preventing any reimposition of censorship. By passing the 1789 and 1793 Declarations, these journalist-printers were protecting not just their political freedom, but their economic self-interest too (Censer 1976: 6).

As publishers, the revolutionaries exercised their political right of media freedom through their natural right to own their own printing presses as private property. Under the Girondin model, the political citizen and the 'natural man' were united in one person: the journalist-printer. The revolutionaries not only shaped the policies of the National Assembly through their arguments in print, they also sold their publications to their fellow citizens as commodities. Just as 'trade and commerce' bound together civil society, so competing newspapers and book-sellers contributed to the creation of the 'general will' of all citizens. In the same way as the division of labour between individuals produced social wealth, so the printing of publications with different viewpoints created a common political culture. In the Girondin model, therefore, the ideological rivalry between different journalist-printers was underpinned by a common consensus to respect the natural laws of bourgeois society.

The Republic of Property-owners

The Girondin model of media freedom was derived from the optimistic vision of humanity proposed by the Enlightenment philosophers. In their view, society was composed of autonomous property-owning individuals. When the rule of natural laws was instituted, the desires of these individuals and the policies of the state would be in harmony. But in these theories the only individuals defined as 'natural men' were the owners of private property: the bourgeoisie. Therefore, for the Enlightenment philosophers, each individual was simultaneously a moral, social citizen and an egoistic, self-sufficient bourgeois (Marx 1970: 76–82).

The natural law theories of the Enlightenment philosophers were an abstraction of radical changes occurring within contemporary French society, caused by the spread of the money economy. Under the absolute monarchy, the feudal system had slowly disintegrated. At the centre of this social change there was a profound transformation in the nature of property. Instead of being enmeshed within familial relationships, land and other goods were turned into commodities: the absolute and unconditional property of specific individuals. In turn, the growth of individual property ownership paralleled the dominance of the money economy over social production. As more and more necessities were produced only for exchange, so society itself became constructed through money. As more people worked only to obtain money, so the social division of labour was produced through commodity exchanges (Marx 1973: 221–8).

As the concrete peculiarities of each individual's labour were abstracted in monetary exchanges, so the traditional division of labour derived from inherited privileges became difficult to perpetuate. For the revolutionaries, the surviving feudal rights were anachronistic vestiges of an earlier era. Instead, they believed that the protection of private property-ownership was the only precondition needed for the exercise of political rights by all citizens (Sièyes 1982: 14–17). 'The abolition of privileges created free and equal citizens; the transformation of property empowered them to act as genuinely independent individuals' (Sewell 1980: 136).

After the abolition of the absolute monarchy and the feudal orders, France became a republic of property-owners. Under the new order, social existence was divided between the public sphere of the constitutional state and the private worlds of property-owning individuals. The abolition of familial property relations created a dialectical separation between the private and public spheres of human existence. On the one hand, the social production of necessities was increasingly privatised by the individual property-owners. On the other, the rise in commodity production undermined the private control of the state by the absolute monarch. When social production was organised through market competition, an impartial legal framework was needed to regulate the monetary relations between individuals. In everyday circumstances, isolated producers were linked together in civil society by an endless series of reciprocal business deals. But when these individuals argued over contracts, civil law emerged as the public means of settling conflicts between the atomised members of civil society (Sièyes 1982: 85; Pashukanis 1978: 93, 137).

By overthrowing the absolute monarchy, the revolutionaries completed the process of changing the state into the instrument of the collective needs of individual private property-owners. Under feudalism, private wealth and political power were simultaneously combined in the hands of the aristocracy. By contrast, the advent of modernity required a clear separation between the private world of individual property-owners and the public sphere of the constitutional state. By turning the state into an impartial umpire of civil society, political power could no longer be directly connected with economic relationships between individuals. Instead, the dominance of some individuals over others was established through the impersonal relations of exchange, backed by the impartial sanctions of the law. By implementing the 1789 and 1793 Declarations, the constitutional state emerged as the sole regulator of the separation between the private sphere of individuals within civil society and the public sphere of citizens of the republic. The reorganisation of social life around monetary relations had led to a simultaneous increase in the rights of individuals and the power of the state.

After their 1879 election victory, the republicans' constitutional settlement was based on the principles of the 1789 and 1793 Declarations. The primary task of the new government was the provision of the legal framework needed for market competition between the members of civil society. In their settlement, the republicans reflected the social reality of late-nineteenth-century France. The majority of the population were or wanted to be autonomous individual property-owners. In the countryside, most people were land-owning peasants or members of such families.

Within the towns, the professions, artisans and shopkeepers jealously guarded their personal economic autonomy. Even the majority of French industrial companies were small, family-centred concerns. In both countryside and city, the majority of French people were united in believing that 'the individual property-owner was master in his own house' (Gauron 1983: 43). This widespread ownership of private property provided the economic foundation for the constitutional settlement introduced by the republicans. In the Third Republic, most individuals could be simultaneously citizens and bourgeois. As predicted by Gambetta, the adoption of the political programme of the Paris Commune did not create the conditions for a social revolution. On the contrary, in a society of individual property-owners, the democratic republic brought 'order and stability'.

For the republicans, the establishment of the Girondin model of media freedom was a crucial part of their constitutional settlement. Under the 1881 press law, the libertarian principles of article 11 of the 1789 Declaration and article 7 of the 1793 Declaration became a specific piece of legislation guaranteeing freedom of publication. After the passing of this legislation, individual citizens could now directly participate in political decision-making by publishing their own newspapers or books. The views of individual citizens were not only indirectly represented in the legislature, they were also directly expressed in print. But this political right of media freedom was dependent on the natural right of the property-ownership of printing presses. Underlying the diverse opinions published in rival newspapers or books, the Girondin model of media freedom was based on a common consensus over the protection of the ownership of private property. In the republic of property-owners, the right of media freedom was confined to the members of the bourgeoisie.

THE MENTAL MAP OF THE GIRONDIN MODEL

Figure 1.1 shows the psychogeography of the Girondin model of
media freedom. This is an ahistorical and abstract model of the
concepts found in article 11 of the 1789 Declaration, article 7 of
the 1793 Declaration and the 1881 press law. Media freedom is
exercised in a society of atomised individuals. As a pre-social
natural right, every individual enjoys the freedom of speech,
including in print. The success or failure of publications depends
on market competition between individual journalist-printers.
Publishers are not censored, but they are barred from infringing
the rights of other individuals or republican institutions. These
restrictions are regulated by clearly defined laws passed by the constitutional government. By legally regulating media freedom, the
constitutional state implements the 'general will' of the citizens.
In turn, the decisions of the republic are created by the participation of its citizens in political discussions in print. *Since they have
the natural right to ownership of private property and the political right
of free speech, all citizens can express their views by becoming journalist-
printers.*

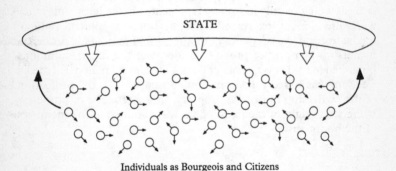

Individuals as Bourgeois and Citizens

Figure 1.1: The Mental Map of the Girondin Model

→   Information flows   ➤   Elections and political controls

⇨   Regulation and legal controls   ○   Individuals

2

The Liberty of the Nation

The Decline of the Girondin Model

Under the 1881 press law, the Girondin model of media freedom
was transformed into the legal framework for the private owners
of printing presses to publish newspapers and books. The continued
existence of this model depended on the widespread ownership of
individual private property among the French population. As with
other aspects of the republican constitutional settlement, the victory
of political radicalism within publishing was also a triumph for social
conservatism. Before the First World War, there were few external
or internal pressures for radical social change on the Third Republic.
France was a leading military power in Europe and had an extensive
overseas empire. More importantly, the constitutional settlement
had established 'order and stability' internally. After the victory of
the republicans, a democratic and prosperous society was created
by the combined efforts of small capitalists, artisans, professionals and peasants. Reinvigorated by republican freedoms, Paris
soon became the intellectual and artistic capital of Europe.

These achievements of the Third Republic were threatened by
the further development of capitalism. In both town and countryside, individual property-owners resisted the spread of more
collective forms of economic organisation, such as joint-stock
companies or direct investments by banks. Above all, they feared
that full-scale industrialisation would lead to their descent into the
ranks of the propertyless working class. Therefore, in defence of
their individual private property, the majority of French voters
supported politicians advocating restrictive economic policies. But
despite this social conservatism, it was impossible to stop the
evolution of capitalism altogether. Over time, there was a steady
increase in the productivity of both labour and capital. After
successive restructurings, the most innovative companies discovered
Fordism: the mass production of commodities, using wage-workers
on assembly lines or in offices. In turn, the resulting rise in the
number of workers created consumers for the increased amount
of commodities produced on the assembly lines (Aglietta 1979).
Despite the need for modernisation, the new techniques of Fordism
were only slowly adopted in France. Under the Third Republic,

even the largest French companies were less than a tenth of the size of their British or German competitors (Kuisel 1981: 85).

In common with most other French manufacturers, most book-publishers in France remained small businesses. By contrast, newspaper-publishers were pioneers of industrialisation. The introduction of Fordism in newspaper publishing was encouraged by the specific nature of production in this sector. When a newspaper was published, the majority of the costs of production were incurred by its journalists and printers in the creation of the first copy of a print run. However, as one copy of a publication could be easily reproduced, the costs of each individual newspaper fell rapidly as further copies were printed. Because of these economies of scale, the industrialisation of printing dramatically lowered the price of each copy of a paper. As prices fell, almost everyone could afford to buy a copy of newspapers produced by mechanised printing presses. By the 1920s, the costs of both morning and evening newspapers were included as part of the basic necessities required by every French worker in a minimum daily budget proposed by the main trade union federation (Bellenger et al. 1972: 80–94, 140–1; Bernard and Dubief 1985: 262).

As in any other sector, the industrialisation of newspaper production involved the simultaneous mechanisation of production and the proletarianisation of the direct producers. While individual journalist-printers in the 1789–99 Revolution had created their own publications, in the newspapers of the Third Republic the roles of journalist and printer were separated. Moreover, with the need for large capital investments in mechanised printing presses and the hiring of staff, no single individual could afford to start a newspaper. Instead of owning their own publications, journalists and printers became the employees of joint-stock companies and financial institutions controlling the mass-circulation newspapers (Bellenger et al. 1972: 137–40, 239, 297; Zeldin 1980: 144–63, 178–92).

During the 1789–99 Revolution, the publications of the journalist-printers were only available to the inhabitants of Paris and a few major cities. In contrast, by the late nineteenth century a combination of growing literacy, better transport and republican freedoms had created a nationwide readership for newspapers within France. In response, the industrialisation of newspaper production proceeded quickly. From 1872 to 1884, the daily circulation of the first newspaper printed on mechanised presses rapidly rose from 220,000 to 825,000 copies. The success of this first mass-circulation newspaper encouraged other publications to introduce mechanised production. But the increased capital costs of producing a daily publication with mechanised printing presses and wage-workers soon created an oligopoly within the French newspaper industry. By 1912 there were only four major national newspapers: two morning and two evening publications. With a combined sale of 4.5 million copies, these papers not only obtained over two-fifths of the total readership, they took most of the advertising as well (Bellenger et al. 1972: 221, 297–315). In the provinces, these national newspapers were complemented by many successful local and regional publications. But even within the local press, a nationwide oligopoly dominated newspaper publishing: Hachette controlled the distribution of most publications across the country, while Havas provided agency reports of domestic and foreign events to most provincial newspapers and sold their local advertising space to national advertisers (Bellenger et al. 1972: 235–8, 288–94, 461–72).

In contrast with the publications of 1789–99, the first mass-circulation papers avoided identification with the policies of individual politicians. As they became a commodity like any other, these newspapers tried to attract a large audience of people holding many different political positions. Another strategy for winning readers from all parties was the avoidance of divisive political issues altogether by only covering human interest and crime stories in a sensational manner. But the depoliticisation of the mass-circulation newspapers was limited by their dependence on advertising. Under the Third Republic, both national and local newspapers sold 'editorial advertising' to interested companies or governments. For example, the Panama Canal Company paid for articles in leading newspapers encouraging readers to purchase shares in its fraudulent enterprise. Because publishing was a business, newspaper-owners were as interested in selling their products to advertisers as to their readers. By the 1920s and 1930s, a slow decline in the sales of the major nationals further increased their dependence on advertising and bribes. In return for money from the financial oligarchy and foreign fascist regimes, the mass dailies launched a bitter campaign of smears and personal abuse against the leaders and supporters of left-wing parties (Bellenger et al. 1972: 266–75, 492–522). 'On the whole, the French press was corrupt, biased, anti-parliamentarian and xenophobic, and much of what it printed was noxious' (Bernard and Dubief 1985: 264).

During these campaigns against the parties of the Left, the mass-circulation newspapers remained protected by the Girondin model of media freedom. However, these papers were now supporting fascist politicians who wanted to abolish the republic and its democratic rights. The extreme Right's bribery of the newspapers was the final stage in the decline of the Girondin model. Under the 1881 law, the liberty of the press was underpinned by individual ownership of printing presses. But once publishers had to purchase mechanical presses and employ wage-workers, only joint-stock companies or financial institutions possessed enough capital to compete in the newspaper market. Although more people now had access to political information, it was impossible for most individual citizens to express their views in print by becoming owners of newspapers. Instead, they were confined to being the passive readers of newspapers. The democratisation of the availability of the media had actually eliminated the possibility of individual participation within newspaper publishing. Because of widespread bribery and advertising, readers could not even exercise much influence over the content of newspapers through their choice of publications. However, because the freedom of the press from arbitrary censorship was a central tenet of republicanism, the growth of the mass-circulation newspapers did not lead to the abandonment of the Girondin model. Yet for the majority of individual citizens the exercise of this interpretation of media freedom was no longer possible in the era of Fordism.

Wireless Telegraphy

When it first appeared in the early 1920s, radio broadcasting was at the cutting edge of the 'second industrial revolution' of new electronic technologies and Fordist methods of production (Braverman 1974: 155–67). Using a combination of Taylorist labour discipline, scientific research and assembly-line production methods, manufacturers were able to lower the price of radio receivers until almost everyone could afford a set. During the 1930s, rising living standards among the proletariat were symbolised by the slow spread in working-class households' ownership of radio sets. The successful adoption of Fordism by radio-set manufacturers encouraged companies in other sectors to reorganise their methods of production. By forcing more individual private property-owners to become wage-workers, the economic modernisation pioneered by the radio manufacturers weakened the social foundations of the constitutional settlement underpinning the Girondin model.

The mass production of radio sets by Fordist methods created the conditions for the mass consumption of radio programmes. In response, radio broadcasting also rapidly developed along Fordist lines. The industrialisation of publishing had been encouraged by the rapid obsolescence of the political news printed by daily newspapers. The advantages of economies of scale in media production were intensified in radio broadcasting. In this new technology, the transmission of music and speech over the airwaves simultaneously produced and distributed the same programme to many different receivers. Instead of printing many individual copies of a paper, a radio station broadcast a constant stream of instantly obsolete programmes. With many hours of airtime to fill, the radio stations needed paid workers to create programmes for their listeners. Because the skills of musicians and journalists were difficult to mechanise, the radio stations displaced the costs of their workers through the repeated reproduction of the products of their labour. Despite its high costs, the productivity of skilled labour was dramatically increased by transmitting one programme to millions of listeners. As with the mass-circulation newspapers, radio stations needed the maximum possible audience for each programme to increase their economies of scale.

However, the Fordist logic of radio broadcasting took some time to become apparent. As in other countries, most people in France initially believed that radio broadcasting was simply a new form of point-to-point communications. Hence the first French term for radio broadcasting was tsf, an abbreviation of *télégraphie sans fil* (wireless telegraphy). Before 1914 the French government had encouraged some limited experiments in radio broadcasting for military purposes. Once the First World War started, the military uses of radio broadcasting were quickly developed for the struggle against Germany. Therefore, in the interests of national security, the first laws dealing with radio broadcasting included the new medium within the existing state monopoly over telegraphy (Millerand 1923: 6,174).

The creation of a legal framework for radio broadcasting protected not only the military use of radio communications, but also the telegraph monopoly of the Ministry of the PTT (Poste, Télégraphie et Téléphone). Ever since Louis XI had set up a national postal service in the late fifteenth century, the French state had controlled all point-to-point communications. During the eighteenth and nineteenth centuries, monarchical regimes and republican governments had both extended this monopoly by placing the use of the mechanical and electrical telegraph systems under state control as well (Cazenave 1984: 9–10). Under the Third Republic, whether for reasons of military security or economic efficiency, parties of both Right and Left strongly supported the continuation of the state monopoly over postal and telegraphic communications. As long as radio broadcasting was believed to be a type of point-to-point communications, the new technology was condemned to remain part of the postal and telegraph monopoly.

By defining radio as a form of telegraphy, the new laws effectively expropriated all radio frequencies. This primary act of nationalisation justified all subsequent state interventions within the electronic media. But at first the French state only used the ownership of the airwaves to introduce basic technical regulations to prevent interference between two stations that might use the same frequency. In 1921 the Ministry of the PTT began licensing a few enthusiastic amateurs to experiment with the new technology of radio. After a few months, these *sans-filistes* soon discovered the joys of broadcasting music and speech to each other over the airwaves. Within this small world of engineers, radio broadcasting became an electronic version of the Girondin model of media freedom. Because everyone owned a transmitter, these broad-caster-engineers could simultaneously produce and receive radio programmes (Bourdon 1988: 12). Like the journalist-printers of 1789–99, each individual could directly exercise the right of media freedom through two-way communications over the airwaves. However, this limited version of the electronic agora did not last long. Using mass-production techniques, radio-set manufacturers soon started producing simple receivers as consumer commodities. Under Fordism, the democratisation of the availability of radio broadcasting meant that most individuals could only be listeners.

In 1922, inspired by the boom in set sales in the US, the CSF-SFR electronics company began to manufacture basic radio receivers. As France's most powerful electronics company, CSF-SFR easily obtained permission from the Ministry of the PTT to start its own station, which was called Radio Radiola after the brand name of its receivers. However, the company soon discovered a major problem facing the new electronic media: the reception of radio programmes by listeners was entirely free. In the 1920s there was no technical way of selling radio programmes at the point of con-sumption. The new electronic medium faced an entirely social problem: how to turn radio programmes into commodities. Initially, CSF-SFR funded Radio Radiola out of the sales of its own receivers to the station's listeners. But because other set manufactures were not willing to contribute money for the service, Radio Radiola soon began to sell limited advertising within its programmes. By discovering this method of transforming programmes into com-modities, Radio Radiola pioneered the development of commercial radio broadcasting in France (Duval 1979: 40–9).

Once Radio Radiola started transmitting, it was obvious that radio broadcasting was no longer only a wireless version of telegraphy. However, despite the advent of the new mass medium, the Girondin model was still not extended to radio broadcasting. Under a decree proclaimed in 1923, anyone could buy a licence for a receiver, but only a small minority of individuals were allowed to own radio trans-mitters. As long as the PTT monopoly over point-to-point communications was preserved, private individuals and companies were able to obtain licences to run their own radio stations. However, the potential power of news or current affairs radio programmes worried many leading politicians. As direct censorship of the media was against republican principles, the French government quietly prevented 'subversives' from gaining access to the airwaves through the licence-granting process. Thus, although a few favoured radio-station owners were granted freedom of speech over the airwaves, the majority of French citizens were restricted to being listeners (Ledos et al. 1986: 41).

'A Regime of Liberty Controlled by the State'

In 1926, following the success of Radio Radiola, the French government decided to treat tsf as a medium in its own right by introducing a specific decree-law on radio broadcasting. As a preamble to this legislation, an official report was produced examining the development of the new electronic medium in Great Britain, the US and Germany. During the early 1920s these three countries had adopted very different approaches to the organisation of radio broadcasting. In the US, anyone could set up a radio station without needing permission from the state. But because this free access to the airwaves had created a 'cacophony' of interference between rival radio stations, the French report concluded that an undiluted version of the Girondin model could not be applied to radio broadcasting for technical reasons. Therefore, in contrast to the opening clause of the 1881 press law, the first article of the 1926 decree law emphasised the legal powers of the state over the transmission and reception of all types of radio signals (Poincaré 1926: 13,795).

In contrast with the US, the 1920s British state had resolved the technical problems of radio broadcasting by establishing a nationalised monopoly to control the airwaves. However, because of its liberal economic policies, the French government was unwilling to finance a state radio broadcasting monopoly out of public taxation. More importantly, republican politicians also feared that the complete nationalisation of radio broadcasting would contravene the principles of the Girondin model by creating 'a State monopoly of thought and propaganda' (Poincaré 1926: 13,795–6). Therefore, although the airwaves remained nationalised, the French government was prepared to grant licences to commercial radio stations.

Following their rejection of the American and British examples, the French republican politicians looked to Germany for a solution which overcame the technical problems of radio broadcasting without leading to a state monopoly. In Germany, the state retained control over the transmission of radio signals, but allowed private control over programme-making. For conservative republicans in France, the German system of radio broadcasting provided a middle way between the extremes of no government regulation and too much state intervention.

According to the Minister of Commerce and Industry, the 1926 decree-law created 'a regime of liberty controlled by the State'

(Cazenave 1984: 16). Although they could be closed down for threatening 'public order' or 'national security', commercial radio stations
could obtain broadcasting licences from a commission composed
of representatives from the main government ministries. Even if
they did not enjoy the same autonomy as the newspapers,
commercial radio stations were still free from any direct control
by the government. In addition, the 1926 decree-law tried to
implement elements of the Girondin model within radio broadcasting. Because most citizens were unable to own their own radio
transmitters, the new legislation envisaged the making of programmes
by 'intellectual or artistic groups, the press and listeners' (Poincaré
1926: 13,798). For republican politicians, the creation of these
programme-making groups was a means of overcoming the technical
limitations on the implementation of the Girondin model within
the new electronic medium. By participating in programme-making
groups, individual citizens could now directly exercise their right
of freedom of speech in radio broadcasting. As well as being
listeners, citizens would also be speakers over the airwaves.

By the late1920s, a successful commercial radio sector had been
established within France. With a rapid increase in advertising,
commercial radio broadcasting soon became very profitable. As a
consequence, large banks and joint-stock companies started buying
up the shares of the commercial radio stations. These new owners
were primarily interested in radio broadcasting as a business.
Therefore they quickly ousted the founders of the commercial
stations, who had been radio enthusiasts in the early 1920s.
Similarly, the programme-making groups were excluded from the
airwaves. Instead, the commercial radio stations provided entertainment programmes, which were designed to attract a mass
listenership for their advertisers. Once the programme-making
groups were abolished, the last vestiges of the Girondin model in
commercial radio broadcasting disappeared (Ledos et al. 1986: 33).

By providing popular programmes, the commercial stations soon
turned radio broadcasting into the dominant sector of the mass media
in France. In 1930 there had been only 500,000 radio sets in a
population of around 20 million people. But by 1939 the number
of receivers had rapidly risen to 5.5 million. At the outbreak of the
Second World War, most urban households owned a radio set
(Bellenger et al. 1972: 472). When the commercial radio stations
began to attract large audiences, their news and current affairs
programmes were heard by most voters. Therefore, as with the mass-
circulation newspapers, the parties of the Right were determined
to control these stations' political coverage. Although they had
extensive legal powers over the new medium, leading right-wing
politicians preferred more direct methods of influence over the
commercial radio stations, such as owning their shares or bribing

them with public funds. In addition, they also had many corrupt links with the major shareholders of these stations. Controlled by right-wing politicians and their financial backers, the commercial stations avoided any favourable coverage of the parties of the Left in their news bulletins (Bernard and Dubief 1985: 175–6).

During the late 1920s, Trémoulet, an aspiring media magnate, created a network of several commercial radio stations covering southern France. As in the US and Britain, economies of scale in programme-making and engineering encouraged the centralisation of production across many different radio stations (Cazenave 1984: 18). In 1931 the success of Trémoulet's network inspired a minor drug-dealer to set up Radio Luxembourg. Like its founder, Radio Luxembourg operated outside the law from the beginning. For instance, the station started broadcasting on a frequency assigned to another operator under international treaties. Furthermore, Radio Luxembourg transmitted entertainment programmes for the inhabitants of northern France, funded by advertisements and sponsorship from French companies. But as it was based in the Grand Duchy of Luxembourg, this commercial station could ignore all the provisions of the French laws on radio broadcasting.

When Radio Luxembourg began to transmit programmes in English and German, the British and German governments launched an international campaign against the pirate radio station for violating treaties on the international division of frequencies and for broadcasting programmes to their domestic listeners without their permission. However, the French government refused to support these protests. On the contrary, leading French politicians and banks were closely involved in the project. As with other commercial radio operations, the pirate station was owned by the financial oligarchy. Thus, although it was not legally regulated by the French state, Radio Luxembourg was under the control of the financial backers of the French government. Moreover, as with many mass-circulation newspapers, Havas was appointed to provide the news and current affairs programmes for Radio Luxembourg. Not surprisingly, these programmes provided favourable coverage of leading right-wing politicians (Duval 1979: 255–67).

The creation of Radio Luxembourg signified the end of the Girondin model of media freedom. During the 1789–99 Revolution, individual journalist-printers directly expressed their own views in print by owning their own newspapers. In the early 1920s, when they simultaneously transmitted and received radio programmes, a small minority of broadcaster-engineers had briefly re-created this two-way form of communications over the airwaves. But with the wider availability of radio broadcasting, individual citizens could no longer directly exercise their right of freedom of speech over the airwaves. For both technological and economic reasons, radio broadcasting had developed a complete separation between the trans-mitter and receiver of programmes. Although a limited number of workers actually made the radio programmes, these individuals were employed to reproduce the views of the station-owners, who were right-wing politicians or members of the financial oligarchy. The Fordist development of the new electronic medium had restricted the right of freedom of speech in radio broadcasting to a minority of shareholders and their political friends. In a Fordist mass medium, there could only be a one-way flow of communications. As neither listeners nor employees of the radio stations could express their own views over the airwaves, no version of the Girondin model of media freedom was possible within radio broadcasting.

When Citizens are not Bourgeois

By the 1930s, the Girondin model of media freedom had been made obsolete by the industrialisation of newspaper publishing and radio broadcasting. Under Fordism, the natural right of private property-owners (owners of printing presses or radio transmitters) prevented most citizens from exercising the political right of media freedom. Once each individual was no longer simultaneously bourgeois and citizen, the Girondin model of media freedom disappeared. This contradiction between natural and political rights was only exacer-bated by the development of Fordism. Even before its advent, there had been large numbers of propertyless individuals in France. Before the expropriation of the aristocracy and the church, the majority of the French population in the countryside were landless peasants or tenant farmers. Within the city, there were large numbers of propertyless servants and day-labourers (Thompson 1943: 83).

During the 1789–99 Revolution, the key dispute between the different republican factions centred on the extension of political rights to individuals without property. In the 1789 Declaration, every individual was granted the rights of citizenship, regardless of feudal rank or religion. Yet these political rights could only be effectively exercised through the ownership of private property. Many revo-lutionary leaders feared that the granting of political rights to propertyless people would lead to the wealthy being deprived of their natural right to private property (Cobban 1963: 166–7). In 1789 Emmanuel Sièyes, a philosopher involved in the drafting of the Declaration, advocated the creation of two tiers of citizenship. In his view, all individuals possessed natural rights, which allowed them to live within civil society. But as peasants or workers, the majority of the French population were confined to being simply 'passive' citizens. By contrast, individuals with sufficient private property were allowed to become 'active' citizens with full political rights. Sièyes justified the exclusion of all propertyless individuals from the political rights of 'active' citizenship because the state was a social contract between private property-holders. In his view, only private property-owners were 'true shareholders in the great public enterprise' of the state. In his refusal of full citizenship to all propertyless individuals, Sièyes suppressed the inherent contradiction between bourgeois and citizens' rights (Sewell 1988: 107–10).

This division of the French population into 'passive' and 'active' citizens was vigorously opposed by Robespierre and the Jacobins as perpetuating the feudal privileges of the absolute monarchy in a new form. For them, the rights of full citizenship had to be extended equally to all male members of civil society, regardless of whether or not they owned private property (Soboul 1974: 180–3). Inspired by Rousseau, the Jacobins believed that individuals acquired political rights by personally participating in the formation of the 'general will'. According to Rousseau, the members of civil society became citizens by participating in the public meetings of the agora. But because of physical limitations, it was impossible to realise this vision of direct democracy within France. Despite extending the franchise, the Jacobins could not create the conditions that would enable all citizens to be actively involved in political decision-making. In practice, only citizens of Paris were able to influence the policies of the French government through a series of revolutionary demonstrations and uprisings (Cobban 1963: 214–18).

During the 1789–99 Revolution, both Girondins and Jacobins were faced by the emergence of a contradiction between participation and democracy within modern society. For the Girondins, this could be resolved by restricting political rights to a minority of property-holders. Within this small group, all could participate in political decision-making by becoming politicians or by publishing their own views in print. Yet without the widespread ownership of private property, this constitutional settlement rested upon the exclusion of the propertyless majority from political decision-making. In response, the Jacobins called for the separation between natural and political rights to be overcome by granting full citizenship to all male individuals. However, after the abolition of the property qualification, direct participation in political decision-making by all citizens became impossible. For example, without private property individuals could not express their views by publishing newspapers on their own printing presses. Instead, the 'general will' of all citizens had to be represented through the institutions of the democratic republic. Thus, when bourgeois and citizens' rights came into contradiction, the Jacobins privileged the involvement of citizens within the democratic republic over market relationships between individuals within civil society.

The Republic of the Nation-People

The separation of natural and political rights reflected the division between civil society and the state within early capitalism. As market relations developed, the state emerged as the defender of the impersonal interests of the individuals within civil society. Even under the absolute monarchy, the state provided an impartial legal framework for market relationships between individuals. After 1789 the revolutionaries accelerated the de-privatisation of political power. Under their constitutions, the state was controlled by the representatives of individual citizens. However, as it became more democratic, the autonomy of the state grew. During the 1789–99 Revolution, the state's independence from the control of civil society increased. In the period of national emergency, the revolutionaries gave precedence to the defence of the political rights of all citizens over the protection of the natural rights of particular individuals. Under attack from internal and external enemies, political democracy was protected by the power of the authoritarian state.

The autonomy of the republican state was inherited from the absolute monarchy. France was one of the first modern nations in the world. Created as a distinctive political unit by the military conquests of the French kings, a national market had been carved out of the medieval system of continental trade routes. Although it undermined the self-sufficiency of the different provinces by providing better communications and levying national taxes, the absolute monarchy was unable to complete the unification of the country by imposing a common system of administration, customs, taxes, law or local government. Crucially, most of the population of France inhabited self-sufficient village communities. Living outside the money economy and state controls, the majority of these peasants did not even speak French (Weber 1977: 34–6, 44–9). Responding to this fragmentation, the leaders of the 1789–99 Revolution accelerated the political and economic centralisation of the country. The revolutionaries not only abolished the remaining feudal privileges of the aristocracy and the clergy, they also swept away the autonomous provinces of monarchical France. Under the new order, individuals within civil society were guaranteed natural and political rights in return for their recognition of the authority of the centralised state. In the 1789 Declaration, the revolutionaries proclaimed that: 'The nation is essentially the source of all sovereignty; nor can any caste, or individual, be entitled to any authority which is not expressly derived from it' (Jaume 1989: 13).

During the revolution, there was a fundamental transformation in the nature of political power. Under the absolute monarchy, the state had been the personal property of the king. After the monarchy's fall, political power passed to the elected representatives of the citizens. According to the Jacobins, the state now represented the 'general will' of the whole population. By participating in political decision-making, the atomised individuals of civil society were transformed into a sovereign nation-people (Hegel 1975: 197–8). As the state was the 'general will' of all citizens, the actions of the government necessarily reflected the wishes of the whole population. Because the revolutionaries had no experience of multi-party politics, opposition to the particular policies of the Jacobin government soon became synonymous with treason against the republican state. The leaders of the Jacobins attacked their opponents as aristocratic or foreign plotters, rather than as democratic rivals. As the political rights of individuals were created by participation in the state, no single individual possessed the right to resist the 'general will' of the entire nation-people:

> The greater harmony that reigns in the public assemblies, the more, in other words, that public opinion approaches unanimity, the more the general will is dominant; whereas long debates, dissensions and disturbances bespeak the ascendance of particular interests and the decline of the state. (Rousseau 1968: 151)

Despite the Jacobins' theories, the majority of the population still could not participate in the creation of the 'general will' of the French nation-people. Not only did the peasants live outside the money economy of the towns, they avoided any contact with the state. Even within the urban areas, the Jacobins excluded the female majority of the population from political decision-making. The active participation of men in the public sphere of the democratic republic was only made possible by women caring for the private sphere of home and children (Marand-Fouquet 1989). Instead, the Jacobin government increasingly believed that the 'general will' was formed by the revolutionary clubs which had been set up in every major town in France. As the revolutionary crisis intensified, the clubs successively supported the constitutional monarchy, the Girondins and, eventually, the Jacobins. Under the impact of foreign and civil wars, the clubs were transformed from open debating societies into a narrow fraternity of the revolutionary faithful. Using this national network of supporters, the Jacobin government replaced the fragmented and corrupt administration of the absolute monarchy with a centralised and efficient bureaucracy of its loyal agents in each town across the country. The revolutionary clubs passed from local agoras to servants of the republican state (Soboul 1974: 590).

The Jacobin dictatorship was established in 1793–4 for pragmatic reasons. The civil war and foreign invasions created an acute political crisis. In response, the legislature delegated its political powers to a strong executive body: the Committee of Public Safety.

Because of the emergency, the new executive was not restrained by the provisions of the two Declarations of the Rights of Man and the Citizen. Robespierre, the leader of the Jacobins, defended the violation of these fundamental rights by distinguishing between societies at peace and at war. After the victory of the Jacobins, the republican government would defend the political and natural rights of all members of civil society. However, during the war the revolutionary dictatorship could violate these rights to preserve civil society from its internal and external enemies. The imposition of a dictatorship in the short term would be justified by the creation of a democratic republic in the long term. While monarchs were condemned for violating individual rights, the revolutionary dictatorship could legitimately repress its citizens in defence of the republic (Robespierre 1967: 58-67). For Robespierre, this distinction was clear: 'Revolution is the war waged by liberty against its enemies; a constitution is that which crowns the edifice of victory once victory has been won and the nation is at peace' (Robespierre 1967: 59).

After Robespierre's overthrow by the Directory, the wartime expediencies of his government were transformed into a distinct political position by the Conspiracy of Equals. Led by Gracchus Babeuf, these radical Jacobins called for a social revolution against the new rulers who had taken over the power and wealth of the old aristocracy. According to Babeuf, the contradiction between bourgeois and citizens' rights had caused the fall of the Jacobin government. Although it had privileged political over natural rights, the government had only taken limited measures against the ownership of private property, such as restricting price rises. Nonetheless, because they wanted to prevent the imposition of any further controls, the owners of private property had conspired to overthrow the Jacobins. Under the Directory, universal male suffrage was abolished and replaced by a property-based franchise. Babeuf claimed these events proved that the individual ownership of private property was incompatible with the preservation of political democracy. In his view, the only method that could end the contradiction between bourgeois and citizens' rights was the nationalisation of all private property. For Babeuf, private property was 'an invention of civil law, and may, like it, be modified or abolished' (Buonarroti 1836: 151). Therefore the natural right of private property had to be suppressed to protect the political rights of citizens.

Like the Jacobins, Babeuf believed that individuals became citizens by participating in the affairs of state. But, drawing his support from the poorest areas of Paris, Babeuf wanted this political right of all citizens to be realisable in practice. Therefore he called for the state to provide a 'frugal state of comfort' for all citizens

(Buonarroti 1836: 422). As the owner of all property, the state should organise housing, clothing, food and medical aid for the citizens of the republic. In return, they would have to work, serve in the military and participate in political decision-making. According to Babeuf, the state's expropriation of all natural rights would create the conditions under which the real exercise of political rights by all citizens within the democratic republic could be achieved. But, like Robespierre, Babeuf also believed that this democratic republic could not be established immediately after the revolution. He advocated restricting political power to a minority of 'vigorous and revolutionary' activists in the short term (Buonarroti 1836: 102). The longevity of this revolutionary dictatorship was open-ended. In Babeuf's view, the French people needed to be morally regenerated through state education before fully exercising their political rights as citizens. Once again, the revolutionary dictatorship in the short term was justified by the need to create a democratic republic in the long term.

Under the absolute monarchy, the French state was never able to unify the whole country. However, under the Jacobins the fragmented royal administration was transformed into a centralised bureaucracy. During the period of civil war and foreign invasions, the state suppressed the rights of particular individuals in order to defend the interests of all citizens. Despite its commitment to representative democracy, the Jacobin revolutionary dictatorship completed the separation of the state from civil society. The programme of Babeuf's Conspiracy of Equals represented the logical theoretical conclusion of this process. By sacrificing their natural right of private property, the atomised individuals of civil society would be emancipated as citizens of the republic of the nation-people. By abdicating their political rights in the short term, these citizens would aid the long-term transition to a democratic republic. Thus the Conspiracy of Equals simultaneously advocated the real participation of all citizens in political decision-making and the complete autonomy of the revolutionary state from the members of civil society.

'Sound Writings'

Although they championed the principles encapsulated in article 7 of the 1793 Declaration, in practice the Jacobins never respected this radical version of the Girondin model. Under attack from internal and external enemies, the Jacobins reintroduced press censorship and suppressed opposition newspapers. Despite his defence of the unconditional liberty of the press in the debates on the 1789 and 1793 Declarations, Robespierre refused to respect this right for newspapers and book-sellers opposed to his own regime. When resistance to the Jacobin government grew, he denounced the journalists of the opposition newspapers as 'the nation's most dangerous enemies' (Hampson 1988: 227–8). As with other clauses of the 1793 Declaration, article 7's protection of media freedom was suspended for the duration of the national emergency. The exercise of the right of freedom of publication by particular individuals was removed in the public security interests of all citizens. As one leading Jacobin put it: 'In England, liberty of the press is necessary against a despotic government, but in France, the press is not free to curse liberty – i.e. democratic government' (Brinton 1961: 146).

By rejecting the link between political rights and private property, the Jacobins privileged the active participation of citizens in the democratic republic over market relationships between individuals within civil society. Therefore media freedom was no longer created by the individual ownership of printing presses. Instead of becoming journalist-printers, citizens indirectly exercised their right of media freedom through participation in the republic of the nation-people. As the representative of the 'general will' of all citizens, the Jacobin government was entitled to control the content of every newspaper and book. Because it was developed under Robespierre's government, this is called *the Jacobin model of media freedom*. 'The censorial office sustains morals by preventing opinions from being corrupted, by preserving their integrity with wise rulings, and sometimes even by settling points on which opinion is uncertain' (Rousseau 1968: 175).

Alongside the censorship of opposition newspapers and book-publishers, the Jacobin model of media freedom also involved the active promotion of republican opinions among the French population. According to Robespierre, 'mercenary writers' were taking advantage of people's ignorance of the benefits of republicanism to mislead them into opposition to the Jacobin government. Therefore he called for the direct support of 'sound writings' by the state (Hampson 1988: 227–8). During their rule, the Jacobins not only introduced subsidies and other forms of help for pro-government newspapers and book-publishers, they also aided theatres and organised public festivals across the country. Using these different means, the Jacobin government tried to indoctrinate the French people in republican virtues. For instance, in the 1793 Declaration the Jacobins proclaimed that the 'progress of public reason' depended upon the education of all citizens (Jaume 1989: 301).

The subsidising of newspapers and book-publishers was an integral part of a wider policy of remoulding the population into citizens of the French nation-people. In the late eighteenth century, most people lived in autarchic village communities, were illiterate and only spoke their own local dialects. Together with measures encouraging economic and political centralisation, the Jacobins were committed to creating cultural homogeneity across France. For example, Robespierre's government was determined that French should become the single 'republican language' of all citizens. In combination with a policy of 'linguistic terrorism' against rural vernaculars, the government subsidised the publication of French newspapers and books to ensure that most reading could only be carried out through the official language. According to the Jacobins, French citizens needed a common language to participate fully in political decision-making. In the republic of the nation-people, the 'general will' of all citizens could only be expressed in French (Hegel 1975: 138; Soboul 1974: 592–3).

As in other areas, the expediencies of the Jacobin government were only theorised into a coherent programme by Babeuf's Conspiracy of Equals. Like Robespierre, Babeuf rhetorically accepted that freedom of publication was essential for citizens to participate in political decision-making. However, after the experience of the civil war, Babeuf was also concerned about 'delivering the Republic to interminable and disastrous discussions' (Buonarroti 1836: 210). According to Babeuf, the revolutionary government did not just have to subsidise 'sound writings' and censor opposition publications. Crucially, he also called for the complete nationalisation of all printing presses. In his version of the Jacobin model, the government of the democratic republic expressed the views of the citizens in the newspapers and books published on the nationalised printing presses. As employees of the revolutionary state, journalists and printers could only reflect the views of the people as defined by their elected representatives. In the programme of the Conspiracy of Equals, Babeuf proposed the following rules for the nationalised newspapers and book-publishers:

1. No one may promulgate opinions directly contrary to the sacred principles of equality, and of the sovereignty of the people.
2. All writings on the form of Government, and on its administration, are to be printed and sent to all the libraries. ...
3. No writing about any pretended revelation [i.e. religion] whatever can be published.
4. All writings are printed and distributed, if the conservators of the National Will shall judge that their publication may be useful to the Republic. (Buonarroti 1836: 210)

These rules were not simply measures of political and religious censorship. Inspired by the Jacobin government, Babeuf also wanted the systematic state education of all citizens. By imposing a republican morality on the population, citizens would be saved from the temptations of 'effeminate manners, false ideas of happiness, dangerous examples, and incentives to pride and vanity' (Buonarroti 1836: 210). The Conspiracy of Equals argued that only virtuous citizens could rule themselves. After the nationalisation of private property, lack of moral education was the only barrier to the effective participation by all citizens in political decision-making within the democratic republic. The revolutionaries had to use political power to transform the people into moral citizens through education, especially using state control over publishing. As with the Jacobin government, the publications of Babeuf's revolutionary dictatorship would not directly reflect the opinions of all citizens, who were still under the corrupting influence of the old order. Instead, in the long-term interests of the people, newspapers and book-publishers would remain separated from the control of the citizens during the initial phase of the revolution. For Babeuf, the only form of media freedom which served the interests of all citizens was the revolutionary dictatorship's absolute control over publishing.

During 1789–99, the French revolutionaries developed two contradictory models of media freedom. In the Girondin model, individuals expressed their opinions in print using their own printing presses. In the Jacobin model, citizens elected the republican government, which expressed their views in newspapers and books printed on the state-owned printing presses. While the Girondin model limited the exercise of this right to a few individual property-owners, the Jacobin model extended media freedom to all male citizens within the republic. But under the Jacobin model, newspapers and book-publishers could only act as a one-way flow of communications from the republican government to its citizens. Even when political rights were not restricted by a revolutionary dictatorship, newspapers and book-publishers did not offer individual citizens a diversity of views. Instead, these publications had to reflect the single 'general will' of the republic of the nation-people. The price of more democracy within the media was the removal of any individual participation within newspaper publishing. Like an audience watching a theatre play, individual citizens could only read the printed opinions of others: 'in the spectacle, the spectator is in the grip of an invincible passivity: he has nothing to do but look and listen' (Ozouf 1988: 208).

THE MENTAL MAP OF THE JACOBIN MODEL

Figure 2.1 shows the psychogeography of the Jacobin model of media freedom. This is an ahistorical and abstract model of the practice of the Robespierre regime of 1793–4 and the programme of Babeuf's Conspiracy of Equals of 1795–6. Media freedom was exercised in a society composed of atomised individuals and the democratic republic. As long as they were male, all individuals possessed political rights. The citizens expressed their opinions by participating in political decision-making. Through the republican government, citizens' opinions were reflected by the newspapers and book-publishers. The state not only censored all publications opposing the policies of the government elected by the people, but also subsidised those newspapers and book-sellers promoting republican virtues. If all printing presses were nationalised, the newspapers and book-publishers could only reflect the opinions of the government of the democratic republic. As citizens, individuals could be readers only of the publications controlled by the democratic republic. *Since they had the vote, all citizens determined the opinions of their newspapers and books by electing the government of their choice.*

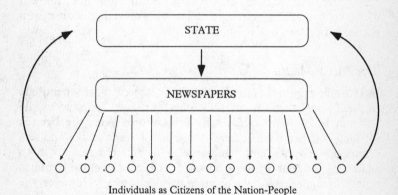

Individuals as Citizens of the Nation-People

Figure 2.1: The Mental Map of the Jacobin Model

→ Information flows

➤ Elections and political controls

O Individuals

3

The Liberty of the Party

The Revival of the Jacobin Model

Once the French media had been industrialised, the Girondin model was obsolete. Under Fordism, the right of media freedom was now restricted to the financial oligarchy and its right-wing political allies. Because they benefited from this situation, the parties of the Right were determined to preserve the economic basis of the Girondin model. They claimed that there could be no media freedom without the private ownership of printing presses and radio transmitters. In contrast, the parties of the Left revived the Jacobin model. In their view, the nationalisation of all newspapers and radio stations was necessary so that all citizens could indirectly exercise their right of media freedom through their political representatives. Among the parties of the Left, the only question was which version of the Jacobin model was the most democratic form of media freedom under Fordism.

The Mass Media as 'Transmission Belt'

In 1920 the majority of the French Socialist party voted to affiliate to the Third International, which had just been founded by the Russian Bolsheviks. Before the First World War, the French working class had been organised in anarchist trade unions and represented by Marxist political parties. For different reasons, both anarchists and Marxists were opposed to the policies of the Jacobins, especially the need for a revolutionary dictatorship. However, the outbreak of war completely transformed French working-class politics. In 1914 the leaders of both anarchist trade unions and Marxist political parties rallied to the defence of the democratic republic against the German invasion. But as casualties mounted and living standards fell, these left-wing supporters of the war were increasingly discredited. Moreover, while the French anarchists and Marxists were collaborating with bourgeois parties in a coalition government, the Russian Bolsheviks had not only opposed the war but also had seized power in a revolution. In 1920, therefore, most members of the French Socialist party voted to reject the failed ideologies of their traditional leaders and to follow the new course

38

towards the future advocated by the Bolsheviks. Crucially, in place of the parliamentary parties of pre-war Marxism, the French Communists were now committed to building a disciplined revolutionary conspiracy (Bernard and Dubief 1985: 152–3).

Although this political strategy was presented as an innovation, the formation of the Communist party was actually a return to the past for the French Left. During the late eighteenth century, Babeuf and his followers had called for the creation of a new Jacobin dictatorship. After the 1848 French Revolution, the revolutionary socialist Auguste Blanqui advocated that the emerging working-class movement should also adopt this conspiratorial political strategy. Inspired by the Jacobins, he believed that this conspiracy should enjoy unfettered power during a transitional period after the revolution. According to Blanqui, the failure of the 1848 Revolution had been caused by the immediate introduction of universal male suffrage. Corrupted by false ideas disseminated by the church and bourgeois newspapers, the workers and peasants had voted a new monarch into power (Rebérioux 1963: 278–9). Because of this experience, Blanqui believed that the primary function of the revolutionary dictatorship was the implementation of an authoritarian version of the Jacobin model. Once all newspapers and other publications had been nationalised, the media would be used to educate people in the republican values of the new society. Only after this process of indoctrination was completed would democracy be allowed. In this version of the Jacobin model, the long-term interests of the people were best served by propertyless individuals abdicating their right of media freedom to the revolutionary dictatorship in the short term (Villepontoux and Le Nuz 1986: 105–27).

Despite being rhetorically committed to Marxism, the Bolsheviks were much more influenced by the tradition of French Jacobinism. While European Marxists had built their parties as mass organisations of workers, the Bolsheviks were an elite conspiracy of intellectuals (Kondratieva 1989: 51–69). Like his Jacobin predecessors, Lenin, the leader of the Bolsheviks, argued that a revolutionary conspiracy was needed to direct the popular struggle for democracy against the absolute monarchy. Under authoritarian rule, it was impossible for individuals to exercise their democratic rights within the revolutionary movement (Lenin 1973: 137–76). After they seized power in 1917, the Bolsheviks quickly transformed their conspiratorial party into a revolutionary dictatorship. Under threat from civil war and foreign invasions, the Bolsheviks rebuilt the centralised bureaucracy and the armed forces to defeat their internal and external enemies.

The conspiratorial structure of the Bolshevik party facilitated its fusion with the hierarchical structures of the state bureaucracy inherited from the absolute monarchy. In time, this led to the emergence of a new ruling class of party officials and state functionaries: the nomenklatura (Voslensky 1984: 26–52). When one-party rule was established, the Bolsheviks used the historical example of the 1793–4 Jacobin dictatorship to justify their own authoritarian rule. Like Rousseau, Lenin rejected representative democracy in favour of direct participation by workers and peasants in political decision-making. Echoing Blanqui, the Bolshevik leader argued that a short-term 'democratic dictatorship' was needed to create the economic conditions for the establishment of participatory democracy in the long term (Lenin 1933: 36–40, 73–9).

Alongside this economic justification, the Bolsheviks also used the Jacobin model of media freedom to defend their revolutionary dictatorship. As his Jacobin predecessors had done, Lenin believed that the majority of the population needed educating in revolutionary ideas. Before the 1917 Revolution, he had asserted that 'the press is the core and foundation of political organisation' (Lenin 1965: 505). As a consequence, the Bolsheviks were founded as a newspaper-party, which used its clandestine publications to claim leadership over the different groups fighting the absolute monarchy. For Lenin, the Bolshevik newspaper was a 'transmission belt' for the one-way flow of ideas from the professional revolutionaries to the Russian population. Although he called for the recruitment of 'worker-correspondents', Lenin believed most individuals would remain only readers of the party newspapers. Even before the 1917 Revolution, the Bolsheviks believed that media freedom had to be confined to a minority of professional revolutionaries (Lenin 1973: 98; 1976: 53).

For Lenin, the exclusion of the propertyless majority of the population from media freedom was inevitable within an industrialised society. The private ownership of printing presses by a minority of shareholders prevented most people from exercising their right of media freedom directly. Moreover, because they were only readers, workers and peasants had fallen under the ideological domination of the newspapers owned by the bourgeoisie. Like Blanqui, Lenin believed that the ruling class used its ownership of the printing presses to control the minds of the propertyless majority of society: 'All over the world, wherever there are capitalists, freedom of the press means freedom to buy up newspapers, to buy writers, to bribe, buy and fake "public opinion" for the benefit of the bourgeoisie' (Lenin 1965: 505).

Immediately after their seizure of power, the Bolsheviks reimposed press censorship and closed down several right-wing newspapers. During the civil war and foreign invasions, the Bolsheviks also suppressed the publications of their socialist and anarchist rivals.

Once again, the defence of media freedom for opposition newspapers was equated with supporting the struggle against the revolution (Bettelheim 1977: 267–9). Implementing the ideas of Babeuf and Blanqui, the Bolsheviks did not only closed down the publications of their opponents, but also used the nationalised media for the 'political education' of the Russian people in Bolshevik ideas (Kenez 1985: 121–8). In the Bolshevik adaptation of the Jacobin model, propertyless individuals were not merely unable to express their own political opinions in print or over the airwaves, they also could not exercise their right of media freedom indirectly through elected representatives.

Because they had been indoctrinated in the false ideas of the old order, the workers and peasants were seen as being incapable of freely electing their own political representatives. Lacking the natural rights of private owners, propertyless individuals had to abdicate all their political rights to the minority of professional revolutionaries, who represented the long-term interests of the people. Under this version of the Jacobin model, the state-owned media expressed the opinions of the propertyless majority of the population by producing propaganda for the ruling party. As it was developed by the one-party dictatorship of the Bolsheviks, this definition is known as *the totalitarian model of media freedom*.

> Down with the non-partisan writers! Down with the literary supermen! Literature must become part of the common cause of the proletariat, 'a cog and screw' of one single great Social-Democratic [i.e. Bolshevik] mechanism set in motion by the entire politically-conscious vanguard of the entire working class. (Lenin 1979: 180)

From its formation, the French Communist party was committed to this new model of media freedom. In its view, the Girondin model was a ruse to cover the self-interest of the owners of the media and their right-wing political allies. Using evidence from the USSR of bribes paid to the mass-circulation newspapers by the Russian absolute monarchy, the French Communists exposed 'the abominable venality of the rotten press' behind the rhetoric of media freedom (de la Haye and Miège 1982: 10). Echoing the Jacobins, the French Communists argued that 'there must be no freedom [of the press] for the murderers of freedom'. As well as advocating the suppression of right-wing publications, they also wanted the media to educate the population in revolutionary ideas. According to the party leadership, media freedom had to be restricted to the 'liberty to go ahead on the road of progress' (Duclos 1962: 50).

For the French Communists, the party's own newspapers and book-publishers were precursors of the totalitarian media of the future. As its first condition of membership, the Third International declared that: 'the periodical and other press and all the Party's publishing institutions must be subordinated to the Party leadership' (Comintern 1980: 93). Therefore the political leadership of the Communist party appointed the editors of its publications and purged journalists with dissident opinions. By employing journalists and printers as wage-workers, the party hierarchy could directly control the content of all Communist publications. From 1920 onwards, the principal activity of the French Communists consisted of distributing their propaganda among the workers, especially through sales of their daily newspaper (Kriegel 1985: 190–8, 248). As in the USSR, the French Bolsheviks believed that their party media were not only educating the people in Leninist ideology, but also pioneering the organisational structures of the future communist society. For the Communists, the totalitarian model was the most democratic form of media freedom.

The Crisis of the Liberal Republic

Before the 1930s, Jacobin forms of state intervention in France were limited to the provision of universal education and improved transport facilities. Under the Third Republic, the state mainly acted as a 'nightwatchman' defending the individual ownership of private property. As a consequence, there were very few nationalised industries, little regulation of factory conditions and limited welfare benefits. For most of the time, economic policy-making was delegated to the Finance Ministry, which was dedicated to 'balanced budgets' and 'sound money'. The deflationary policies of the Finance Ministry reflected the social conservatism of the Third Republic. Because the development of Fordism threatened the constitutional settlement, successive republican governments were much more interested in protecting the individual ownership of private property than in promoting the economic modernisation of France (Kuisel 1981: 10–21, 94–6).

During the First World War, the French government was temporarily forced to abandon economic liberalism. As an emergency measure, the production of military supplies was placed under close state supervision and limited welfare benefits were introduced (Bernard and Dubief 1985: 21–6). However, after the final victory of France and its allies, these wartime innovations were quickly ended. But with the slow spread of Fordism, the traditional policies of deflation and non-intervention became increasingly obsolete. As the new technology and working methods were adopted, state economic intervention was needed to synchronise the simultaneous growth in production and consumption. Without the regulation of industry, controls over the banks and more welfare spending, the expansion of production remained limited by the speculative activities of the financiers and the low living standards of the working class (Lipietz 1987: 34–5). Under Fordism, the state could no longer simply provide the legal framework for market competition between independent producers. Instead, the state and the joint-stock companies had to collaborate in the management of the national economy. As in other industrialised countries, an 'industrial productive bloc' of bureaucrats and industrialists was needed to carry out the economic modernisation of France (Gramsci 1971: 291; Negri 1988: 24–8).

During the 1920s and 1930s, the formation of this 'industrial productive bloc' was hampered by the constitutional settlement of the Third Republic. In France, the process of dividing the individual property-owners into a minority of shareowners and a majority of wage-workers was only partly completed. Although there was a significant working-class electorate, the parties of the Left still could not win the support of the majority of the French population (Lacouture 1977: 256–7). Instead, the growth in the size of the working-class electorate created political instability within the Third Republic. Unable to win enough support to govern on their own, the parties of the Left were also not able to create an 'industrial productive bloc' with other sections of French society. As they benefited from the spread of Fordism, both left-wing parties and industrial corporations opposed liberal deflationary policies and supported greater state economic intervention. However, these two potential members of the 'industrial productive bloc' were bitterly divided over the control and ownership of the means of production. This class polarisation also undermined any long-term alliance between the parties of the Left. In defence of the democratic republic, both socialists and republicans were united against the threat of fascism. However, the republicans were vehemently opposed to any measures weakening the ownership of private property, including the nationalisation of large industries. Because of these fundamental divisions, France was governed by a series of unstable coalition governments (Bourdé 1977: 15–20, 161–6; Bernard and Dubief 1985: 295–8).

In the 1920s and 1930s the Socialists and Communists were the two major parties of the French working class. When they formed an alliance with left-wing republicans, the parties of the Left won the 1936 general election. For the first time since the Paris Commune, the existence of political democracy threatened the survival of the rights of private property in France. During the 1930s, the two left-wing parties supported an updated version of Babeuf's programme for the nationalisation of all private property. This revival of Jacobinism was greatly encouraged by the perceived success of

the industrialisation policies of the Soviet government. In contrast
to the do-nothing policies of the French Finance Ministry, the
Bolsheviks had seized control of the 'splendidly equipped
mechanism' of the industrial corporations. Freed from private
ownership, the productive power of modern industry was now
supposedly being directed by the revolutionary state to raise the
living standards of all sections of society, especially the working class
(Lenin 1970: 59–60; 1978: 92–101). Inspired by this example, the
French Left called for the nationalisation of all private companies
to create the missing 'industrial productive bloc' in France. By
the mid-1930s, both Socialists and Communists believed that the
French state could carry out the Fordist modernisation of the
country in the interests of the working class (Lipietz 1984: 102–3).

The Birth of the Nationalised Radio
Broadcasting Corporation

During the early twentieth century, state economic intervention
within the media slowly grew. Before the First World War, the mass-
circulation newspapers remained protected by the Girondin model.
During the war, the French government not only introduced
military censorship and suppressed pacifist newspapers, but also
published its own propaganda and subsidised patriotic newspapers.
For most politicians, however, this revival of the Jacobin model was
only a wartime emergency measure. When Germany was defeated,
therefore, both military censorship and overt political subsidies were
quickly abandoned and French newspaper- and book-publishers
were once again regulated by the Girondin model of media freedom
(Bellenger et al. 1972: 412–27; Mayeur 1984: 236–7, 248).

However, for technical and economic reasons, the Girondin
model could never be fully applied to radio broadcasting. Although
the first stations were set up by commercial companies, the French
government was closely involved in the early development of radio
broadcasting for military purposes. In 1921 the PTT began its own
research into radio as a new technology for point-to-point communications. At the same time, this nationalised corporation also
became interested in radio broadcasting. By 1923, L'École
Supérieure des PTT had established a state-owned radio station
in Paris to compete with the existing commercial services. Because
this local experiment was successful, the PTT started lobbying for
permission to create a nationwide radio broadcasting system. By
1926 it had obtained authorisation for its proposals and quickly
opened the first national radio station in France. Using one powerful
long-wave transmitter to cover the whole country, the PTT realised
the full potential of radio broadcasting for Fordist mass production.

From one central studio, a small team broadcast the same radio programmes to millions of listeners across the country. Alongside the commercial stations, the PTT had created a powerful nationalised radio broadcasting system in France (Poincaré 1926: 13,797; Ledos et al. 1986: 33).

By the mid-1930s the PTT radio network had expanded to 14 national and local stations, including three in Paris (Duval 1979: 316). Under the 1926 decree-law, the PTT only provided the technical and administrative services for state-owned local radio stations. As in the commercial sector, republican politicians wanted to preserve a limited version of the Girondin model within the nationalised radio broadcasting system. Because it was impossible for everyone to be a broadcaster-engineer, individuals were encouraged to join programme-making groups organised by the PTT stations. However, in practice this extension of the Girondin model to radio broadcasting was limited to those people acceptable to the PTT bureaucrats and the republican politicians. According to the decree law of 1926, the PTT radio stations were to recruit their programme-making groups from among the 'respectable' sections of French society:

1. central or local public services;
2. general or national interest associations or corporate groups;
3. authors, composers, professors, lecturers, musicians, artists and performers;
4. constructors and dealers in radio equipment;
5. groups of amateurs and listeners;
6. representatives of the press. (Poincaré 1926: 13,797)

By the late 1920s, while these amateurs had lost their airtime on the commercial channels, the programmes of the PTT radio stations continued to be largely made by voluntary organisations. As a consequence, the two radio systems provided quite different types of programmes. On the one hand, the commercial stations transmitted mainly entertainment programmes designed to attract a large audience for their advertisers. On the other, the state radio stations concentrated on cultural and educational programmes to please their paymasters in the National Assembly. Because they chiefly listened to the PTT services, republican politicians were easily influenced by lobbying against the further expansion of the commercial radio sector. According to the supporters of the PTT, the application of the Girondin model to commercial radio broadcasting had failed. By the late 1920s, individuals could only exercise free speech over the airwaves by participating in the programme-making groups of the PTT stations. Ironically, the survival of the Girondin model within the new electronic medium now depended on the state ownership of radio broadcasting (Ledos et al. 1986: 33).

In 1933 the PTT took over Radio Paris, the leading commercial station in France. Although the rest of the privately owned stations kept their licences, the French government decided to halt any further expansion of the commercial radio sector. Protected from any further commercial competition, the principal problem faced by the nationalised radio stations was how to raise revenue. Initially, while the PTT paid for technical and administrative expenses, the costs of programme-making were raised by the voluntary organisations from advertising and listener donations. But in 1933 the French government decided to end this dual system of fundraising. Inspired by the British example, all advertising on the state radio stations was abolished and the licence fee for radio sets was substantially increased. In effect, the French government had overcome the technical limitations on the commodification of broadcasting by imposing the compulsory sale of radio programmes on the owners of receivers. Because almost everyone tuned into its programmes at some time, the republican politicians decided that all French listeners should be forced to contribute towards the costs of the nationalised radio broadcasting system. After the passing of this measure, the PTT was able to finance both the running costs of its radio stations and the expansion of its network (Duval 1979: 312–16; Bourdon 1988: 14).

However, this new form of funding for the PTT radio stations removed the financial autonomy of the programme-making groups. With their increased revenue, the PTT stations could now employ workers to make their programmes. As a consequence, the *sans-filistes* were once again excluded from the airwaves (Duval 1979: 314–19). Crucially, by the mid-1930s republican politicians no longer believed that radio enthusiasts were citizens exercising their right of media freedom over the airwaves. Dismissing the possibility of implementing any version of the Girondin model within the radio broadcasting system, the French government announced its intention to substitute 'responsible individuals for irresponsible collectivities' in the management of the nationalised stations (Doumergue 1934: 10,492). During the early 1930s, the management boards of the state radio stations were repeatedly reorganised. In each restructuring, republican politicians tried to find a system of selection for the management boards which combined local and national accountability.

In 1935 Georges Mandel, the minister responsible for the PTT, introduced a series of decrees removing the last *sans-filistes* from the management boards and replacing them with members appointed by central government or with representatives elected by an electoral college of local licence-holders (Duval 1979: 318). With the adoption of Mandel's scheme, the last remnants of the Girondin model within radio broadcasting finally disappeared. Although

radio had been pioneered by the broadcaster-engineers, the industrialisation of the new medium ensured that there would be no form
of two-way communications across the airwaves for most people.
Because individuals were unable to exercise their media freedom
directly over the airwaves, Mandel was determined to encourage
the participation of the entire listenership in electing the management
of the state-owned radio stations.

In Mandel's variant of the Jacobin model, individuals indirectly
exercised their media freedom by voting in elections for both
licence-holder representatives and members of the National
Assembly. On 26 May 1935, the first elections for the licence-holder
representatives on the management boards of the state-owned
radio stations were held. The voters had to choose between the
candidates of the Catholic church's Radio Famille organisation and
the Left's Radio Liberté group. In most state radio stations, the
right-wing Catholic list won the majority of seats for licence-holder
representatives on the management boards. However, Radio
Liberté's left-wing candidates were victorious in some major cities,
such as Toulouse and Marseilles (Duval 1979: 318–19). Although
more than 220,000 voters took part in this experiment in listener
democracy, the exercise was never repeated. As the political crisis
intensified, both right-wing and left-wing parties wanted to exercise
undivided control over the nationalised radio broadcasting system.
In their view, local licence-holder representatives should not be able
to obstruct central government, which represented the 'general will'
of the whole electorate. Because Mandel's version of the Jacobin
model was discredited, many French politicians now advocated the
introduction of the totalitarian model within radio broadcasting.

The Right Jacobins

During the 1920s, the French Communists created a disciplined
organisation of professional revolutionaries. Despite being controlled
by the Third International, the Communists managed to gain
support from a revolutionary minority of the French population.
Because they were propertyless, many workers felt excluded from
the republic of property-holders. For example, the decline of the
Girondin model demonstrated how the protection of private
property restricted the political rights of propertyless individuals.
For Communist voters, the totalitarian dictatorship of their party
was the democratic expression of the propertyless members of civil
society.

However, after the Nazi seizure of power in Germany in 1933,
the Third International abandoned its outright opposition to parliamentary democracy. As was the case in other countries, the

French Communists joined the Popular Front coalition with Socialists and left-wing republicans to defend the democratic republic against the threat of a fascist coup (Dimitrov 1938: 108–11; Danos and Gibelin 1986: 11–27). Ever since the foundation of the Third Republic, supporters of extreme Right parties had opposed the constitutional settlement. As the restoration of the monarchy became impossible, these organisations began to advocate the establishment of a right-wing version of the Jacobin dictatorship. As long as the ownership of private property remained widespread, however, there was little support for anti-parliamentarianism from the French petit-bourgeoisie and peasantry. But in the 1930s the Great Depression not only bankrupted many individual property-owners, it also created a widespread fear of proletarianisation among the petit-bourgeoisie and peasantry. Some individual property-owners therefore abandoned their traditional support for the democratic republic and sought radical solutions for their economic difficulties. For them, the seizure of power by a right-wing dictatorship would not just prevent the election of a Left government, it would also provide them with financial help and employment (Milza 1987: 44–6; Burrin 1986: 27).

Aided by Italy and Germany, the campaign for the overthrow of the democratic republic was led by the fascist parties. In many ways, the anti-parliamentarianism of the extreme Right echoed the criticisms of the democratic republic made by the Communists. For example, the Parti Populaire Française (PPF) also claimed that the power of the financial oligarchy had destroyed any real democracy within the Third Republic. As a consequence, the PPF called for the creation of a right-wing dictatorship to institute a new political and economic order. The PPF promised that under fascist rule small property-owners would be protected from excessive competition by the industrial corporations and expropriation by the Left parties. At the same time, the PPF also advocated the state's creation of employment for its supporters. If they could not hold on to their private property, the petit-bourgeoisie and peasants would be able to preserve their social status by becoming the functionaries of a fascist dictatorship (Brunet 1986: 256–8).

The rise in support for fascism paralleled the decline in the social basis of the constitutional settlement of the Third Republic. Fearing or experiencing a loss of their individual private property, many members of the petit-bourgeoisie and peasantry abdicated their political rights to the fascist parties. Instead of basing citizenship on the ownership of private property, the fascists claimed that individuals participated in political life through their membership of the nation-people. In place of elections, the 'general will' of the atomised members of civil society would be created by a totalitarian dictatorship, especially through the will of a charismatic leader. According to the fascists, this 'democratic dictatorship' would be the representative of the endangered individual property-owners of French society. 'In substance, the totalitarian leader is nothing more or less than the functionary of the masses he leads ... Without him, they would lack external representation and remain an amorphous horde; without the masses, the leader is a non-entity' (Arendt 1968: 23).

At the centre of this right-wing anti-parliamentarianism was the fascist version of the totalitarian model. In France, the fascists' media policy was largely derived from the example of Nazi Germany. After seizing power, the Nazis had set up a Ministry of Propaganda to control the mass media and the arts. From the beginning, this ministry did not merely purge all opponents of the regime from the newspapers and radio stations, it also used the media to impose Nazi beliefs on the German population. Realising the centralising possibilities of the new electronic medium, the Nazis created nationwide radio stations, manufactured cheap receivers and built 'loudspeaker pillars' in public places (Zeman 1964: 51–2). Crucially, the Nazis believed that the development of radio broadcasting was a technical fix for the physical limitations of public rallies, which were their supposedly participatory replacement for representative democracy. For the Nazis, the broadcasting of these political mass meetings over the airwaves created a limited form of electronic agora. By coming together to listen to Hitler's radio speeches, the atomised members of civil society were fused into a single German nation-people through collective worship of the charismatic leader. In Goebbels' view, radio broadcasting had become the most important 'intellectual weapon of the total state' (Bramsted 1965: 55, 209; Heiber 1972: 151).

In most countries, when the newspapers were first industrialised, the political opinions of their owners were muted to attract the largest possible readership. However, after this process of concentration ended in a state monopoly, the content of both newspapers and radio programmes could be determined by the ruling party. Despite drawing support from different classes, both fascists and Communists supported the totalitarian model of media freedom. For both parties, the Girondin model was no longer possible in the emerging Fordist society. Instead, the dispossessed petit-bourgeoisie or propertyless workers had to abdicate their political right of media freedom to a charismatic leader or the ruling party. By seizing control of the media, the totalitarian state could then express opinions in print or over the airwaves 'on behalf of' the people.

The Creation of the Totalitarian Media System

When the Popular Front won the 1936 election, the Third Republic entered its terminal crisis. Because political democracy threatened individual property rights, the parties of the Right called for the creation of an authoritarian regime to roll back the social reforms of the Popular Front. In 1938, after the resignation of the Socialist prime minister, a right-wing republican government was formed. When the trade unions resisted an extension of the working week, this administration broke the subsequent strikes by force. In this conflict, the government openly used news bulletins on both state and commercial radio stations to put out propaganda aimed at demoralising the protestors and encouraging waverers to go to work. Radio broadcasting had been turned into 'a remarkable instrument for maintaining order' (Bourdé 1977: 211).

The opportunity for government control over both state and commercial radio stations had been created by the threat of invasion by Nazi Germany. As in the past, an external threat justified the suppression of internal dissent. Reviving the Jacobin model, the right-wing republican government not only purged opposition supporters from the state-owned radio stations, but also took direct control of the news bulletins on both nationalised and commercial stations. Soon afterwards, censorship was imposed on all other programmes on the commercial stations too. In the government's view, radio broadcasting had to be turned into 'a strong instrument of moral defence' for the French people (Duval 1979: 321–2). During the 1938 Munich crisis, this 'moral defence' led to both state and commercial radio stations urging their listeners to support the disastrous agreement with Hitler on the partitioning of Czechoslovakia (Duval 1979: 321–2).

As war approached, the French state completed its take-over of the airwaves. All news programmes on the nationalised and commercial stations were under the control of the Centre Permanent de l'Information Générale, which was an embryonic Ministry of Information. Once this bureaucracy was in place, a committee of government ministers met each day to decide the content of all radio news bulletins. At the same time, the remnants of listener democracy disappeared with the merger of the local and national PTT stations into a single national radio broadcasting corporation under a director-general appointed by the government (Eck 1985: 19–20). In a similar fashion, military censorship was also applied to all national and local newspapers. When the Nazi-Soviet pact was signed, the popular newspapers of the Communist party were banned altogether (Bellenger et al. 1972: 583, 616–22).

After the defeat of France in 1940, this authoritarian version of the Jacobin model was quickly transformed into the totalitarian model. Under the terms of the armistice, the German army established an occupied zone in the north and west of France. However, the rest of the country was run by the Vichy regime based in southern France. When the French army was defeated, the National Assembly abdicated all its powers to Pétain, who had been a successful general during the First World War. Under his rule, the democratic republic was abolished and replaced by a fascist dictatorship (Azéma 1984: 44–55). In imitation of Nazi Germany, Pétain's dictatorship rapidly imposed the totalitarian model on the French mass media.

By creating its own Ministry of Information, the Vichy government asserted its authority over the newspapers and radio stations operating in the half of the country that it controlled. The new propaganda ministry issued daily guidance notes suggesting how sensitive topics should be covered by these media. At the same time, the regime nationalised the Havas press agency to distribute pro-government articles and subsidised the owners of collaborationist newspapers (Rossignol 1991: 18–25; Institut Hoover 1957: 930–1). Above all, the Vichy regime was determined to control its own radio stations. After obtaining permission from the occupiers, the new government reopened the main PTT radio station. As Radio Vichy, this national station was soon providing regular news bulletins from the new capital for listeners across France. When commercial radio stations wanted to restart broadcasting in southern France, the Vichy regime outlawed all advertising on them. Instead, their owners were paid to broadcast the news bulletins and other propaganda programmes of the fascist government (Duval 1979: 327–9; Ragache and Ragache 1988: 60–1).

For the Vichy regime, the distribution of fascist propaganda was a substitute for democratic elections. Under the old order, the 'general will' of the citizens had been expressed through their elected representatives. By contrast, under the Vichy government, the 'general will' of the French people was now expressed through the totalitarian dictatorship of the charismatic leader. Therefore, when he appeared on the radio, Pétain spoke as the 'voice of France'. As most individuals could only be listeners, Pétain expressed their opinions on the airwaves for them. The Ministry of Information issued guidance notes on these radio talks to all newspaper and radio journalists, who explained the dictator's message in subsequent articles or programmes. As in Nazi Germany, the atomised members of civil society were supposedly united into a single nation-people by the radio speeches of the leader of the totalitarian dictatorship (Rossignol 1991: 103–5).

Using Pétain's radio talks, the Ministry of Information created the fascist ideology of the National Revolution. Instead of being derived from the ownership of private property, Vichy based individual citizenship on membership of the French nation-people. The collaborationist newspapers and radio stations urged the French population to unite against the threat from the 'extra-national' conspiracies of Jews, freemasons and Marxists (Rossignol 1991: 14–15, 119). In particular, the Vichy media promoted the ideals of Catholic fascism. According to Pétain, the defeat of France could only be reversed by a return to the traditional peasant values of 'work, family and country' (Faure 1989: 16–17, 248–9; Nolte 1969: 51–189). While the Bolsheviks adopted the totalitarian model to modernise the Russian Empire, Pétain wanted to use the same methods to lead the French people back into a mythical rural past.

Because of the division of the country, the Vichy regime was never able to impose complete control over all newspapers and radio stations in France. In the occupied zone, the French media came under the authority of the Propaganda Staffel of the German army. After purging the political and racial enemies of the Nazis, the army enforced rigid censorship, controlled paper supplies, took over the Havas press agency and nationalised all printing presses. In addition, the Propaganda Staffel turned the PTT's Radio Paris into the national radio station for the occupied zone. Although it also broadcast entertainment programmes, this station was primarily used to transmit Nazi news and information programmes. Critical of Vichy's Catholicism, Radio Paris became the mouthpiece of the PPF and other radical fascist parties. Under the supervision of the Propaganda Staffel, every French newspaper and radio station in the occupied zone had to support collaboration in their articles or broadcasts (Duval 1979: 334–9; Ragache and Ragache 1988: 55–7, 227).

When the Allies invaded North Africa in 1942, the Germans occupied the southern half of France. As a consequence, Radio Vichy, several local radio stations and the southern newspapers came under the control of the German army (Institut Hoover 1957: 932–5). As the Allies advanced, the official French newspapers and radio stations became instruments of the Nazi totalitarian state. For example, the collaborationist newspapers and radio stations not only censored all information about the forced deportations of Jews to the death camps, they also promulgated violently anti-semitic propaganda to justify their mass murder. Fearing the consequences of a German defeat, many French fascists actively supported this Nazi version of the totalitarian model (Rossignol 1991: 216–19).

As the defeat of Nazi Germany became increasingly inevitable, the construction of a fully totalitarian state within France was speeded up. According to the French fascists, growing opposition

to the German occupation of France could only be eliminated by
a combination of physical repression and state propaganda. But by
collaborating with the Nazis, the Vichy media had lost the support
of the majority of the French population. Without the citizens'
voluntary abdication of their political rights, the totalitarian model
collapsed. In its final stage, the fascist media could no longer unite
the individual members of civil society behind the charismatic
leader. Since 1940, Radio Vichy and Radio Paris had been involved
in a 'battle of the airwaves' against the French-language services
of the BBC and Radio Moscow, which called for armed resistance
to the occupation. Without a complete monopoly over all radio
broadcasting, the Vichy regime and the Nazis could not prevent
the French population from listening to these 'anti-national' radio
stations (Ragache and Ragache 1988: 223–4; Rossignol 1991:
304–5). By 1944, the advocates of totalitarianism had lost their
propaganda war with the defenders of the democratic republic. In
liberated France, a new model of media freedom was now needed.

THE MENTAL MAP OF THE TOTALITARIAN MODEL

Figure 3.1 shows the psychogeography of the totalitarian model of media freedom. This is an ahistorical and abstract model derived from the one-party dictatorship over the mass media exercised by the Bolsheviks in the USSR, the Nazis in Germany and the Vichy regime in France. Because they were only listeners to the radio or readers of the newspapers, individual citizens abdicated their political right of media freedom to the 'democratic dictatorship' of the ruling party or the charismatic leader, who expressed their opinions for them. In turn, the radio stations and newspapers were nationalised under the control of the ruling party or charismatic ruler. Under state ownership, the mass media simultaneously censored all opposing opinions and promoted the ideology of the ruling party. By placing the mass media under the control of the totalitarian state, the atomised individuals in civil society were united as members of the working class or the nation-people. *Since they had political rights, all citizens controlled what they heard on the radio stations or read in the newspapers by abdicating their political rights to the ruling party or the charismatic leader.*

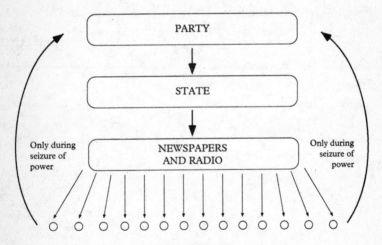

Figure 3.1: The Mental Map of the Totalitarian Model

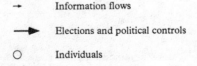

4

The Liberty of Many Parties

The Marxists of the Republic

During the late nineteenth century, the constitutional settlement of the Third Republic was created through the collaboration of republicans and socialists. In the two-round, first-past-the-post election system used in France, the monarchist parties could only be beaten in the second round if the republicans and socialists combined their votes in favour of their best-placed candidate in the first round (Mayeur and Rebérioux 1987: 260–1). Backed by a left-wing majority in the National Assembly, the republicans were able to implement the political programme of the Paris Commune: the creation of a democratic republic. Because of this common belief in political democracy, many republicans regarded the socialists as wayward members of their own movement, rather than as ideological adversaries: 'socialism is ... the logical consequence, extreme, dangerous (if you wish it), of the principles [of the Declaration of the Rights of Man and the Citizen] of 1789' (Aulard 1926: 48).

For Gambetta and the republicans, the democratic republic was needed to establish 'order and stability' in France. By contrast, the socialists thought that political democracy was the precursor of the social revolution. In contrast to their Blanquist and anarchist rivals, the Marxists believed that the creation of the democratic republic had ended the era of insurrectionary politics. In their long-term strategy, the workers would overthrow the capitalist system through the creation of a mass political party. By winning a parliamentary majority, the socialists would be able to use the democratic republic to implement the social programme of the Commune. While both Blanquists and anarchists retained a belief in direct democracy, Marxists assumed that the workers could only express their opinions through the election and supervision of their own representatives (Nicolaievsky and Maenchen-Helfen 1976: 297–390).

During the late nineteenth century, the French Marxists were divided into various squabbling factions. In 1905, however, the Second International cajoled the different groups into forming a single socialist party: the Section Française de l'Internationale Ouvrière, or SFIO (Candar 1988: 32). This new political party adopted the interpretation of Marxism championed by the leading member of the Second International: the Sozialedemokratische Partei

Deutschlands (SPD). In its 1891 Erfurt Programme, the SPD emphasised the Marxist commitment to working within the institutions of the democratic republic. While Marx had retained some reservations about the parliamentary road to socialism, the SPD asserted that the social revolution could only be achieved through the winning of a general election by a socialist party. According to the German Socialists, their electoral victory was inevitable in the long term. As the industrialisation of capitalism slowly forced small property-owners to join the propertyless working class, the Marxist political party would almost automatically win political power through the ballot-box (Salvadori 1990: 32–41).

In reality, the electoral strategy of the Erfurt Programme was unachievable within the autocratic constitution of imperial Germany. By contrast, the SFIO could potentially take power by winning a general election within the French constitutional settlement. According to Jean Jaurès, the first leader of the SFIO, this proved that the imminent social revolution was the culmination of the long struggle for democracy begun by the bourgeoisie in the 1789–99 Revolution (Jaurès 1968: 63–8). Because of this analysis, the orthodox Marxists refused to join the Communist party at the SFIO's 1920 Congress of Tours. During the Congress' debates Léon Blum, the SFIO leader at that time, argued that there was no need for a violent revolution in the countries of western Europe. Restating Jaurès' view, he claimed that the political revolution had already been victorious in France. Because all male workers had the vote, Blum believed that the Socialists now had to wait until the industrialisation of capitalism created an electoral majority for the social transformation of society. Criticising the Bolsheviks for their premature seizure of power, the leader of the orthodox Marxists warned that there could be no social revolution without the necessary economic preconditions (Blum 1972b: 452–3).

By committing itself to this long-term electoral strategy, the SFIO faced the problem of whether or not to participate in coalition governments with the republican parties in the short term. Although its supporters sometimes had to vote for republicans in the second round of elections, the SFIO initially refused to act as the minority partner in a coalition government. Fearful of being absorbed by the Left of the republican movement, the SFIO only wanted to come to political power with an absolute majority in the National Assembly. But this fundamentalist strategy was quickly abandoned at the outbreak of the First World War. As in the 1870–1 Franco-Prussian war, the Socialists joined in a coalition government with the bourgeois parties to defend the democratic republic against foreign invasion (Bernard and Dubief 1985: 4–6).

At first, the SFIO leadership believed that the wartime coalition was only a temporary arrangement for the duration of the war. But once the conflict was over, the SFIO emerged as the largest political party in the National Assembly. This electoral success created a major dilemma for the party leadership. On the one hand, the wartime industrialisation of production had increased the size of the working-class electorate. It thus became increasingly difficult to form a left-wing government without the support of the SFIO. On the other hand, however, the majority of the French population were still small property-owners. The SFIO therefore could not win an absolute majority in a general election. By the early 1920s, this contradiction within the SFIO's political strategy became acute. After the 1924 general election, the left-wing republicans could only form a government with the tacit support of the SFIO deputies in the National Assembly (Lacouture 1977: 191–7).

During the early 1930s the threat of fascism removed the SFIO leadership's final inhibitions against participation in a peacetime coalition government. Under pressure from their supporters, the SFIO, left-wing republicans and Communists formed the Popular Front, which achieved victory at the 1936 general election. Because the SFIO emerged as the largest party within the coalition, Blum became the first Socialist prime minister of France (Danos and Gibelin 1986: 11–41). Although the Popular Front government soon collapsed, the occupation of France by Nazi Germany revived the alliance between the different anti-fascist parties. In 1945 the SFIO reemerged as one of the four main groups within the Resistance coalition. For a brief month, Blum even became prime minister of France again (Lacouture 1977: 534–42).

In the post-war period it was very difficult to form any government without the participation of the SFIO. Yet, confined within these coalition governments, the Socialists were unable to launch the promised social revolution. For Blum, the political dilemma of the SFIO was explained through the distinction between the long-term 'conquest of power' and the short-term 'exercise of power' by a Marxist party. In his view, the 'conquest of power' described the orthodox electoral strategy of the 1891 Erfurt Programme. With an absolute majority in parliament, the Socialists could carry out the social revolution. But in Blum's view this strategy was not applicable to the Popular Front and Resistance coalition govern-ments. Because it was allied to parties representing other classes, the SFIO had to accept limitations on the implementation of its maximum programme. In these situations, Blum believed that the SFIO could only carry out the 'exercise of power' (Blum 1958: 428–31).

During the 1936–8 Popular Front government, the left-wing republicans were allowed to veto the mass nationalisation of leading firms and banks. Similarly, after liberation the presence of Christian

Democrats and Gaullists in the coalition government also prevented the introduction of more radical economic measures (Bourdé 1977: 44–7; Rioux 1989: 56–62). Without an absolute majority in the National Assembly, the preconditions for the social revolution were not present. Although it was in power, the SFIO could not radically change society. During this 'exercise of power', the Socialists committed themselves to the enlightened administration of capitalism, rather than the radical transformation of society. 'The Socialist party ... exercises legal power conforming to the institutions which govern it and in the framework of the social system which exists, that is to say in the framework of a capitalist system' (Blum 1958: 428).

The Modernisation of France

During the period of the 'exercise of power', the SFIO wanted to introduce real changes to satisfy the needs of its working-class electorate. As its numbers and living standards increased, Blum hoped that the working class would acquire the self-confidence needed to carry through the final transformation of French society (Blum 1958: 431–2; 1972b: 455–7). Under the Popular Front government, reflationary fiscal policies and limited industrial planning were adopted to realise this goal. However, it was not until after the defeat and occupation of France that the economic liberalism of the Third Republic was completely discredited. By 1945 all anti-fascist parties were committed to both political democracy and interventionist economic policies. When the Fourth Republic was founded in 1946, the political reforms of the new constitution, including female suffrage, were complemented by the adoption of Fordist economic policies, such as welfare spending, nationalisations and a reform of the civil service (Cobban 1965: 203–10). Crucially, the right-wing parties in the Resistance coalition also supported these new economic policies. For the Gaullists, state intervention was needed to rebuild France's economic and military strength. For the Christian Democrats, the government had a duty to create the material basis of a moral life, especially for families. With support from both Left and Right, the democratic republic became the public service state (Bernard and Dubief 1985: 43–4, 73; Choisel 1987: 91).

After the collapse of the Third Republic, the right-wing political parties accepted that the economy could no longer be regulated by market competition alone. In the immediate post-war period, the different political parties only disagreed on the extent of state control that should be exerted over the economy. Under Fordism, state intervention was needed to create a virtuous circle of rising production and consumption. As in the other major industrial countries, the French state had to adopt interventionist economic policies, such as the creation of a welfare system, minimum wage laws and controls over the financial sector (Lipietz 1987: 35–9). Above all, the Resistance coalition government wanted the French state to create the missing 'industrial productive bloc'. With all-party agreement, individual property-owners were to be turned into wage-workers employed by joint-stock companies.

Following liberation, the Resistance coalition government national-ised the major financial institutions, the utilities and several leading companies, such as Air France and the Renault car company. In addition, the government created the Commisariat Général du Plan (CGP) to plan the French economy and to direct the savings of the population towards industrial investment. Although most companies remained privately owned, the Jacobin state was now the leader of the 'industrial productive bloc' in France (Kuisel 1981: 180–90; Gauron 1983: 92–3, 117–18). For the Socialists, the state's acceptance of responsibility for the social and economic welfare of its citizens was needed to abolish the low wages, long hours and bad conditions which the French working class had suffered for decades. In the 1946 Declaration of the Rights of Citizens, the founders of the Fourth Republic promised that: 'The Nation guarantees the necessary conditions for their development to the individual and the family' (Jaume 1989: 333).

According to Blum, state regulation of the economy was also needed to protect citizens' democratic rights from being undermined by industrialisation. In the past, the democratic republic had only to guarantee the juridical and constitutional rights of property-owning individuals. But as Fordism developed, the political rights of the propertyless workers were threatened by the property rights of the financial oligarchy. However, although they could no longer exercise their political rights directly, the propertyless citizens still elected representatives from different political parties to national and local assemblies. During the period of the 'exercise of power', Blum believed that the parties of the Left had to use their power over state institutions to create the social and economic conditions under which all citizens could exercise these political rights. As under the Jacobins, the 'general will' of the nation-people took precedence over particular individuals' right of private property. According to Blum, individual citizens influenced the policies of the democratic republic through the electoral competition between the political parties. For him, the 'general will' of the citizens could only be created by the elected representatives of several different political parties (Blum 1965: 498–503).

By stressing the importance of electoral democracy, the SFIO's revival of Jacobinism differed from the version supported by the

totalitarian parties. For both Communists and fascists, the disappearance of individual property-ownership led to the abdication of
all political rights to the revolutionary conspiracy or charismatic
leader. By contrast, in Blum's version of Jacobinism the propertyless workers preserved their political rights through the competition
between different parliamentary parties. According to Blum, citizens
expressed their opinions not only by voting in elections, but also
by participating as members of political parties. Hence he strongly
criticised the lack of internal debates within the Communist party
for weakening democracy in France (Blum 1972b: 454; Lacouture
1977: 133–8). Within the SFIO, this multi-party version of the
Jacobin state was closely identified with the 'exercise of power' by
the Socialist party in a coalition government. According to leading
Socialists, the conflict between the contending classes had been
institutionalised by a combination of political democracy and
interventionist economic policies.

In the 1870s Marxists had believed that the organisation of
production by co-operatives would lead to the diminution of the
role of the state: 'the Commune made that catchword of bourgeois
revolutions, cheap government, a reality' (Marx 1933: 43). But by
the late 1940s the Socialists were leading advocates of the interventionist state. Caught within the limitations of the 'exercise of
power', the SFIO had quietly abandoned the social revolution in
favour of a multi-party version of the Jacobin state. Under the Third
Republic, the Socialists had supported not only the constitutional
settlement but also the creation of an impartial legal system and
the introduction of public education. With the foundation of the
Fourth Republic, they believed that the economy had now been
emancipated from the control of the financial oligarchy. Reflecting
on these changes, most Socialists could no longer believe that the
Fourth Republic was simply the 'committee for managing the
common affairs of the whole bourgeoisie' (Marx 1965: 35). Instead,
with all-party acceptance of political democracy and economic
intervention, they claimed that the public service state now served
the interests of all citizens alike: 'In the majority of European
countries, the state has ceased to be the pure and simple expression,
the exact expression of capitalism' (Blum 1958: 435).

This new public service state needed a well-paid and highly
trained bureaucracy to run its activities. Under the Third Republic,
the majority of civil servants had been badly paid and poorly
educated. Breaking with the past, the Resistance coalition
government founded the École Nationale d'Administration (ENA)
and other colleges to educate the new type of state bureaucrat. Above
all, these officials were trained to work for coalition governments
made up of both Right and Left parties (Wickham and Coignard
1988: 125–6, 149). However, although they were supposed to act

as impartial umpires between the competing parties in political and economic matters, these bureaucrats soon began to identify their own self-interest with the needs of the entire country. Alongside the traditional bourgeoisie, the public service state had produced its own section of the ruling class: the nomenklatura of leading bureaucrats.

The Left Invents Public Service Media

At the centre of the construction of the public service state was the development of a new interpretation of media freedom. For Blum, this freedom was 'the foundation of political liberty' (Blum 1972a: 500). Inspired by the 1891 Erfurt Programme, Blum believed that citizens exercised their political rights within the democratic republic by choosing between the competing candidates of different parties. By providing political news to the voters, the newspapers and radio stations played a key role in sustaining the democratic republic. However, Blum feared that media freedom was rapidly disappearing in France. Because of the high costs of production, the independent journalist-printers had been replaced by mass-circulation newspapers owned by the financial oligarchy. According to Blum, these media monopolists were using their newspapers to mislead the population with right-wing political propaganda. '[T]he freedom of the press, in the present phase of capitalism, is only a lying appearance; like all free trade or free competition' (Blum 1972a: 496–9).

During the 1920s and 1930s, there was a sustained campaign of slander and vilification by the French media against the leaders and activists of the Left parties (Lacouture 1977: 402–6). Not surprisingly, both Socialist and Communist parties were extremely hostile to private owners' continued control of the mass-circulation newspapers and commercial radio stations. But although both supported the nationalisation of the mass media, the two parties were divided on the future organisation of newspaper publishing and radio broadcasting. While the Communists advocated the introduction of the totalitarian model, the SFIO wanted a more democratic version of the Jacobin model of media freedom.

Crucially, although he rejected the Girondin model, Blum still wanted to preserve the right of citizens to express their opinions through the media. During the 'exercise of power', Blum believed that the public service state would have to create the social and economic conditions to enable all citizens to exercise the political right of media freedom. For example, in the newspaper industry media freedom was being undermined by the inequality of means between different publications. Blum therefore advocated the nationalisation of all mass-circulation newspapers to free them from the influence of the 'money powers'. Under his proposals, the public service state would organise the printing, distribution and sale of advertising for all national or local newspapers. As in other areas, Blum believed that the French state could administer the newspaper industry in the interests of all citizens. For him, the ideological conflict between competing political parties would be institutionalised through the public service state's monopoly ownership of all newspapers (Blum 1972a: 500–2).

But Blum did not advocate the government's editorial control of newspapers. Unlike the Communists, Blum opposed the monopoly ownership of the press by a single ruling party. Instead, he proposed that the editorial control of the different newspapers be divided between the various political parties represented in the National Assembly. Under this scheme, newspapers would compete for readers by providing contrasting political viewpoints, rather than through the wealth of their financial sponsors. After the national-isation of the press, Blum believed that all citizens would indirectly exercise their right of media freedom by voting for representatives from the different political parties. In proportion to their success in elections, the public service state would provide printing presses and other resources to the competing parties. Although the public service state could not re-create the two-way communications of the journalist-printers, individual citizens would indirectly influence the one-way flow of communications provided by the mass media through their political representatives (Blum 1972a: 501–2). As it was developed for the 'exercise of power' by the SFIO, this definition is known as *the public service model of media freedom*.

The Popular Front's Media Reforms

Alongside its political and economic reforms, the Popular Front government wanted to raise the cultural awareness of the French population. Inspired by the Jacobins, the government believed that educating all citizens in republican virtues would weaken support for the authoritarian solutions of the extreme Right. Before 1936, the Communist party had already set up the Maisons de Culture – arts centres where radical intellectuals and workers could collaborate in the anti-fascist struggle. After its election victory, the Popular Front government financially supported various radical cultural organisations involved in theatre, cinema, libraries, sports and music. Following the introduction of paid annual holidays, the new government even organised tourist trips for its working-class supporters. For the parties of the Left, these initiatives were needed not just to recruit intellectuals and artists to the anti-fascist movement, but also to extend the provision of cultural and leisure activities to citizens of all classes (Jackson 1990: 1,118–26, 131–4).

Because of the support of the mass-circulation newspapers for the extreme Right, the parties of the Left saw the introduction of the public service model of media freedom as a central part of this ideological struggle against fascism. In the election programme of the Popular Front, state intervention within the media was included as part of a series of measures in defence of the democratic republic, such as the suppression of fascist paramilitaries and the extension of trade union rights. By 1936 the public service model was not only being promoted by the SFIO, it was being formally supported by left-wing republicans and Communists too. In its section on the press, the coalition agreement of the parties of the Left called for:

> Reform of the newspapers by legislative measures ... which will guarantee the normal means of existence to newspapers, which compel publication of their financial resources, which end the private monopoly of commercial advertising and the scandal of financial advertising, and which finally prevent the formation of newspaper trusts. (Rassamblement Populaire 1964: 227)

After its 1936 election victory, the Popular Front government attempted to implement some of Blum's proposals for reforming the mass-circulation papers. Although it did not nationalise them, its new law tried to limit the bribery of newspapers by financial interests and foreign governments. But even without proposals for the nationalisation of newspapers, the limited reforms of the Popular Front government were bitterly opposed by the parties of the Right. Although they could not stop the bill in the National Assembly, conservative politicians were able to block the press reforms in the Senate (Bellenger et al. 1972: 36–9, 491–2). Ironically, the continued ownership of the mass-circulation newspapers by supporters of the financial oligarchy helped the publications of the Left parties. After the Popular Front coalition's election victory, the daily circulation of the SFIO's newspaper rose to 300,000. The Communists benefited even more from the abandonment of political neutrality by the mass-circulation newspapers. By 1936, *L'Humanité*, their morning newspaper, had become the fourth most popular daily and their evening publication was the sixth largest seller (Bellenger et al. 1972: 574–50, 581).

While its press reforms were blocked, the Popular Front government was more successful in reorganising radio broadcasting in France. As a pioneer of the 'industrial productive bloc', an important section of the new electronic medium was already owned by the state. As in newspaper publishing, the Socialists assumed that radio broadcasting could only be freed from the control of the

financial oligarchy through state ownership. Therefore, within the
Popular Front coalition, the Socialist and Communist parties
called for the nationalisation of the remaining commercial radio
stations. In their view, the PTT and commercial stations had to
be merged into a single public service broadcasting monopoly
along British lines.

In the early 1920s, the British Broadcasting Corporation (BBC)
had been set up by a cartel of radio-set manufacturers. Fearing the
chaos of the deregulated American airwaves, the British government
had decided to grant a monopoly over radio broadcasting to a single
company. Because newspaper-owners opposed the funding of
radio broadcasting by advertising, the licence fee was transformed
into the compulsory sale of BBC programmes to all owners of radio
receivers. In 1926 a parliamentary committee condemned the
funding of a private monopoly through a form of public taxation.
Following its recommendations, both major political parties
supported the nationalisation of the BBC (Crawford 1926: 5, 13).
Although the Labour party believed that the BBC was the 'socialist
model' of the future, the nationalised corporation was not controlled
by elected politicians (Dalton 1935: 102–3). In contrast to Blum's
public service model, the BBC management was independent of
day-to-day controls exercised by both government and opposition
parties. Through skilful lobbying, Reith, the BBC's first director-
general, persuaded the major political parties to rely on the neutrality
of the corporation's bureaucracy to ensure the impartial presentation of their views (Reith 1924: 122).

Yet, within the balanced programmes of the BBC, there were
strict limits on political pluralism. During the 1926 General Strike,
the leaders of the trade unions and the Labour party were prevented
from broadcasting. Even when there was no civil unrest, Communists
and other left-wingers were systematically excluded from the
airwaves (Briggs 1961: 361–84; Middlemas 1979: 366–7). Despite
these authoritarian features within the British radio system, the
Popular Front government still tried to introduce a BBC-style
public service broadcasting monopoly in France. But, as with the
press reforms, opposition from the right-wing parties prevented the
licences of the commercial radio stations from being revoked
(Miège et al. 1986: 17–18). However, by introducing decrees to
remove PTT officials and reduce the number of listener representatives, the government was able to assert its authority over the
management boards of the existing state-owned radio stations.
Instead of electing listener representatives, citizens now influenced
the output of the nationalised stations through the intermediary of
the political parties. As an institution of the emerging public service
state, the PTT radio network was committed to the impartial presentation of the views of the competing parties within the National

Assembly. In its electoral programme, the Popular Front coalition had called for the 'Organisation by the State of radio broadcasts with a view to assuring the accuracy of the news and the equality of airtime for political and social organisations' (Rassamblement Populaire 1964: 227).

In reality, however, the PTT radio network remained the prize of the ruling parties' electoral victory. In the late 1930s the political polarisation between Left and Right was too deep to allow a permanent consensus between the government and opposition over the management of the state broadcasting system. In contrast with the BBC, neither right-wing nor left-wing parties were willing to grant autonomy to the management of the PTT radio network. At the same time, as was the case under the Jacobins, it was believed that there could be no freedom of speech for the enemies of liberty. Faced with the threat of fascism at home and abroad, the Popular Front government could legitimately exclude the parties of the Right from the airwaves and organise propaganda in defence of political democracy (Duval 1979: 312–13, 319). While the BBC was committed to the balanced coverage of both major parties, the PTT radio stations mostly reflected the diversity of opinions within the Popular Front parties and their affiliated cultural, educational or trade union organisations (Jackson 1990: 130). Thus, although the public service model created the economic conditions for the expression of opinions by the citizens' elected representatives, media freedom on the state-owned radio stations was effectively limited to the supporters of the Popular Front.

The 'New Press' of the Liberation

After the fall of the Popular Front government, the French media were rapidly reorganised on the totalitarian model. During the period of occupation, the media of the German army and the Vichy regime were challenged by the clandestine publications of the Resistance groups. When France was liberated, the persecution of democratic and socialist opinions came to an end. The Vichy newspapers were summarily closed down by the victorious Resistance coalition. Facing no competition, the 'new press' of the different Resistance groups quickly became the primary source of information in the country. In the immediate post-war period, the most successful publications were the newspapers of the parties of the Left. After liberation, the combined circulation of the two major left-wing newspapers reached almost 50 per cent of the total daily readership. By 1947 L'Humanité was the largest selling daily newspaper in France (Bellenger et al. 1975: 301, 357).

Despite the success of their own publications, the Communist and Socialist parties still called for the introduction of the public service model within newspaper publishing. Just before liberation, the Resistance's clandestine newspapers had issued a programme for the post-war reconstruction of the mass media in France. Inspired by Blum, they had called for the nationalisation of all mass-circulation newspapers and radio stations. For them, the independence of the mass media from the 'money powers' could only be guaranteed through state ownership. Alongside state-led educational and cultural activities, the nationalisation of the media would help to defend the democratic republic against its internal enemies (Bellenger et al. 1975: 175).

In contrast, the victorious Resistance coalition initially simply restored the 'republican legality' of the pre-war period. Although military censorship was still in force, the Girondin model protected the Resistance newspapers from the government assuming direct control over their content (Bellenger et al. 1975: 183–4). Furthermore, the provisions of the 1881 press law were strengthened by the adoption of a new Declaration of the Rights of Citizens as a preamble to the first constitution of the Fourth Republic. In article 14, the 1946 Declaration promised that:

> All men are free to speak, to write, to print, to publish; they are able, by means of the press, or any other means, to express, distribute and defend all opinions up to the point where they do not abuse this right, notably by violating the liberties guaranteed by the present declaration [of the Rights of Citizens] or by undermining the reputation of others.
>
> No expression of opinion can be enforced. (Jaume 1989: 328)

However, there was no Girondin media freedom for the opponents of the democratic republic. Following liberation, many Vichy publishers and journalists were executed or imprisoned as traitors (Bellenger et al. 1975: 192–3, 322–5). In a law of 1946, this purge was completed by the transfer of ownership of the assets of the collaborationist publications to the Société Nationale des Entreprises de Presse (SNEP), a nationalised company run by representatives of the state, the Resistance newspapers and the print-workers' union (Gouin 1946: 4,095–8). As in Blum's proposals, the SNEP provided the use of printing presses and other services to newspapers owned by political parties or Resistance groups. At the same time, the Resistance government also helped the 'new press' with financial subsidies, including tax exemptions, cheap railway distribution, low-priced telephone calls and reduced postal charges. In the aftermath of the defeat of fascism, Blum's public service model had been partly realised within French newspaper publishing (Bellenger et al. 1975: 403–5; Queuille 1944).

This model of media freedom was also applied to the Havas press and advertising agency. Because its private owners had been hostile to the parties of the Left, the Resistance government turned the press agency part of Havas into the state-owned Agence France-Presse (AFP). After its nationalisation, AFP was given the legal duty to provide an independent and impartial news agency service to all national and local newspapers. By working for all political tendencies without favour, AFP embodied the principles of the public service state (de Gaulle 1944; Bellenger et al. 1975: 230–4, 386–91):

> The Agence France-Presse is not able in any circumstances to take account of influences or considerations of a nature to compromise the accuracy or objectivity of the news; it is not able under any circumstances to pass under the influence in law or fact of any political, ideological or economic group. (Coty 1957: 582)

Yet the implementation of the public service model never extended to the nationalisation of all newspapers owned by joint-stock companies. Immediately after liberation, some Resistance groups did call for the ownership of newspapers to be restricted to political parties, voluntary organisations or workers' co-operatives (Bellenger et al. 1975: 221–2). But, in practice, only the publications of collaborators were expropriated and the worst abuses of the newspapers under the Third Republic outlawed. With the 1881 press law still in force, the 'new press' soon faced fierce competition from the old-style mass-circulation newspapers owned by financial and industrial interests. When the cold war broke out, there was a rapid decline in the popularity of the newspapers of the parties of the Left. Within a decade, the Communist party's morning newspaper lost over half its readership. More disastrously, the daily circulation of the SFIO's newspaper collapsed to only 13,500 (Bellenger et al. 1975: 453).

Although they never completely regained their pre-war influence, four major publications once again dominated newspaper publishing in France. Along with their provincial rivals, these mass-circulation newspapers won readers by muting their political loyalties or concentrating on human interest and crime stories (Bellenger et al. 1975: 355–7, 410–11, 438–55). With the decline in the publications of the parties of the Left and the revival of the mass-circulation papers, the press reforms of the Resistance coalition government had failed. As the cold war intensified, both right-wing politicians and newspapers attacked the SNEP as the final obstacle to the full restoration of the Girondin model. In 1954 their campaign resulted in the printing presses and other assets owned by the SNEP being either returned to their previous owners or sold to the newspapers using them (Coty 1954: 7,555–9). With the privatisation of the

SNEP, the attempt to introduce the public service model of media freedom to newspaper publishing was over.

The Creation of Public Service Broadcasting

When they drew up their proposals for the reorganisation of the post-war media, the Resistance groups proclaimed their determination to prevent 'the businessmen, who arrive in the baggage-train of the armies of liberation, putting their hands on our radio' (Duval 1979: 358). But because of the ease with which transmitters could be detected by the occupation forces, there were no Resistance pirate radio stations waiting to take over the equipment of the Vichy broadcasters. Instead, after liberation, the Resistance groups looked to the new government to organise the reconstruction of radio broadcasting in France. Under the occupation, most commercial radio owners had actively collaborated with the Vichy regime and the Nazi occupation forces. As in newspaper publishing, these treasonable activities justified the new government's expropriation of the commercial radio stations' assets. When the Allied forces landed in France, one of the first decisions of de Gaulle's administration was the revocation of all commercial radio licences (Duval 1979: 359).

During the war, the Resistance groups had relied on the French-language services of the BBC and Radio Moscow for their propaganda against collaboration with Nazi Germany. Following the liberation of Paris, the Resistance government decided to set up its own nationalised radio system. After purging collaborators and employing new staff, the facilities of the state and commercial radio stations were merged into a single nationalised radio broadcasting monopoly, which became Radiodiffusion-Télévision Française (RTF). Inspired by Blum, the Resistance coalition government created the RTF to emancipate radio broadcasting from the control of the financial oligarchy. As with AFP, nationalisation was also designed to secure the equal treatment of all political parties by the news services of the radio stations. Ironically, by placing the commercial stations under tight state control, the Vichy regime and the Nazi occupation forces had prepared the way for the creation of a public service broadcasting monopoly. The expropriation of the commercial stations and the creation of a single state-owned network was the culmination of a long process of concentration within French radio broadcasting.

Like its PTT predecessor, the RTF was provided with a secure source of income from the licence fee. But, in contrast to the pre-war period, the state-owned corporation only provided national radio channels for French listeners. By the early 1950s, the RTF was also transmitting a regular television service for a limited number of viewers. Despite its growing responsibilities, the RTF was never given a clear legal status by any government of the Fourth Republic. Like the AFP, the RTF was nominally run by an independent management council composed of representatives from the government, the National Assembly and its audience. However, real power was wielded by the minister of information, who appointed the director-general of the RTF. From the late 1930s onwards, there had been a withering away of the laws governing the electronic media. While the pre-war commercial radio stations had been controlled by a series of laws, there was little need for detailed legal regulation of a state-owned broadcasting corporation. In place of a juridical relationship, there existed a bureaucratic hierarchy descending from the minister of information down to the lowest employee of the RTF.

Under the Fourth Republic, there were at least ten attempts to create a more pluralist structure for the RTF. These proposals would have granted the nationalised broadcasting corporation BBC-style autonomy from control by central government. However, the different political parties in the National Assembly could never agree on how the director-general and management board of the RTF were to be appointed. On the one hand, each political faction wanted to have as much influence as possible over the management of the state broadcasting corporation. On the other, the parties were not willing to abandon control of the RTF to unaccountable bureaucrats (Bourdon 1988: 10, 17–18).

Crucially, in Blum's public service model citizens expressed their opinions over the airwaves through their elected representatives. Unlike the BBC, the French advocates of public service broadcasting assumed that the RTF could only be accountable to its audience through the political parties' direct control over the corporation. In Belgium and some other west European countries, the sharing of party control over the state broadcasting corporation culminated in the 'pillarisation' of the electronic media. For example, all jobs within Belgian radio and television broadcasting, from top managers to doorkeepers, were divided among the competing political parties in accordance with their level of electoral support. By having their own supporters within the workforce of the electronic media, both government and opposition parties could use their members to express the views of their supporters on the news and current affairs programmes of the nationalised broadcasting corporation. In Belgium, the public service model was successfully turned into a stable institutional structure through this 'pillarisation' of the nationalised broadcasting monopoly (Burgelman 1989).

The Formation of the Mediaklatura

After nationalisation, all RTF workers became members of the civil service. As in other institutions of the public service state, the broadcasters were expected to work for both Left and Right parties. For many RTF employees, this commitment to political impartiality was a continuation of the unity of the Resistance coalition. But idealism was not the only reason for RTF employees' support for the public service state. For the first time, all workers in the electronic media were treated as professionals, with their skills recognised by their social peers. Just as the ENA was educating a new generation of civil servants, the RTF formed its own cadre of loyal administrators and broadcasters. Moreover, because the National Assembly was unable to agree on how to implement the 'pillarisation' of the corporation, the RTF temporarily avoided direct party involvement in the management of its radio and television stations. Alongside the nomenklatura of the public service state, the nationalised broadcasting corporation had produced its own unaccountable bureaucracy: the mediaklatura.

Like other officials of the public service state, the mediaklatura of the RTF was committed to the modernisation of France. With a monopoly over radio and television broadcasting, the RTF centralised all programme-making in the hands of a small number of professionals, almost all of whom were based in Paris. By the end of the 1950s, the productivity of labour within the electronic media allowed just 7,500 RTF workers to provide one national television station and three national radio services to over 40 million French people (Bourdon 1990: 56). Following the Jacobin tradition, the RTF management believed that this electronic media monopoly had to be used for the political and cultural enlightenment of its listeners and viewers, rather than simply to entertain its audience. By the late 1950s, the RTF had become known as the *télé des profs* (television of the teachers). 'Etienne Lalou said that he'd prefer to give a lesson to all of France rather than to a class of thirty children' (Ledos et al. 1986: 50).

But, as in other industrialised countries, there were major cultural differences between the various classes within French society. With the industrialisation of the country, wage-workers were increasingly divided by their different levels of educational achievement (Bourdieu 1984). By filling its schedules with educational and cultural programmes, the RTF primarily served the cultural needs of the most privileged sections of French society. In contrast, the majority of the population would have preferred more mass-entertainment shows for their amusement. In the public service model, however, citizens were only involved in the electronic media through their elected representatives. Because media freedom was a political right, the provision of entertainment programmes was largely ignored in the public service model. Instead, as a means of educating the citizens in republican values, the dissemination of high culture was encouraged by this model of media freedom.

The Collapse of Public Service Broadcasting

By imposing high culture on French audiences, the RTF demonstrated its independence from the wishes of most listeners and viewers. However, as an institution of the public service state, the RTF never won complete autonomy from the political parties. For example, the director-general and other leading officials of the RTF were appointed by the Ministry of Information and the licence fee needed annual approval from the National Assembly (Bourdon 1986: 46). Because of these bureaucratic and financial controls, the nationalised broadcasting corporation's news coverage had to serve the interests of the political parties in power. Each day, officials from the main government ministries met to decide how the current controversial issues would be handled by the news bulletins of the state-owned radio and television channels (de Tarlé 1979: 47).

> As Information Minister ... Mitterrand ... told the National Assembly, '[Radio] makes policy every day and its policy is defence of French national interests.' As the government, he added, represented the popular will, it had every right to oversee what was being broadcast. (MacShane 1982: 48)

When the Resistance coalition was in power, all anti-fascist parties were given airtime on the radio and television stations of the RTF. Yet this sharing of party control never evolved into the formal 'pillarisation' of the nationalised broadcasting corporation. With the outbreak of the cold war, the consensus between the political parties soon broke down. On the Left, the Communists attacked France's involvement in the NATO alliance as threatening the Soviet Union. On the Right, the Gaullists opposed the loss of national sovereignty under the new treaties. But because of French dependence on American economic aid, the Gaullists and Communists failed to prevent the incorporation of France within the US sphere of influence. Therefore, from 1947 onwards, French governments could only be formed by political parties loyal to the American alliance, who became known as the Third Force (van der Pijl 1984: 138–62).

With the break-down of agreement between the political parties, the public service model of media freedom rapidly declined within the RTF. After Stalin's take-over of eastern Europe, all Communists were excluded from the RTF's programmes. Once again, there were no political rights for the enemies of the democratic republic. Similarly, when he campaigned for a new constitution, de Gaulle was also banned from the airwaves in 1949 (Rioux 1989: 158). With a monopoly on political power, the Third Force political parties shared control over the RTF by rotating the ministry of information among the different coalition partners. Yet in the 1951 elections almost half the electorate had voted for either Communist or Gaullist candidates (Rioux 1989: 165). Under the Third Force governments, the supporters of these two parties were not allowed to express their opinions in the electronic media through their elected representatives. With the end of the consensus between the different political parties of the Resistance, the public service model in the French electronic media was severely weakened.

This decline of the public service model was accelerated by the internal and external crises faced by the SFIO. With the Communists and Gaullists excluded from power, the Third Force governments had to be constructed around an alliance of the SFIO with conservative parties. However, the Socialists had already lost their position as the largest workers' party to the Communists. With American money, the Socialists partly rebuilt their party and union organisations, but never regained their electoral majority among working-class voters (Johnson 1981: 33–4). At the beginning of the cold war, the SFIO had joined the Third Force coalition government in order to obtain American economic aid for its supporters. But instead of carrying out the 'exercise of power', the SFIO leaders rapidly abandoned their remaining radical policies to stay in office. By the time the Fourth Republic ended in 1958, the Socialists had not only organised the suppression of strikes, they had also supported the brutal war against the Algerian nationalists. Because of this political opportunism, the SFIO failed to recruit new supporters and steadily lost votes to other political parties. When the Fourth Republic was finally overthrown by de Gaulle, the Socialist party had almost collapsed as a political organisation (Johnson 1981: 35–6, 42; Rioux 1989: 159–61, 255).

In the last years of the Fourth Republic, the degeneration of the SFIO led to the party's abandonment of the public service model. In 1956, despite their anti-colonial policies, the Socialists decided to continue the French army's occupation of Algeria. As a wartime emergency measure, censorship of the mass media was imposed in both Algeria and France. During the crisis, editions of major newspapers were seized, anti-imperialist publications were closed down, journalists were imprisoned and the director-general of the RTF was sacked for opposing the repressive policies of the Socialist prime minister. The mass media were prevented not just from reporting military operations, but also from criticising the war. Inspired by the Resistance, left-wing activists set up clandestine publications to distribute uncensored information about the war, especially reports on French army atrocities against the Algerian population (Bellenger et al. 1975: 247–8, 449–500). By the time of the demise of the Fourth Republic, the Socialists had completely abandoned the aims of the 'exercise of power'. Instead of using state power to protect political rights, the SFIO was restricting the fundamental liberties of all citizens in order to hang onto office. When de Gaulle came to power, the public service model had already been destroyed by its Socialist originators. As president of a new republic, de Gaulle was now free to impose his own model of media freedom.

THE MENTAL MAP OF THE PUBLIC SERVICE MODEL

Figure 4.1 shows the psychogeography of the public service model of media freedom. This is an ahistorical and abstract model of the theories of Léon Blum, as well as the practice of the Popular Front, Resistance coalition and Fourth Republic governments. Media freedom was exercised in a society composed of the democratic republic and atomised individuals with political rights. Because they did not own printing presses or transmitters as private property, citizens expressed their opinions by participating in political decision-making through internal party debates and voting in general elections. By nationalising private property, the democratic republic became the public service state, which created the social and economic conditions for the exercise of the political rights of citizens. In the mass media, the nationalisation of newspapers, radio and television stations guaranteed media freedom for all political parties. The different political parties' access to the mass media was decided according to the number of deputies they had in the National Assembly. The opinions of the citizens were expressed in the mass media by their elected representatives from the competing parties. *Since they had the vote, citizens controlled the content of the mass media by voting in elections for candidates from the competing political parties.*

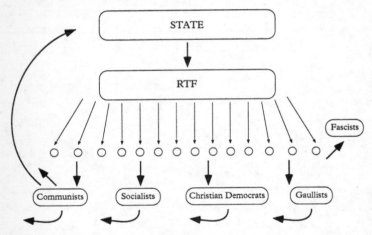

Individuals as Citizens of Multi-Party State

Figure 4.1: The Mental Map of the Public Service Model

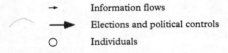

→   Information flows

➡   Elections and political controls

○   Individuals

5

The Liberty of the President

The Fifth Republic

In 1958 a revolt by the army in Algeria led to the collapse of the
Fourth Republic. The weak Third Force governments had been
unable to accept the end of French rule over Algeria. Faced with
the threat of a military dictatorship, the ruling parties abdicated
their political power to General Charles de Gaulle. Since the 1940s,
he had been campaigning for the creation of a strong executive. In
his new constitution, de Gaulle separated the powers of the executive
and the legislature. Under this 'democratic dualism', the president
appointed the government and dominated the National Assembly.
In all previous republican constitutions, the 'general will' of the
citizens had been created by the deliberations of their representatives in the National Assembly. By contrast, under the constitution
of the Fifth Republic the 'general will' of the citizens was expressed
by both an elected legislature and an elected executive (Avril 1987:
28–32, 64–6).

More importantly, the new constitutional settlement immediately
ended the fractured party system of the Fourth Republic. Under
his leadership, the General united the various right-wing republican
parties into a single organisation, which won a large majority of seats
in the National Assembly. By allowing voters to elect the head of
state, de Gaulle also tried to create an intimate link between the
president and the citizens. Influenced by both Jacobinism and
Christian Democracy, the General claimed that the Fifth Republic
would defend the interests of all citizens against the demands of
particular groups or individuals. For his followers, the charismatic
leadership of de Gaulle guaranteed the unity of the nation-people
against external and internal dangers, such as economic competition from the US or a political take-over by the Communist party
(Johnson 1981: 73–82).

'The Thirty Glorious Years'

Under its 'republican monarch', the French state could now be more
decisive in its economic policies. Following the collapse of France's
empire and the formation of the European Economic Community

in the 1950s, there was no longer any colonial or domestic protectionism for French companies (Kuisel 1987: 21). Because of their
small size and technological backwardness, these enterprises encountered great difficulties in competing successfully with more advanced
foreign corporations, especially from the US. Ironically, the international free-trade system imposed by the Americans led to the
adoption of interventionist economic policies in France. In the
General's view, the state had to organise the economy to prevent
French national sovereignty from being eroded by American
hegemony over the world market (Choisel 1987: 87): 'we will be
overtaken and dominated, for the first time in our history, by a more
advanced civilisation' (Servan-Schreiber 1968: 65).

Under de Gaulle, the state actively promoted the economic
modernisation of French society. In all forms of Fordism, the state
had to regulate the simultaneous growth in production and consumption. But in France the interlocking of public and private
initiatives was taken much further. In response to the 'American
challenge', the General was determined to carry through the social
transformation of French society. As leader of the 'industrial
productive bloc', the French state had to use its fiscal and financial
resources to develop its own domestic Fordist corporations: 'The
danger is not in what the Americans can do, but what the Europeans
cannot do' (Servan-Schreiber 1968: 54).

During de Gaulle's presidency, French society was in the middle
of the '30 glorious years' of rapid industrialisation from 1945 to
1975. Once the state was able to co-ordinate the economy, Fordism
created a virtuous circle of growth within the French economy. In
turn, this process of industrialisation completely transformed
French society. In 1945 France was still a mainly rural society made
up of small property-owners. But by the end of the period of rapid
industrialisation, the overwhelming majority of French people
lived in urban areas and were employees of public or private corporations. Despite the unequal distribution of wealth, these new
wage-workers enjoyed a steadily increasing standard of living
(Mendras and Cole 1991: 6–21). During the 1920s and 1930s, the
new consumer culture of Fordism had been pioneered by the
radio-set manufacturing industry. With rising wages, workers also
started buying other consumer goods produced by the industrial
corporations, such as refrigerators, record players, vacuum cleaners
and washing machines. By the late 1950s, the ultimate American
consumer commodity became available to the French people: the
television set.

As with the radio receiver, the ownership of television sets spread
rapidly among the population. In 1957 only 6 per cent of homes
owned a television. But by 1968 this had risen to over 60 per cent
of households (Bourdon 1990: 11). As the ownership of sets spread,

watching television programmes quickly became the most popular leisure activity of the French population. Although they could not escape from the need to work, people were now able to buy consumer goods for their leisure time. In the 1960s, above all other commodities, this newly acquired affluence of French workers was symbolised by the purchase of a television set.

The Gaullist RTF

After he came to power, de Gaulle rapidly asserted his leadership of France by placing his own supporters in charge of all major institutions. At the same time, his new administration began lifting the censorship imposed on newspaper publishing by the last governments of the Fourth Republic. After independence was granted to Algeria, the newspapers were once again regulated by the Girondin model (Bellenger et al. 1976: 172–5, 182–3). For the Gaullist government, the renewed independence of the newspapers was a useful justification for asserting control over the more influential electronic media. Echoing the arguments of the Left, the Gaullists claimed that the national and local newspapers merely represented partial interests. According to Peyrefitte, a Gaullist minister of information, this imbalance could only be corrected by the dissemination of the government's views through the electronic media (Bourdon 1990: 106). The creation of a stable government had ended the nationalised broadcasting corporation's limited independence from the politicians. As soon as he came to power, de Gaulle appointed his supporters as managers and news journalists at the RTF. In contrast with its public service past, the corporation could now only express the viewpoints of the executive. Invoking the Jacobin model, a Gaullist manager of the RTF explained: 'A [RTF] journalist must be a French journalist before being an objective journalist' (Bourdon 1990: 83).

Under the Fifth Republic, political pluralism across all forms of mass media was to be created by the domination of the RTF by the Gaullist party. Controlling both executive and legislature, the new government exerted its power over the RTF by appointing its top management and deciding the level of the licence fee. This subordination of the RTF to the Gaullist party was institutionalised through the formation of the Service de Laisons Interministérielles pour l'Information (SLII), which supervised the contents of news programmes on the nationalised radio and television stations. In particular, this committee ensured that the opinions of the opposition parties were almost completely excluded from the RTF's news and current affairs programmes. At the same time, the SLII also encouraged the electronic media to promote the achievements of the new republic (Bourdon 1990: 100–3). Despite the passing of various laws and decrees, there was still no real juridical relationship between the RTF and the government. On the contrary, in a bureaucratic hierarchy, de Gaulle controlled the nationalised radio and television stations through a chain of command running from the minister of information through the SLII to the management of the RTF. The General even personally supervised any programmes featuring himself (de Gaulle 1987: 67).

Although he abandoned the political pluralism of the public service model, de Gaulle continued the pedagogical mission of the RTF. As a Jacobin, de Gaulle embraced the potential for cultural centralisation inherent within the Fordist media. For example, because it helped to create a common national identity for all French citizens, he welcomed the decline in local dialects caused by the dominance of Parisian French on the state-owned radio and television stations (Dreyfus 1983: 32). At the same time, the General also wanted the RTF's programmes to reduce the cultural differences among its audience. The RTF broadcast only a limited number of popular entertainment shows and instead concentrated on its high-culture programmes. According to Andre Malraux, the minister of culture, the promotion of classical music and theatre by state-run institutions would not only restore national pride, it would also unite the French people in a common appreciation of traditional culture (Bourdon 1990: 130–3; Forbes 1987: 133).

The Périphériques

Although commercial broadcasting was banned within its borders, the government was powerless to stop radio stations transmitting French-language programmes from outside France. After the Second World War, Radio Luxembourg and other commercial radio stations started broadcasting, from neighbouring countries, services aimed at French audiences. Because they were sited on the borders of France, these stations were called the *périphériques*, or peripherals (Duval 1979: 365–98). During the Algerian war, the RTF's news service rapidly lost credibility among French listeners. As they were independent of the French government, the news bulletins of the *périphériques* quickly attracted this disgruntled audience. Soon almost three-quarters of the French population were listening to the news programmes of the commercial radio stations in preference to the service provided by the RTF. By 1958, even government ministers were tuning into the *périphériques* (Bourdon 1990: 81, 98).

When it came to power, the Gaullist government wanted to remove any competition for the RTF news programmes by closing down the *périphériques*. But because these stations were based in foreign countries, this policy was unrealisable in practice. Instead, the government attempted to take over the commercial radio stations by purchasing their shares. Under the Fourth Republic, SOFIRAD, a nationalised radio holding company, had already acquired a majority stake in two of the *périphériques*. After he became president, de Gaulle continued this policy by purchasing shares in the remaining stations (Duval 1979: 380–3). Although a take-over of Radio Luxembourg by SOFIRAD was initially blocked by the Grand Duchy, the French government was eventually allowed to become a major shareholder through Havas, the nationalised advertising agency (Defrance 1979: 39). By purchasing their shares, the Gaullist government hoped to influence the news and current affairs programmes of the *périphériques*. However, because they were selling commercials, these stations needed high ratings for their advertisers. In contrast with the 1930s, the funding of broadcasting by advertising now protected the independence of news bulletins from control by right-wing politicians. Ironically, in the early 1960s the only radio stations implementing the public service model within the French electronic media were commercial operations.

'The Government in the Dining Room'

On 18 June 1940, one week after Pétain had announced over the airwaves the armistice with the Nazi invaders, de Gaulle made his first speech on the BBC external service calling for the continuation of resistance to German occupation. Because of the popularity of his broadcasts, de Gaulle was soon transformed from an obscure army general into the undisputed leader of the Resistance movement. For the next four years, de Gaulle and Pétain competed over the airwaves to win the loyalty of the French people (Rossignol 1991: 23, 302). Even before the Second World War, French political leaders had used radio broadcasting to make personal appeals to the population. Similarly, under the Fourth Republic Prime Minister Mendès-France had given weekly radio talks explaining his government's policies (Rioux 1989: 227–30). With the creation of the Fifth Republic, the speeches and activities of the new president became the main items on most news bulletins. When he appeared on television, de Gaulle did not use notes for his speeches and refused to wear his glasses. On screen, he was determined to portray an image of authority and confidence (Bourdon 1990: 21; de Gaulle 1970: 301–2).

During a coup attempt in 1961, de Gaulle demonstrated the power of his personal appearances over the airwaves. After one speech by the General on radio, soldiers refused to follow the orders of their mutinous officers and the putsch by the French army

in Algeria collapsed (Guichard 1985: 151). Under the Fifth
Republic, everyday politics were also centred around the president's
radio and television appearances. Instead of new policies being
presented to the National Assembly, most important initiatives were
announced in live press conferences from the presidential palace
(de Gaulle 1970: 304). Traditionally, the central government had
communicated its policies to local communities through the
members of the National Assembly. In contrast, de Gaulle believed
that the electronic media could now be used to speak directly to
individual citizens in their own homes: 'By sound and by image,
I am close to the nation' (de Gaulle 1970: 304).

Because it created an intimate relationship between the president
and the citizens, de Gaulle believed that the television set had become
'the government in the dining room' (R. Thomas 1976: 16). Under
the Fifth Republic, the 'general will' of all citizens was personified
by the executive president. Therefore, in de Gaulle's version of the
Jacobin model, the collective labour of the RTF workers had to
be concentrated on the dissemination of the 'sound and image' of
the General. The media freedom of all citizens was now transformed
into the personal appearances of one man: de Gaulle. As the
elected representative of all citizens, the president used these radio
and television appearances to explain the policies of his government
to the voters. 'On each occasion, I aimed at showing where we are
collectively before the problem of the moment, at indicating how
we are able and must solve it, to encourage our will and our
confidence to succeed' (de Gaulle 1970: 302).

Because of the centralisation of broadcasting, almost all citizens
could simultaneously hear or watch the same speech by the president
on the RTF stations. When they were brought together as a
homogenous radio and television audience, de Gaulle believed
that the atomised members of civil society had been united into
the single nation-people. As in an agora, all citizens could now
personally hear and see their chosen leader. Yet although this
personal relationship was seen as an electronic agora, citizens could
not really participate in two-way communications with their elected
leader. On the contrary, as listeners or viewers, they could only
passively listen or watch the speeches of the president. Under the
General's control, the electronic media could only be a one-way
flow of communications from the elected leader. As this version
was developed by de Gaulle, this definition is known as *the Gaullist
model of media freedom.*

The ORTF: the High Point of the
Gaullist Model

With increasing ownership of television sets, the nationalised broadcasting corporation enjoyed a rapid increase in its licence fee

revenue (Bourdon 1990: 11–12). Because of this expansion, de Gaulle decided that there should be a reorganisation of the corporation's management. Therefore, in the 1964 broadcasting law, the RTF was transformed into the Office de Radiodiffusion-Télévision Française (ORTF). Under this legislation, the nationalised broadcasting corporation remained completely subordinated to the Gaullist party. The minister could still appoint party loyalists and civil servants to be managers or members of the ORTF management board. At the same time, the ministry of information directly controlled the corporation's expenditure (de Gaulle 1964: 5,636–7).

Under the 1964 law, all 'principal tendencies of thought and great currents of opinion' were promised access to the radio and television programmes of the ORTF stations (de Gaulle 1964: 5,637). However, this promise to implement the public service model within the electronic media was completely hypocritical. Like other nationalised industries, the ORTF was a servant of the Gaullist party-state (de Tarlé 1979: 49–50). As with many other institutions of the Fifth Republic, the loyalty of the ORTF was tested by the May 1968 Revolution (see pp. 95–6). When the ORTF workers went on strike, the government was forced to use Gaullist sympathisers among the management to produce a minimal news service (Bourdon 1990: 260–1). Under Gaullist control, the ORTF censored news favourable to the strikers and only broadcast information approved by the government. As a contemporary wall poster put it: 'the police speak to you every night at 8 o'clock [on the evening news bulletin]' (Mésa 1984: 88). By retaining control over the ORTF, de Gaulle was able to defeat the insurrection through one crucial speech over the electronic media. Rallying his supporters against the threat of a Communist seizure of power, de Gaulle was able to go on to win a landslide victory in the subsequent legislative elections (Joffrin 1988: 292–300).

With the May 1968 Revolution defeated, the Gaullist government quickly purged the strike leaders from the staff of the ORTF (Bourdon 1990: 263–6). Yet despite this further tightening of political controls over the ORTF, the long-term survival of the Gaullist model within the electronic media was undermined by a pragmatic decision made by the General in the same year. Wishing to avoid large rises in the licence fee, de Gaulle permitted the sale of brand-label commercials on the ORTF television stations. Within three years, the ORTF was selling twelve minutes of advertising every day and receiving extensive sponsorship for its most popular game shows (Bourdon 1990: 276–7).

In the long term, this diversification of the funding of the ORTF weakened the political control of the Gaullist party over the electronic media. After 1968, the ORTF had to provide contrasting styles of programmes to satisfy both types of funders. For the

Gaullists, the principal task of the state broadcasting system was the promotion of the political views and cultural policies of the government. In contrast, the advertisers simply preferred neutral news bulletins and lots of entertainment shows to attract large audiences for their commercials. Despite the purges, the creation of an independent source of revenue increased the ORTF's political autonomy from the ruling party.

The Exclusion of the Left

Under the Fifth Republic, the strength of the Gaullist party was paralleled by the marginalisation of the parties of the Left. After the failure of its Algerian policies, the SFIO went into a rapid decline and was soon reduced to a few dozen deputies and control over a handful of local councils. In contrast, the Communist party became an essential part of de Gaulle's constitutional settlement. On the one hand, the bitter rivalry between the Communists and Socialists split the left-wing electorate into two. On the other, fear of the Communists rallied the right-wing electorate behind the Gaullists. As a consequence, the parties of the Right were able to remain in power for over 20 years (Johnson 1981: 53–4, 136).

During the Nazi occupation of France, the Communist party had led the armed resistance to the invaders and collaborators. As the 'party of the rifles', the Communists emerged from the war as the largest left-wing party in the country, with 28 per cent of the vote in the 1946 general election (Johnson 1981: 137–8). After the outbreak of the cold war, the Communist party was forced into permanent opposition. Because of its minority support, the party could neither carry out a revolutionary transformation of French society nor deliver reforms to its voters. Instead it became a 'tribune party', which articulated the hostility of its supporters to the existing order (Johnson 1981: 25–6, 142–50). When de Gaulle came to power, this role of permanent opposition was consolidated within the new constitutional settlement, especially after the collapse of the SFIO. While the Gaullists dominated the government and major industries, the Communists controlled the parliamentary opposition and the trade union movement.

In permanent opposition, the Communist party created its own 'counter-society' inside France. Using its professional activists, the party leadership built a network of unions, societies, publications, festivals and other activities to sustain its supporters. Excluded from French society, many workers transferred their loyalties to the self-proclaimed champion of the international proletariat: the USSR. Alongside its social and union organisations, the Communist party's most important method of recruiting new supporters was the sale of its newspapers and other publications. As well as promoting its ideas and policies, the revenue from these publications provided a large part of the funding of the Communist party. Under the Gaullist model, the division of the political system between the two main parties was reflected in the unequal distribution of influence within the mass media. While the Gaullists dominated the ORTF, the Communist party was allowed to publish its own newspapers for members of its 'counter-society' (Kriegel 1985: 143–7, 187–9, 203–6).

The Left and the ORTF

Ever since the 1920s, the Communists and Socialists had been opposed to the private ownership of the electronic media. Above all, they believed that the nationalisation of broadcasting was needed to ensure left-wing opinions had access to the airwaves. Under the Fifth Republic, however, the state-owned electronic media systematically excluded the two Left parties from the airwaves. Not surprisingly, both Communists and Socialists were disorientated by the Gaullist party's implementation of a version of the Jacobin model. Many left-wing ORTF workers were willing to accept the Gaullists' control of the corporation as a lesser evil than private ownership. In particular, both types of Jacobins could agree that the principal task of the ORTF was to educate the French people in high culture (Bourdon 1990: 118–22, 286–7).

The Communist party leadership could never clearly decide which other version of the Jacobin model should replace the Gaullist model within the mass media. At different times, the Communists actively supported both totalitarian and public service models. For instance, the party leadership tolerated the rehabilitation of the totalitarian model by its leading theoretician: Louis Althusser. Influenced by the Chinese Cultural Revolution, Althusser was convinced that the principal obstacle to a Communist revolution in France was the ideological domination of the working class by the bourgeoisie. According to his analysis, the workers were culturally controlled by a number of different institutions, which he called ideological state apparatuses (ISAs). Crucially, alongside the educational, political and legal system, the most important source of ideological domination was: 'the communications ISA (press, radio and television)' (Althusser 1971: 137).

Inspired by Mao Zedong, Althusser called for the destruction of the bourgeoisie's ISAs. In his view, the workers could only be rescued from their ideological errors by submitting to the leadership of the French Communist party, which kept faith with the revo-

lutionary science of Leninism. By reintroducing the totalitarian model
to the French media, the Communist party would reeducate the
workers in revolutionary ideas through its own 'communications
ISA' (Althusser 1971: 155–9). For Althusser, the nationalised
broadcasting monopoly was the only possible structure for the
electronic media. The ORTF was inevitably an ideological *state*
apparatus. According to this analysis, a Communist management
of the ORTF would simply have to change the political content of
the news bulletins and other programmes. Never questioning the
hierarchical management structure of the nationalised broadcasting corporation, Althusser only attacked de Gaulle for placing the
ORTF at the service of the wrong party: 'no class can hold State
power over a long period without at the same time exercising its
hegemony over and in the Ideological State Apparatuses' (Althusser
1971: 139).

Although Althusser's revival of the totalitarian model was popular
among radical students and academics, his approach was never
supported by the Communist trade unionists working for the
ORTF. Instead, along with their Socialist colleagues, they
campaigned for the implementation of the public service model.
Above all, the unions wanted to end direct Gaullist party control
over the ORTF's news and current affairs programmes (Bourdon
1990: 49–50, 252–3). During the May 1968 Revolution, the ORTF
strikers called for the introduction of 'impartial and truthful news
broadcasts' which would present the views of all political parties
(Fisera 1978: 305–7).

After the defeat of the strike at the ORTF, the campaign for the
reintroduction of the public service model to the electronic media
was continued by both Communists and Socialists. When the two
parties formed an electoral alliance in 1972, their Common
Programme contained a media policy centred around the defence
of all French citizens' 'right to information'. Inspired by Blum, the
Communist and Socialist parties defended the right of all citizens
to a diversity of political opinions within the mass media. Rejecting
private ownership, the two parties of the Left called for the creation
of a 'true public service' within the electronic media. Unlike the
biased Gaullist ORTF, a reformed nationalised broadcasting corporation would present 'the expression and confrontation of currents
of opinion and thought' within its news and current affairs
programmes (Parti Communiste et Parti Socialiste 1972: 163–6).
Yet, at the same time, the Communists and Socialists wanted to
purge the Gaullist party loyalists from the ORTF. Ironically, despite
their advocacy of the public service model, the Gaullist model had
also been implicitly accepted by the parties of the Left.

The Slow Revival of Public Service Broadcasting

Under the Gaullist model, the opposition parties were prevented from expressing their views on ORTF news and current affairs programmes. Even at election times, the Gaullist government restricted the amount of airtime available to its political opponents. During a referendum in 1962, while each opposition leader was given only two minutes on television to present their views, the Gaullist prime minister received over 20 minutes for his presentation (Cotta 1986: 140). When he was attacked for this censorship, the minister of information replied that 'access to radio and television broadcasting [for the opposition parties] isn't a right, but a favour' (Bourdon 1990: 109). Ironically, in order to attract left-wing listeners, the commercial radio stations preserved elements of the public service model within their programmes. For example, during the same referendum, one *périphérique* ran a series of 'duels' between two leading politicians from the contending political parties. In these confrontations, the representative of the Gaullist party was forced to debate on equal terms with the spokesperson of the opposition parties (Bourdon 1990: 109).

During the debates on the 1964 law, the parties of the Left renewed their demand for more coverage on the news bulletins of the nationalised broadcasting corporation. Although the Gaullists rejected the reintroduction of the public service model, pressure from the opposition forced one major concession from the government: an all-party committee of the National Assembly to monitor the ORTF (de Gaulle 1964: 5,637). Using this opportunity, left-wing members of the committee started negotiations with the ORTF management over the coverage of presidential and legislative elections. After a series of meetings, the ORTF management agreed to allow more appearances by opposition parties over the airwaves at election times. Despite the subordination of the ORTF to the Gaullist party, the Assembly committee had successfully revived the public service model for presidential and legislative elections (Bourdon 1986: 47–8).

During the 1965 presidential elections, each candidate received 2 hours of airtime on the ORTF's radio and television stations. Because of his appearances on the ORTF's radio and television stations, Mitterrand, the candidate of the Socialist and Communist parties, was able to win enough votes to force de Gaulle to a second ballot. Shocked by this result, the government quickly reimposed the Gaullist model on the nationalised broadcasting corporation. During the second round of the contest, the news and current affairs programmes actively supported de Gaulle's campaign for reelection. With this help from the ORTF, de Gaulle defeated Mitterrand in the second round and was reelected president (Bourdon 1990:

109–11). But during the May 1968 Revolution, Gaullist control over the electronic media was severely shaken by the ORTF strike. In response to this crisis, the government introduced some minor reforms to the ORTF, such as the abolition of the SLII and the appointment of new members to its management board. More importantly, this episode had severely discredited the reputation of the ORTF among the French people. As had been the case during the Algerian war, the audiences of the *périphériques* grew rapidly during the period of unrest. Ironically, with their public service style, these commercial radio stations had covered the left-wing revolution more objectively than the nationalised broadcasting corporation had (Bourdon 1990: 265–9). The dramatic fall in the ORTF's audience threatened the continued existence of the Gaullist model. Without viewers and listeners, the president could no longer use the ORTF to unite the atomised citizens of the nation-people around his leadership.

Following his defeat in a referendum in 1969, de Gaulle resigned from office. After the subsequent elections, Georges Pompidou became the new president. As his first prime minister, Pompidou appointed Jacques Chaban-Delmas, who came from the reformist wing of the Gaullist party. Under the slogan of 'participation', Chaban-Delmas initiated a series of political and social reforms to defuse the threat of further social unrest. By overcoming the 'cultural blockage' of the class struggle, the prime minister hoped to unite the French people behind the common goal of prosperity (Lipietz 1984: 69–70). As a central part of these reforms, the new prime minister decided to reintroduce the public service model to the electronic media. As a first step, Chaban-Delmas abolished the Ministry of Information and handed over day-to-day control to the ORTF's own management. Inspired by the 'pillarisation' of other west European public broadcasting corporations, the prime minister also decided that the news programmes of the two ORTF television stations had to reflect the views of both government and opposition parties (Bourdon 1990: 280–1).

In November 1969 the ORTF management was permitted to codify the revival of the public service model. In an internal memo, it was announced that all news bulletins would now have to follow new regulations covering the appearances of politicians on the state-owned radio and television stations. By careful monitoring, the government, the ruling party and the opposition would each be granted one-third of the total airtime allocated to political discussions. Under this 'rule of three-thirds', the ORTF ensured that the government could announce its decisions, its supporters could defend its policies and the parties of the Left could put forward their own proposals. Although the opposition parties still could not directly influence the management of the ORTF, Chaban-Delmas' reforms did restore the public service model within the news and current affairs programmes of the nationalised broadcasting corporation. Under Chaban-Delmas, the ORTF gave access to the airwaves to all political parties represented in the National Assembly (*Le Monde* 1969: 19).

The Reassertion of the Gaullist Model

Under the General, the Gaullist party had won the votes of people from all social classes. But with the disappearance of its charismatic leader, the party began to lose its working-class supporters to the parties of the Left. Chaban-Delmas was appointed prime minister by Pompidou to win back the votes of these defectors. However, his reformist policies were bitterly opposed by the conservatives inside the ruling party. Above all, they hated the abandonment of the Gaullist model within the electronic media. In an argument with Chaban-Delmas, one conservative Gaullist claimed: 'You have given the television to our worst enemies' (Avril 1987: 138). Soon the issue of the implementation of the public service model became a major dispute between Chaban-Delmas and Pompidou. Once his fear of revolution had abated, the president became increasingly dissatisfied with the reformist policies of his prime minister. In particular, Pompidou was convinced that the weakening of the Gaullist model within the ORTF had lost votes for his party. After sacking his prime minister in 1972, the president rapidly reasserted his control over the ORTF. By openly ending the public service model at the corporation, the conservatives demonstrated their victory over the reformists within the Gaullist party (Gauron 1983: 132–3).

That year, a new law resurrected the Ministry of Information. As in the past, the nationalised broadcasting corporation was directly controlled by a cabinet minister, who was a leading member of the Gaullist party (Pompidou 1972: 6,851). After the 1972 law was passed, the 'rule of three-thirds' was abandoned, 200 left-wing ORTF employees were dismissed and a new president-director-general was appointed. Once again the ORTF was subordinated to the bureaucratic hierarchy of the Gaullist party-state (R. Thomas 1976: 39–46). Like the General, Pompidou claimed to control the nationalised broadcasting corporation on behalf of all French citizens. Back in 1970, Pompidou had already expressed his belief in the Gaullist model within the electronic media:

> To be a journalist at the ORTF is not the same thing as being a journalist elsewhere. The ORTF, whether you like it or not, is the voice of France. It is so considered abroad. It is so considered by the public. (Bourdon 1988: 33)

Giscard's Gaullism

In 1974, after the death of Pompidou, Valery Giscard d'Estaing
was elected president. For the first time, the president of the Fifth
Republic was not a member of the Gaullist party. As part of his
reform programme, Giscard decided to reorganise the nationalised
broadcasting corporation. A law in 1974 abolished the ORTF as
a single institution. In its place, the new president established
seven separate broadcasting companies, which included three
television stations and a radio corporation. With this new law,
Giscard appeared to abandon the Gaullist model within the
electronic media. The Ministry of Information was abolished again
and the new broadcasting companies were granted autonomy in
their day-to-day management (Giscard d'Estaing 1974a: 8,355–6).
Under the 1974 law, the nationalised radio and television stations
were given the duty of guaranteeing regular appearances of 'the main
trends of thought and the major currents of opinion' on radio and
television programmes (Giscard d'Estaing 1974a: 8,355). Access
to the airwaves for all political parties was guaranteed by writing
the 'rule of three-thirds' into the licence agreements of the nationalised radio and television stations. As a legal condition of their
existence, these stations now had to implement the public service
model within their news and current affairs programmes (Giscard
d'Estaing 1974a: 8,356).

But behind these public service regulations, the 1974 law
preserved important elements of the Gaullist model within the
electronic media. Because he was only leader of a small right-wing
group, Giscard needed control over the nationalised radio and
television stations to counter the superior party organisations of his
Socialist and Communist opponents, as well as his Gaullist allies.
Therefore the government retained close control over the level of
the licence fee and the appointment of senior managers of the
state-owned media companies (Giscard d'Estaing 1974a: 8,355–7).
Like his predecessors, Giscard placed his political supporters in every
important position within the electronic media, from the ex-ORTF
companies to SOFIRAD, Havas and the AFP. When he showed
too much independence, the head of one *périphérique* was summarily
sacked by the new president (Ory 1983: 74).

As in the past, the nationalised radio and television stations
promoted the policies of the government and attacked the opinions
of its opponents. For example, when Giscard was accused of
accepting a bribe from an African dictator, the subsequent 'diamonds
affair' was hardly mentioned on the news and current affairs
programmes of the state-owned electronic media (Cotta 1986:
41–2). Once again, control over the electronic media was a prize
of electoral victory. When Giscard was defeated by Mitterrand in

the 1981 presidential elections, the Socialist supporters celebrating their victory in the Place de la Bastille began to chant for the dismissal of Jean-Pierre Elkabbach, who presented the news on the main evening news bulletin (Documents Observateur 1988: 120). As a friend of Giscard, this newsreader personified the continuation of presidential control over the electronic media. For the crowd at the Place de la Bastille, the end of the Gaullist model was a necessary precondition for any fundamental social change in France.

THE MENTAL MAP OF THE GAULLIST MODEL

Figure 5.1 shows the psychogeography of the Gaullist model of media freedom. This is an ahistorical and abstract model of the control over the electronic media exercised under the presidencies of de Gaulle, Pompidou and Giscard d'Estaing. The citizens exercised their right of media freedom by electing an executive president, who expressed their opinions for them over the airwaves. Although the Girondin model was preserved within newspaper publishing, the radio and television stations were run by the nationalised broad-casting corporation. Under the supervision of the elected president, the ORTF simultaneously promoted the views of the ruling party and attacked its enemies. Using the electronic media, the president established an intimate relationship with the citizens by making personal addresses through the nationalised broadcasting channels. By hearing or seeing the speeches of the president, the atomised citizens were united into a single nation-people. *Since they voted in presidential elections, citizens controlled what they heard or saw on the nationalised broadcasting corporation by electing the president.*

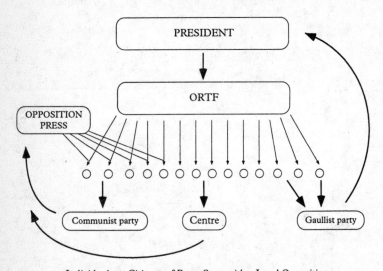

Individuals as Citizens of Party-State with a Legal Opposition

Figure 5.1: The Mental Map of the Gaullist Model

→   Information flows

➤   Elections and political controls

○   Individuals

6

The Liberty of the Co-operative

The Amazement of May

In May 1968 an unexpected revolution took place in France. For
a few weeks, the whole country was convulsed by strikes, occupations and demonstrations. Although it failed to overthrow the Fifth
Republic, the May 1968 Revolution did demonstrate the mutability
of existing society. From this point onwards, many French people
no longer unquestioningly accepted the benefits of economic modernisation. After participating in a social revolution, they now
wanted a greater say in the running of their lives. For the parties
of both Left and Right, this demand for more democracy led to a
major ideological crisis. Ever since 1945, socialists and conservatives had been united over the need for the introduction of Fordism
in France. But in the new hyper-modern world, they were now being
pressurised to introduce some form of participatory democracy.
Crucially, as in the past, both Left and Right believed that this new
type of society would be pioneered by the mass media. Not surprisingly, this led to the emergence of new models of media freedom.

Beyond Modernisation

After 20 years of rapid industrialisation, the everyday lives of the
French people had been fundamentally changed. Instead of being
self-sufficient property-owners, most individuals were now wage-
workers living in a consumer society. Under the Fordist compromise,
ever higher productivity within the workplace was rewarded by
steadily increasing wages. Before May 1968, both right-wing and
left-wing politicians believed that this steady increase in living
standards had removed the main causes of social discontent among
the French people. For example, although they still had to labour,
workers were compensated for their efforts through the provision
of news and entertainment in their own homes by the electronic
media. However, the growth of the consumer society had created
its own social tensions. While their parents saw televisions, fridges
and cars as liberation from poverty, many young people believed
that the desire for consumer goods had trapped society within the
treadmill of wage labour (Gorz: 1970: 256; Lipietz 1984: 68–9).

Although these young radicals were anti-capitalist, there was also a 'generation gap' within the Left. According to the Socialists and Communists, economic modernisation in the short term was needed to create the conditions for social transformation in the long term. However, with the arrival of the consumer society, many young people thought that the programmes of the two left-wing parties were no longer relevant. United by their repudiation of modernisation, young intellectuals and workers started to form their own political movement: the New Left. Before the May 1968 Revolution, the Situationist International (SI) was the most theoretically sophisticated group calling for a revolution against the consumer society. Originally an avant-garde art group, this small band of activists had abandoned painting and film-making for the more demanding task of constructing a new revolutionary programme.

According to the SI, the introduction of Fordism had successfully eliminated the poverty of the past for the majority of the population. Yet, at the same time, workers still exercised almost no control over their own activities in the factories and offices. With the creation of the consumer society, alienation at work had now been extended into people's everyday lives. Under Fordism, the industrial system depended not only on the labour of the workers in factories and offices, but also on the consumption of the commodities produced by the assembly lines. In order to persuade workers to keep on consuming, the large corporations now used the techniques of advertising and marketing to shape the workers' leisure-time. Far from being a place of individual freedoms, the capitalist organisation of civil society ensured that workers were oppressed in both their work and their everyday lives (Debord 1983: theses 25–53).

Using the metaphor of the theatre, the SI described Fordism as the 'society of the spectacle'. As passive consumers, workers could only watch the actions of others without being able to participate themselves. Because of a decline in the extended family and local communities, most individuals were now only connected with each other through the common consumption of the spectacle. Not surprisingly, the Situationists believed that the electronic media were the primary form of the spectacle in modern society. Workers were already spending most of their leisure-time watching their television sets. With its centralised structure, the ORTF only transmitted a one-way flow of communications to its listeners and viewers. For the Situationists, radio and television broadcasting did not simply propagate the false ideas of consumerism and political reformism. More importantly, the electronic media were integrated in the whole daily rhythm of Fordist society. According to a contemporary saying, workers' lives were divided between *métro–boulot–tv–dodo* [underground–job–TV–sleep]. In the SI's analysis, the passive consumption of radio and television programmes was the most dramatic manifestation of the workers' loss of control over all aspects of their lives (Debord 1983: theses 6–53). 'The spectacle is not a collection of images, but a social relation among people, mediated by images' (Debord 1983: thesis 4).

From this analysis of the media, the Situationists deduced that all forms of representation were part of the alienation of life within capitalism. Because they were representative institutions, the parties of the Left were also condemned by the SI for being completely integrated in the 'society of the spectacle'. On the one hand, the Communists' totalitarian model was denounced as the theory of the 'concentrated spectacle'. In the USSR, poverty had confined the control of the mass media to a single bureaucratic hierarchy. On the other hand, the Socialists' public service model was attacked as an apology for the 'diffuse spectacle'. Under Fordism, the abundance of commodities had created a 'false choice' between competing political hierarchies within the mass media. With economic modernisation completed, the Situationists rejected the further need for left-wing political parties, with their long-term strategy for the creation of the socio-economic conditions for a future socialist society. Instead, they advocated an immediate proletarian revolution against the existing order. Above all, this social revolution would end the representation of the workers by the parties and the media (Debord 1983: theses 64–5, 84–124).

After the revolution, the Situationists believed that society would be run by a federation of workers' councils. In place of the totalitarian or public service state, they advocated the introduction of direct democracy in each factory and neighbourhood. As in an agora, the individual workers would participate directly in all decision-making without the mediation of representatives from the political parties. Crucially, the creation of participatory democracy within civil society would lead to the immediate abolition of the state. When workers could directly participate in decision-making, a separate political institution would no longer be needed to mediate the conflicts within civil society (Reisel 1981: 270–82). According to the SI, the rapid abolition of all political and social hierarchies would create 'an immediate rise in the pleasure of living' (Vaneigem 1981: 285).

During the 1789–99 Revolution, Rousseau's admirers had reluctantly accepted that the personal participation of all citizens in a national agora was impossible in a large country, such as France. According to the Situationists, the electronic media now offered a technological solution for overcoming the physical limits on direct democracy. Within the 'society of the spectacle', the centralised radio and television stations only transmitted a one-way flow of communications from the political parties and the mediaklatura to isolated listeners and viewers. But after the revolution, the workers' councils would completely reorganise the electronic media to create two-way communications between the different workers' councils in France and the rest of the world. With the formation of these horizontal links, participatory democracy could then be extended electronically beyond the confines of a general meeting. When participating in decision-making, individual workers would not only attend general meetings of their councils, but would also express their opinions through the electronic media (Vaneigem 1981: 287–8). Using radio and television broadcasting, the Situationists hoped to create a single electronic agora for the entire population. At this point, the contradiction between democracy and participation within the media would have been resolved.

> The abundance of telecommunications techniques – which might at first sight appear as a pretext for the constant control of delegates by specialists – is precisely what makes possible the constant control of delegates by the base, the immediate confirmation, correction or repudiation of their decisions at all levels. (Vaneigem 1981: 288)

The Revolution against the Spectacle

In May 1968, for a brief moment, the revolutionary dreams of the New Left were nearly realised. Although the first protests were started by students, many workers took advantage of the regime's weakness to put forward their own demands in a general strike. Soon, from hospitals to football teams, almost every social institution was convulsed by demands for greater democracy and equality (Joffrin 1988: 193–205). As the old order disintegrated, the New Left revolutionaries called for the implementation of participatory democracy in all political, economic and social institutions. With the abolition of the state and private property, they believed that individuals would be able to transcend the division of social life between politics and economics. 'For the first time since the Commune of 1871, and with a far more promising future, the real individual was absorbing the abstract citizen into his life, his work, his individual relationships' (Viénet 1992: 76).

In May 1968 the electronic media transformed a limited student protest into a general strike. When the police attacked the student demonstrations, live broadcasts from the riots carried on the *périphériques* won support for the protests among the rest of the population. Similarly, when the first protest strike was called, news reports of the subsequent factory occupations encouraged other workers to seize control of their own institutions. While riots or strikes were only directly experienced in one geographical area, the centralisation of the electronic media helped to unite these localised events into a nationwide campaign of protests against the Fifth Republic. Encouraged by the weakness of the Gaullist government, news reporters from the *périphériques* and the ORTF even interviewed the revolutionary leaders on their bulletins. Using the official electronic media, Danny Cohn-Bendit and other New Left activists appealed directly to the French people for their support for the insurrection. In contrast, when de Gaulle made an inept speech over the airwaves, it was widely believed that the Fifth Republic was on the brink of collapse. Far from being the primary form of the 'society of the spectacle', the electronic media were at this moment encouraging their passive audience to participate within the mass movement threatening the whole social system (Joffrin 1988: 114–15, 176–7, 222–9).

As the crisis deepened, the Gaullist government reimposed tight controls over the electronic media, which provoked a strike at the ORTF. Allied with traditional left-wing politicians, the ORTF unions demanded the revival of the public service model within the electronic media (Fisera 1978: 305–7). In contrast, a revolutionary minority within the workforce advocated a more radical restructuring of the ORTF. In imitation of the factory occupation committees, they proposed that members of the ORTF management board should be directly elected by its workers and audience (Fisera 1978: 307). Influenced by the Situationists, Cohn-Bendit and other leaders of the student movement supported this attempt to end the separation of the media professionals from the rest of the population. In their view, the reorganisation of radio and television broadcasting was needed to create two-way communications among the people. Once the electronic agora was formed, then everyone would be able to participate directly in political and social decision-making at both local and national levels (Cohn-Bendit and Cohn-Bendit 1969: 105–6).

During the May 1968 Revolution, these radical proposals on radio and television broadcasting were never implemented. The Gaullist government occupied the ORTF building to stop the strikers from launching their own news service. At the same time, the Situationists were unable to find a suitable transmitter for their proposed pirate radio station based at the occupied Sorbonne (SI 1981: 250). Although the New Left had published its own newspapers and produced many vibrant posters, Danny Cohn-Bendit believed that the fatal mistake of the student revolutionaries was the failure to take over the ORTF. Without their own electronic media, the revolutionaries were unable to speak directly to the population on their own terms (Cohn-Bendit and Cohn-Bendit 1969: 71).

Because he kept control over the ORTF, de Gaulle was able to make a radio speech rallying his supporters against the revolution (Joffrin 1988: 295–7). By dissolving the National Assembly, he managed to move the struggle for power away from the streets and the factories into the electoral arena. Once citizens were able to decide who would form the government, the radicals demanding the dissolution of the state were marginalised. Crucially, in the national election voters were forced to choose between the Gaullists and their only credible opponent: the Communists. From experience, de Gaulle was convinced that the Communists could not unite the divided French Left behind them. In contrast, the General knew that his 'red scare' propaganda would frighten uncommitted voters into supporting his candidates (Johnson 1981: 81–2). In June 1968 the Gaullist party won an overwhelming majority in the elections to the National Assembly. While police repression had provoked a general strike, political democracy had once again created 'order and stability' within the country.

The Birth of the Alternative Media

During the early 1960s, the New Left emerged within the leading industrialised countries. Initially, this movement was mainly involved in solidarity campaigns for Third World national liberation struggles, especially in Vietnam and Latin America. Soon these protests were no longer confined to attacks on American foreign policy. In the industrialised countries, the younger generation resented the cultural and sexual conservatism of their parents. Embracing sexual and chemical hedonism, many young people adopted the bohemian lifestyle of the hippies. By the mid-1960s, this cultural rebellion was increasingly identified with political dissent. Instead of more modernisation, this new generation of revolutionaries wanted to free everyday life from the disciplines of capitalism.

In France, the May 1968 Revolution temporarily transformed this minority of cultural and political revolutionaries into the leaders of an entire generation. Although mass poverty had been eliminated by the advent of Fordism, the student radicals did not protest against continued social inequality alone, but also against the boredom of everyday life. By challenging the Fordist compromise, the students articulated some of the grievances of factory workers from the same generation. Across western Europe, managerial authority was being undermined by absenteeism, wildcat strikes and sabotage (Lipietz 1984: 41). Frightened by unrest in the factories, the Gaullist government was determined to marginalise the political influence of the New Left within France. Excluded from the electoral process, many student radicals soon became involved with the media and other cultural activities. For these New Left activists, the creation of an alternative media was a crucial part of their revolutionary struggle.

Using a Leninist analysis, many members of the New Left believed that the May 1968 Revolution had been defeated by the mass media's ideological domination of the population. Therefore the primary task of the revolutionary movement was to counter the influence of the mass-circulation newspapers and the ORTF by setting up its own alternative media. Because of post-war nationalisation, the New Left was prevented from establishing its own radio and television stations. However, under the protection of the Girondin model, revolutionaries could publish their own newspapers and other publications. Moreover, the costs of publication for small-circulation newspapers had been drastically lowered by the introduction of offset printing and photocopying. During the late 1960s and early 1970s, there was a continual increase in the number of radical publications in France. Deprived of real power, the New Left had to be content to advocate revolutionary ideas in their own alternative newspapers (Boris 1975: 283–6).

At first, most revolutionary newspapers were produced by various small Bolshevik parties. Whether inspired by Mao or by Trotsky, the principal activity of these revolutionary groups was the production of their own newspapers. Following Lenin's example, each party leadership used its publication as a 'transmission belt' to disseminate its revolutionary ideas among the population. Although most Leninist parties had small memberships, a few groups achieved a mass readership for their publications. For example, in 1970 Gauche Prolétarienne's *La Cause du Peuple* sold up to 100,000 copies of each issue (Boris 1975: 220). By creating their own newspaper-parties, the student revolutionaries had successfully renewed the totalitarian model within the French media.

Despite the reemergence of Leninism, most supporters of the New Left were more influenced by their brief experience of popular participation during the May 1968 Revolution. Adopting the slogan of self-management, these young revolutionaries called for direct democracy in all workplaces and social institutions. Above all, New Left activists wanted to apply the principles of self-management within their own revolutionary organisations. By adopting participatory structures, these radicals hoped to prefigure the institutions of the future society. In the US, the American New Left had already begun to create a variety of autonomous social movements, which defended the interests of women, lesbians and gays, ethnic minorities and other communities. In contrast with the Leninist tradition, these groups encouraged participatory democracy within their internal structures. The American New Left activists believed that the new social movements transcended the separation of politics from civil society. By directly participating in decision-making within these movements, individuals would no longer need the state and political parties to mediate the divisions within civil society (Katsiaficas 1987: 204–5).

In the US, these participatory structures were also applied to the emerging alternative media projects. Using cheap offset printing techniques and voluntary labour, radicals had set up underground newspapers to cover events censored by the mainstream media, such as anti-Vietnam war protests, new social movements and the hippie culture. Instead of advocating the policies of a particular sect, these newspapers provided 'counter-information' about the activities of all sections of the New Left. Although some were run by hippie entrepreneurs, many alternative newspapers were organised as co-operatives. In these self-managed newspapers, the journalists not only elected the editors, but also rotated important tasks between themselves. Above all, these radical publications wanted their readers to become directly involved in their different political and cultural activities (Armstrong 1981: 21–2, 32, 43–60).

After May 1968, autonomous movements soon emerged in France as well. Because the traditional Left parties and trade unions were unconcerned about these issues, the leadership of the new social movements was drawn from the veterans of the May 1968 Revolution. Rejecting Leninism, these student radicals believed that the autonomous movements should adopt self-management structures. Like the American New Left, French revolutionaries hoped that the new social movements were prefiguring the future self-managed society. At the same time, the principles of self-management were also applied to the emerging community arts movement. Inspired by the events of May 1968, actors, film-makers and other artists started to involve amateurs in cultural productions (Forbes 1987: 136–44). As in the US, these new forms of politics and culture led to the founding of underground newspapers in France. For example, *Idiot-International* and *Charlie-Hebdo* not only combined coverage of revolutionary politics with alternative culture, but also encouraged readers to contribute their own articles, cartoons and photographs (Boris 1975: 171–2).

Like the autonomous movements and community arts organisations, these early French alternative newspapers were founded as co-operatives. Although they soon collapsed, the two underground papers inspired many different radical groups across the country to set up their own publications. As in the US, a combination of new printing technologies and voluntary labour dramatically reduced the money needed to produce a newspaper. Taking advantage of these low production costs, specialist publications were created for specific regions of France or for the different communities of interest, such as ethnic minorities, pacifists, ecologists, feminists, lesbians and gays, radical scientists and alternative cultural movements (Boris 1975: 226–9, 230–60). By allowing readers to participate in their newspapers, the New Left media activists hoped not only to produce 'counter-information' about the new social movements, but also to create two-way communications between different community organisations. Inspired by the Situationists, these radicals believed that the self-managed newspapers could unite the various autonomous communities into a single revolutionary movement against the capitalist system (Boris 1975: 214–15).

In 1971 some sympathisers of Gauche Prolétarienne created a New Left news agency called Agence-Presse Libération (APL). Although they were Maoists, these radicals did not adopt the total-itarian model for their news agency. Instead, in similar fashion to the underground newspapers, APL was organised as a co-operative of mainly volunteer journalists and photographers. Within the news agency, most management decisions were taken collectively and tasks were rotated among members. Like the American under-ground newspapers, APL wanted to provide 'counter-information' about the activities of the whole New Left. By circulating reports and statements from those directly involved in strikes and other social struggles, APL hoped to facilitate two-way communications among the different groups within the revolutionary movement. Moreover, although its services were free for underground newspapers, APL also sold information and photographs to the mainstream media. During the early 1970s, APL became the principal intermediary between the mass-circulation newspapers and activists involved in industrial disputes or protest movements (Boris 1975: 187–203).

Despite its success, APL was eventually replaced by *Libération*, the first national daily newspaper of the New Left. Like the news agency, *Libération* was a co-operative owned by its staff and sponsors. In its founding statement, the *Libération* collective committed itself not only to equality of salaries among its workforce, but also to the rotation of tasks between journalists and printers (Ory 1983: 53–4). However, the foundation of *Libération* was also a retreat from the more radical experiment of the APL news agency. Although it covered most strikes and protest movements, the new newspaper could not provide the same degree of two-way communications as the news agency had done. By the late 1970s, the employment of paid editors and journalists had further weakened the self-management structures of the newspaper. Even with these problems, *Libération* remained the leading self-managed media organisation in France. The newspaper only survived repeated crises because of the financial support and active participation of its readers (Boris 1975: 201–5; Ory 1983: 54).

By the early 1970s, the New Left revolutionaries had created their own model of media freedom. Like other members of the Left, they believed that the concentration of ownership within the media had rendered the Girondin model obsolete. However, these student radicals did not want to replace the liberal form of media freedom with any version of the Jacobin model. In their view, neither revolutionary conspiracies nor political parties could represent the views of individuals within the media. Instead, they believed that individuals could only exercise their right of media freedom through direct participation in the production and management of the self-managed newspapers. For them, the combination of the political and natural rights embodied by the individual journalist-printers would be reborn through the co-operative ownership of publications by both journalists and printers in conjunction with their readership. Above all, the creation of this self-managed media would overcome the physical limitations on direct democracy. When the agora was built, all individuals and autonomous movements would directly participate in social and political decision-making without the need for representatives. Because it was invented by the veterans of the May 1968 Revolution, this definition is called *the self-management model of media freedom*. According to the advocates of this new interpretation, the contradiction between democracy and participation had now been successfully resolved within the media.

The Video-Militants

For many New Left radicals, the new social movements' final victory over capitalism was viewed as the inevitable result of the evolution of contemporary society. With modernisation completed, individuals were now fighting against their social oppression as women, homosexuals or immigrants, rather than as members of the working class. According to these revolutionaries, the oppressions of sexism, racism and other forms of discrimination were primarily enforced by the mass media. However, with the advent of new computer and media technologies, the dominance of the 'society of the spectacle' was almost at an end. The interactive possibilities of the new information technologies could only be fully realised through the adoption of the participatory forms of organisation pioneered by the new social movements. These radicals believed that the implementation of the self-management model in the electronic media would be the first step towards the creation of direct democracy within all social institutions (Baudrillard 1975: 119–29, 141–51, 160–7).

After the collapse of the May 1968 ORTF strike, the Socialist trade union sponsored the first group of community television activists, who advocated the creation of a television channel controlled by its workers and viewers. In parallel, Godard and other radical film directors experimented with video to produce 'counter-information' programmes (Ory 1983: 66). In 1973 the New Left media activists were given a chance to put their ideas into practice. Using its prototype cable network, Grenoble council decided to set up the Vidéogazette channel. Although it only lasted a few years, this community television station became a symbol of the radical possibilities of the new cheap video and VCR technologies. On the Vidéogazette channel, community groups were not only able to make their own programmes, they also became involved in the management of the station (Simon 1987: 65–6). Inspired by this success, several other groups of 'video-militants' in Paris and elsewhere began producing their own programmes. Denied access to cable networks or the airwaves, these media activists held many successful screenings of their videos at public meetings (Goyet 1987: 58–9; Boris 1975: 296–7).

Echoing the Situationists, the video-militants attacked the one-way flow of communications from the ORTF's television channels. Instead, they wanted to create two-way communications among viewers. Because the skills of video production could be easily learnt by amateurs, almost everyone could express their opinions in a television interview. The major obstacle to this video utopia was the lack of frequencies for interactive television broadcasting. According to the video-militants, this practical obstacle would soon be overcome through the construction of a cable television network in France. Once this system was in place, they believed that every individual would be able not only to receive a wider variety of channels, but also to transmit their own television programmes to each other. Above all, this cable television network was the technological fix for overcoming the physical limits on participatory democracy. When everyone was connected to the cable television networks, individuals would no longer need representatives to exercise their political rights. Instead, they would participate directly in decision-making within the electronic agora created by the community television channels (Flichy and Pineau 1983: 15–16, 103–4; Boris 1975: 291–2).

The Challenge of the Free Radios

While the video-militants were pursuing their high-technology dreams, a new form of alternative media suddenly appeared in France. During the 1977 municipal elections, the Green party set up an illegal radio station in Paris as a publicity stunt. Called Radio Verte, this pirate station was a 'protest-broadcast' against the state's monopoly over the electronic media (Cojean and Eskenazi 1986: 9, 17). In their election manifesto, the Greens called for the licensing of hundreds of local radio stations across France to replace the centralised state-owned electronic media. Under this proposal, small-scale radio stations would provide news about their neighbourhoods, act as community noticeboards and encourage programme-making by local volunteers. Like the underground newspapers and the video-militants, the supporters of Radio Verte hoped to create two-way communications between different individuals and social movements (Haupais 1977; Cojean and Eskenazi 1986: 15–16).

In the US, community radio broadcasting had been permitted for over two decades. As with the underground newspapers, these radio stations did not just provide 'counter-information' about the activities of the New Left, they were also run as self-managed organisations. In Berkeley and other places, the local community radio station played a leading role in the protests against the Vietnam war and in the emergence of the new social movements (Downing 1984: 74–95).

By the mid-1970s, alternative radio stations had also emerged in Italy. As in other industrialised countries, the Italian New Left had founded new social movements, alternative cultural projects and underground newspapers. In 1975 a successful legal challenge by a New Left pirate radio station led to the collapse of the Italian broadcasting laws. Soon afterwards, unlicensed radio and television stations appeared in all parts of the country. Although most were commercial, a minority of the radio stations were run by revolutionary groups. Independent of both state and commercial interests, these radical pirates became known as free radio stations. Adopting the self-management model, the stations not only elected their own administrators, they also encouraged listener participation in their broadcasts. From phone-ins to community programme-making, these stations allowed their audiences to describe their own experiences in strikes or other social struggles. Above all, the free radio stations hoped that an open dialogue over the airwaves would remove any conflicts between the various sections of the Italian New Left (Grimshaw and Gardner 1977: 14–17).

In France, the success of the Italian free radio stations inspired many New Left media activists. Soon they were convinced that such radio stations were not only the most effective method of spreading radical ideas, they were also great fun to be involved with (Collin 1982: 19–24; 198–201). These views were aided by the underdevelopment of radio broadcasting in France. Although there were three Radio France national channels, a few state-owned local radio stations and the *périphériques*, the FM band was almost completely empty. The French New Left soon had the technical means to break the state's monopoly over radio broadcasting. By visiting Italy, French free radio enthusiasts could either buy broadcasting equipment or learn how to build FM transmitters. Following Radio Verte's lead, Green groups and student radicals across the country started setting up their own pirate radio stations too. With these early experiments, the New Left had extended the self-management model into radio broadcasting (Collectif Radios Libres Populaires 1978: 35–9; Cojean and Eskenazi 1986: 19–24).

The Left and the Free Radios

When the first pirate radio stations appeared in France, many supporters of the Left condemned them. For instance, the broadcasting trade unions were afraid that the introduction of competition within the electronic media would lead to job losses at the nationalised radio and television stations (Bourdon 1986: 49). At the same time, many left-wingers were convinced that any breach in the state's monopoly over the airwaves would inevitably lead to the commercialisation of radio and television broadcasting in the country. Fearing a return to the 1930s, both Communists and Socialists denounced the new pirate radio stations, including those run by left-wing activists. For instance, one union official described the free radio stations as: 'generous initiatives, seen as militant, which opened the way for the domination [of the airwaves] by private interests and financial powers tomorrow' (FR-L 1978).

Despite this hostility, the pirate stations gradually silenced their critics within the two parties of the Left. The abandonment of the Jacobin model in radio broadcasting was initiated by members of the Socialist party. During 1977–8, some members of the party became involved in their local pirate radio stations. Soon, these Socialist free radio enthusiasts persuaded their leaders to support their demands for the licensing of local radio stations. Under their proposals, radio licences would only be granted to co-operatives or voluntary organisations (Cojean and Eskenazi 1986: 39). In 1979 the Parisian section of the Socialist party set up its own free radio station as a protest against the bias of the state-owned radio and television channels in favour of the ruling party. After a police raid, Mitterrand, the leader of the Socialist party, was arrested for illegal radio broadcasting. In subsequent interviews, he attacked the use of technical regulations over the airwaves as an excuse for the ruling party's control of broadcasting. For the first time, a leader of a party of the Left had denounced the state's monopoly over the electronic media (FR-L 1979).

Within the Communist party, this change in attitude towards the free radio stations took much longer. Because of its loyalty to the Jacobin models and its union members within the nationalised media companies, the party initially opposed any relaxation of state controls over radio broadcasting. However, in 1978–9 striking steelworkers in Lorraine set up their own pirate radio station: Lorraine Coeur d'Acier (LCA). With its studios in the town hall of the Communist-led local council, LCA soon became the symbol of the steelworkers' strike. When the police tried to close down their radio station the steelworkers successfully defended it in two days of rioting. Because of LCA's role in this important industrial dispute, the Communist party could no longer continue its opposition to the free radio movement (Cojean and Eskenazi 1986: 46).

Yet the existence of LCA weakened the Leninist structure of the French Communist party. Despite being funded by the local Communist trade union, the pirate station adopted the self-management model of the other free radio stations. The members of LCA elected their own administrators, rotated tasks among themselves and made their own programmes. By granting all kinds of people access to the airwaves, LCA successfully won the support of the wider local community for the steelworkers' strike. Rejecting Leninism, one LCA activist proclaimed: 'We have nothing to fear from a debate of ideas, a democratic debate' (Poirier and Serres 1980: 5). However, the Communist party became increasingly worried by the independence of LCA. The national leadership therefore decided to impose the totalitarian model on the heretical pirate station. In its final months on air, even the phone-ins were censored. Alluding to the repression of the Solidarity trade union, one local activist bitterly remarked: 'it's Poland [at LCA], comrade' (Najman 1980a: 1980b).

The Radicalisation of the Pirates

Before the 1978 legislative elections, some leading free radio stations formed the Association pour la Libération des Ondes (ALO). In its campaign for a change to the broadcasting laws, the ALO called for the licensing of dozens of local community radio stations in every city or town (Collin 1982: 117–18). However, the ALO did not advocate a purist version of the self-management model for radio broadcasting. Lobbying a right-wing government, the Association entered into an alliance with some supporters of commercial radio broadcasting within Giscard's own party. United by their dislike of the nationalisation of radio broadcasting, the community and commercial radio enthusiasts were able to agree on a common programme. While the leading commercial pirate station became a voluntary association in 1978, the ALO supported the financing of community radio broadcasting through advertising (Cojean and Eskenazi 1986: 31, 51).

During the 1978 National Assembly elections, Giscard's political party made vague promises in favour of the expansion of radio broadcasting. However, after his party's victory, Giscard failed to fulfil his campaign pledges. Dependent upon the Gaullists for his majority in the National Assembly, he had to pander to their determination to prevent any weakening of the state's control over radio broadcasting. Despite protests from his own supporters, the president decided to introduce new legislation imposing increased fines and prison sentences for unlicensed radio broadcasting (Giscard d'Estaing 1978: 2,935). After this law was passed, the conciliatory strategy of the ALO had failed. Under constant attack by the police, the remaining pirate radio stations were soon radicalised.

During this period, the most articulate defender of the radical free radio stations was Félix Guattari, a New Left philosopher and psychoanalyst. In the mid-1970s he had been heavily involved within the Italian free radio movement. On his return to France, Guattari helped to set up a pirate station in Paris called Radio 93 (Cojean and Eskenazi 1986: 35). Like many New Left gurus, Guattari believed that the mass media were a major method of social control in capitalist societies. As religious and repressive means of enforcing public discipline had declined in effectiveness, Fordist societies had turned to more dispersed and flexible methods of social control, such as the media. By promoting bourgeois 'models of desire', radio and television stations mesmerised their audiences into becoming loyal workers and contented shoppers. Echoing the Jacobin models, Guattari claimed that the majority of the population had fallen under the ideological domination of the mass media (Guattari 1979: 159–60, 228).

However, unlike the Jacobin models, Guattari rejected the abdication of the individual's right of media freedom to the revolutionary conspiracy or the political parties. For this radical philosopher, the new social movements had replaced the traditional parties of the Left as the main opponents of capitalism. With modernisation completed, the contending classes had fragmented into 'different social groups as demarcated by class, age, place of birth, type of job, sexual orientation, etc.' (Guattari 1984: 220). Because of this development, Guattari advocated the replacement of the monolithic political parties with the 'micro-politics of desire', which were based around the participatory democracy of the new social movements. In day-to-day politics, the autonomous movements fought against their own social oppressions, such as racism or sexism. In moments of crisis, the new social movements worked in co-operation against the common enemy, as in the May 1968

Revolution. By combining specific and general demands, the New Left would unite the whole people in the struggle against capitalism (Deleuze and Guattari 1984: 296–322).

Because of the decline in the traditional parties of the Left, Guattari thought that these new social movements were the only force capable of challenging the power of the mainstream media. Above all, he advocated that feminists, ecologists, lesbians and gays, ethnic communities and other autonomous movements should set up their own free radio stations. Inspired by Italian examples, Guattari believed that the individual right of media freedom could only be realised through the collective ownership of FM transmitters by free radio co-operatives. Crucially, instead of being represented by political parties, individuals and autonomous organisations would then speak for themselves over the airwaves (collectif a/traverso 1977: 9).

According to the video-militants, the creation of the electronic agora depended upon the construction of the cable television network in the future. In contrast, Guattari asserted that the contradiction between democracy and participation within the media had already been transcended by the extension of the self-management model into radio broadcasting. Using contemporary radio technology, it was possible for the New Left to build the electronic agora now. Within each autonomous movement, internal discussions were held on its own free radio station. Between the different communities, a common debate was conducted through the diffuse network of alternative radio stations. According to Guattari, these specific and general discussions on the free radio stations formed 'an immense permanent meeting' of the airwaves (Guattari 1979: 159–60). Like the Situationists, the New Left philosopher believed that the electronic media had already provided the technical solution for the physical limits of direct democracy.

By building this electronic agora, Guattari hoped to liberate individuals from the 'models of desire' imposed by the mainstream media. Along with 'counter-information' and political discussions, the free radio stations were also supposed to undermine social and psychic repressions with a 'poetico-frenzied' style of broadcasting (Guattari 1979: 159). The growing popularity of Guattari's 'Mao-Dadaist' philosophy demonstrated the radicalisation of the free radio movement under police repression. After the passing of Giscard's anti-pirate law, most free radio stations believed that the ALO had made too many concessions to the commercial radio lobby without gaining any results. In particular, they disapproved of the ALO's support for the funding of local radio stations through advertising. According to Guattari, the free radio stations had to demonstrate their opposition to the consumer society by refusing the 'intoxication of advertising' (Guattari 1979: 160). Inspired by this analysis, the radical free radio stations decided to break away from the ALO and form a new organisation called the Fédération Nationale des Radios Libres (FNRL). In its statutes, the FNRL specifically banned the use of advertising by any of its member radio stations (Cojean and Eskenazi 1986: 49–50). Despite its New Left politics, the Fédération still hoped for a change in government. With a Socialist victory in the 1981 elections, the FNRL knew that the free radio stations would soon be granted licences.

The Liberation of the Airwaves

As he had been arrested for unlicensed broadcasting, it was obvious that the victory of Mitterrand in the 1981 presidential elections signalled the end of the state monopoly over the airwaves. Trying to establish their claim to a frequency, many different groups quickly set up their own radio projects. Within a few months, the number and variety of pirate stations exceeded the wildest dreams of the New Left media activists. There were unlicensed radio stations catering for ethnic minorities, women, lesbians and gays, religious groups, political parties, local neighbourhoods, pensioners and other communities. By the end of the year, the number of pirate radio stations in Paris alone had risen to 130. In effect, the laws against unlicensed radio broadcasting had completely collapsed (Cojean and Eskenazi 1986: 96–7, 121–5, 134–5, 156).

Before drafting its new broadcasting law, the new administration appointed the Moinot Commission to advise on how its election pledges to reform the media could be honoured. Although it clearly rejected the commercial ownership of the electronic media, the Commission also strongly supported an end to the state's monopoly over the airwaves. While advocating protection of the existing nationalised services, the experts recommended the licensing of local radio and cable television stations. Influenced by the New Left, the Moinot Commission advised that these new services should only be run by co-operatives or voluntary organisations. With close supervision by a regulatory body, the Commission believed that the self-management model could be successfully implemented within the French media. However, the Commission did not support the FNRL's purist version of this model of media freedom. Influenced by the ALO, the experts accepted that the new radio stations could be partly funded by advertising (Moinot 1981: 56–60, 67–8).

Inspired by their pirate experiences, the radical free radio stations rejected this pragmatic view. Although it welcomed the Moinot Commission's support for the self-management model, the FNRL believed that ownership restrictions alone would not prevent a commercial take-over of the airwaves. The only effective deterrent against potential commercial radio operators was a ban on all advertising. Crucially, the radical free radio activists saw the construction of the electronic agora as an act of social will, rather than an economic activity. If advertising was banned, they believed that the free stations could easily be supported by their listeners. Because of the initial popularity of the pirates, the Fédération greatly overestimated the ability of many different stations to survive on voluntary labour and donations alone (Cojean and Eskenazi 1986: 103–8).

As the Socialists prepared their new broadcasting law, the FNRL campaigned for a complete ban on radio advertising. Although it was a New Left organisation, the Fédération had important allies within the Socialist party. The prime minister and other cabinet members were afraid that the legalisation of advertising would lead to a 1930s-style commercial broadcasting system dominated by financial interests and their right-wing friends. Despite a countercampaign by the ALO, the FNRL's lobbying was successful. Under the new law, community radio stations were granted temporary licences for the unused frequencies on the FM band on condition that their services were not funded by advertising (Mitterrand 1981: 3,070–1). For over 40 years, successive French governments had systematically nationalised all radio and television broadcasting inside and outside the country. By contrast, the 1981 radio law ended the state's monopoly over the electronic media. Instead, a purist version of the self-management model was instituted within radio broadcasting.

Despite the granting of licences to local radio stations, the French state did not give up all its controls over the airwaves. Under the new law, the Socialists created the Holleaux Commission to grant licences and supervise the new local stations. When the government eventually introduced comprehensive legislation on broadcasting, this Commission became the subcommittee on radio broadcasting of the media regulatory body: the Haute Autorité de Communication Audiovisuelle (Casile and Drhey 1983: 139–40). Although appointed by the government, the Holleaux Commission was not just composed of political nominees and leading bureaucrats; it also included representatives from the ALO, the FNRL and community arts organisations. Under the new legislation, the Commission was charged with awarding licences to a mix of services, which would allow many different communities access to the airwaves. By imposing promises of performance within licence agreements, the Commission could also stop local radio stations from dropping community programmes in favour of a more commercial format (Mitterrand 1981: 3,070–1; Gavi 1981).

Once it was established, the Holleaux Commission immediately began granting licences to local radio stations. Within two years, over 1,300 licences were issued across the whole country (Cojean and Eskenazi 1986: 203–5). In the provinces, the Commission found no difficulty in finding sufficient vacant frequencies for almost every credible applicant. In Paris, however, there were not enough radio frequencies for all pirate radio stations already on-air. The Commission therefore decided to organise mergers between the different radio groups operating in the capital. For example, rival Zionist, anti-Zionist and orthodox pirates were persuaded to share a single Jewish radio station. Despite their leading role in the free radio movement, Guattari and other radical pirates were also only granted one 'alternative' licence. Forced to combine, their radical free radio station was called Fréquence Libre (Cojean and Eskenazi 1986: 181–5).

Accusing the Holleaux Commission of 'political recuperation', the FNRL attacked these arranged mergers between the pirate radio stations of Paris. In its defence, the regulatory body pointed out that only eight music radio stations had been given licences, while twelve franchises had been awarded to community groups (Prot 1985: 83). However, the Commission still faced angry protests from the supporters of pirate stations which had not received licences. For example, Fréquence Gaie, a lesbian and gay radio station, and Radio Libertaire, an anarchist station, organised demonstrations of their listeners and lobbied the Socialist government. Confronted with these protests, the Commission suddenly discovered two more FM frequencies within the Paris area for these free radio stations. In contrast, the Commission refused to expand the number of top 40 music radio stations. By the time it had finished its deliberations, the Commission had given authorisation to 22 different radio stations within the capital. Before the presidential elections, the airwaves of the city had been almost empty. Only two years later, there was a greater density of radio stations in Paris than in New York. Despite the mergers and limited number of licences, the free radio movement had won its long battle for legitimacy. With their legal status secure, the radical stations could now implement the self-management model of media freedom within the electronic media (Cojean and Eskenazi 1986: 183–8; Prot 1985: 31).

The Collapse of the Radical Free Radio Stations

At the 1982 FNRL Congress, a leading Socialist claimed that the licensing of thousands of free radio stations was 'a symbol of a reviving democracy'. Under the new government, individuals and communities had finally gained access to the airwaves (Cornand

and Villetard 1982). But while the Socialists and the free radio movement were celebrating their triumph, the self-management model had already disappeared in other media. During the late 1970s and early 1980s, the number of underground newspapers had slowly fallen. Reliant on volunteer labour and poorly funded, most radical publications had gone bankrupt. Even in successful publications, the self-management model had been gradually replaced by conventional commercial forms of organisation. In 1980 *Libération*, the only daily newspaper of the New Left, also decided to abandon the self-management model. In place of reader participation and political commitment, *Libération* became a left-of-centre mass-circulation newspaper with professional journalists, different salary levels, specialisation of tasks and corporate advertising. Crucially, managerial power was now concentrated in the hands of the charismatic editor of the newspaper (Ory 1983: 52–4).

By the early 1980s, the self-management model had almost completely disappeared within video production as well. Although the Moinot Commission had supported the licensing of community cable television stations, there were no longer sufficient active groups of video-militants to run these proposed channels (Ory 1983: 101). Because of these failures, the self-management model only continued to exist within the free radio stations. According to New Left activists, the cheapness and technical simplicity of radio broadcasting had protected the ideals of the alternative media from commercial corruption within this sector (Collin 1982: 37–42). Yet, ironically, the longevity of the self-management model within the radio sector also depended upon the state's effective regulation of the airwaves. After they had obtained authorisation, many station operators rapidly began to break the conditions of their licence agreements. For example, they ignored the various restrictions on transmitter power, type of service and position of frequency on the waveband. Above all, the regulatory body was unable to prevent joint-stock companies from acquiring local radio stations, using voluntary organisations as a camouflage. Because the New Left had successfully overturned previous broadcasting legislation, the commercial operators saw no reason why the new regulations should be obeyed (Cojean and Eskenazi 1986: 206–7, 231, 273–6).

February 1982 saw the first major survey of the popularity of the new local radio stations in Paris. This showed that there had been a large increase in the number of radio listeners in the previous year. However, these new listeners were not tuning into the radical free radio stations. Instead, the most popular services were two openly commercial top 40 music stations. Among older listeners, the most successful channel was Radio Service Tour Eiffel, run by the right-wing mayor of Paris. Among the free radio stations, only Fréquence Gaie and a Jewish station had substantial audiences. In contrast, Guattari's radio project received poor ratings. While the weekly audience of the most popular music station was over 500,000, Fréquence Libre only attracted around 30,000 listeners (Gavi and Villetard 1982). During the next three years, these low rating were never reversed by Guattari and his friends. By 1985 Fréquence Libre was twenty-first in the ratings, out of a total of 23 radio stations in Paris (Simard 1985). Although they had obtained licences, the radical free radio activists were unable to build large audiences for their local stations. Without sufficient listeners, their plans for individuals and social movements to participate in programme-making and management were unrealisable.

In the self-management model, individuals exercised their right of media freedom through direct participation within the free radio stations. According to the New Left, individuals directly communicated with one another across the airwaves without the need for representation by either politicians or professional media workers (Collin 1982: 40). However, this electronic agora could only be constructed with the involvement of large sections of the population. But in the early 1980s most listeners did not want to participate in the programme-making and management of the free radio stations. Instead, a small minority of New Left media activists dominated Fréquence Libre and the other radical stations. With their high level of political commitment, they were often culturally separated from their intended audiences. For example, on Fréquence Libre the presenters of many radio programmes refused to adopt professional techniques. Instead, they alienated many potential listeners by 'talking the same way as [they did] in political meetings'. Similarly, when some rappers offered to make programmes for the radio station, the leaders of Fréquence Libre took no interest in the music and were only interested in whether or not the lyrics of the songs were politically correct (Simard 1985). Under the self-management model, all individuals were supposed to be involved in two-way communications over the airwaves. Instead, the radical free radio stations had evolved into a 'transmission belt' for the viewpoints of a small minority of revolutionaries. Despite Guattari's hopes, the contradiction between participation and democracy within the media had not been resolved. Instead, the New Left media activists had unconsciously resurrected the totalitarian model within the free radio stations.

Yet this dependence on a limited number of activists was impossible in the long run. Out of political commitment, free radio enthusiasts had worked for their stations for nothing or for low wages. But as they acquired family responsibilities or other interests, these founding activists slowly started to drift away. Under the self-management model, new workers on a free radio station were supposed to be recruited from among the listeners already participating in programme-making and other tasks. But with their declining audiences, the radical stations were unable to recruit sufficient new activists. Despite their scepticism about the Socialist party, these stations were harmed by the failures of the Mitterrand government. When it was elected, the new government had aroused hopes of substantial changes within French society. However, after the Socialists abandoned their radical policies, there was widespread disillusionment with politics among all sections of the population. Soon this crisis of confidence was damaging not only the parties of the Left, but the new social movements and the alternative media too. With the Left discredited, the radical free radio stations could not attract enough activists or listeners to sustain their services (Simard 1985).

Despite their vision of the electronic agora, the radical stations also could not ignore the economics of broadcasting in the long term. After licences were awarded, the new local radio stations needed premises, studios, transmitters and other equipment. In most cases, they also had to employ some paid staff to carry out essential engineering, broadcasting and administrative tasks. With advertising banned, the stations were supposed to obtain most of their funding from their listeners. But as their audiences remained small, they were never able to raise enough money to cover the minimal costs of radio broadcasting. By the mid-1980s, the radical free radio stations had entered into a vicious circle of decline. While low audiences meant little money was raised, lack of resources hampered attempts to create attractive programming. Without new members joining the stations, the existing activists were increasingly overworked. Under financial and personal pressures, many free radio stations experienced intense internal quarrels, which led to acrimonious splits (Haute Autorité 1983: 36, 39). Although it had beaten the repressive laws of the Giscard government, the free radio movement was unable to survive the problems of legal broadcasting. In 1985 Fréquence Libre, the flagship of the movement, went bankrupt and its frequency was sold to a commercial *périphérique* station (Cojean and Eskenazi 1986: 325). Within only four years, the self-management model had almost completely disappeared from radio broadcasting in France.

The final collapse of the free radio movement ended the struggle for the implementation of the self-management model within the French mass media. Inspired by the May 1968 Revolution, the New Left had called for the overthrow of the 'society of the spectacle'. In the self-managed society, individuals and communities would directly express their own views in print or over the airwaves by participating in the management of newspaper, radio and television stations. While the independence of the journalist-printers and the broadcaster-engineers had been founded on the individual ownership of printing presses and radio transmitters, the autonomy of the self-managed media was based on the collective ownership of the means of communications. Following the introduction of the self-management model, the contradiction between participation and democracy within the media would be finally resolved.

For the New Left, the most important result of the implementation of the self-management model was the provision of a technical fix for the physical limitations on participatory democracy. With the creation of the electronic agora, the views of the people would no longer need to be represented by either the mediaklatura or the political parties. But despite the efforts of the New Left media activists, there was no repetition of the May 1968 Revolution in France. Even the free radio stations were unable to maintain the self-management model in the long term. By the mid-1980s, the widespread disillusionment with politics deprived the radical free radio stations of their potential audience. Lacking mass participation in their activities, these stations could not build the promised electronic agora. The implementation of the self-management model within one sector of the mass media was unable to replace the missing social revolution. Following the failure of the New Left's utopia, the way was now open for the New Right to implement its own model of media freedom.

THE MENTAL MAP OF THE SELF-MANAGEMENT MODEL

Figure 6.1 shows the psychogeography of the self-management model of media freedom. This is an ahistorical and abstract model of the theories of the Situationists and the practice of the underground newspapers, community video groups and free radio stations. This model of media freedom prefigured the reorganisation of society into a direct democracy, which would transcend the separation of the state from civil society. As propertyless workers, individuals exercised their right of media freedom by participating in the co-operatively owned alternative media. Within local communities, individuals spoke to each other about their common interests, such as class, gender, age, ethnicity, sexuality or locality. Between the various workers' councils or social movements, two-way communications were established through the diffused networks of the alternative media. Because everyone could express their opinions in print or over the airwaves, the participatory democracy of the general assemblies of the new social movements was extended beyond the physical confines of a meeting place. With the creation of the electronic agora, the need for individuals' opinions to be represented by politicians or the mediaklatura had disappeared. *Since they could participate in the self-managed newspapers or radio and television stations, all individuals exercised their media freedom by directly expressing their opinions in print or over the airwaves.*

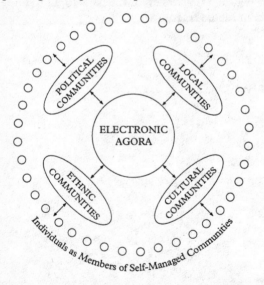

Figure 6.1: The Mental Map of the Self-Management Model

→ Information flows   ○ Individuals

7

The Liberty of the Corporation

The Crisis of Fordism

For '30 glorious years' France enjoyed continuous economic growth. In the early 1970s, however, the economy suddenly went into crisis. In part, this slow-down was caused by the revolt of young workers against the disciplines of the assembly lines. Although they were unable to institute direct democracy within the workplace, these New Left radicals successfully hampered attempts to raise productivity in many factories. At the same time, the rapid rise in world oil prices not only created severe balance-of-payments deficits for the industrialised countries, it also precipitated a serious recession within the world economy. Because higher energy costs deflated their economies, governments across the globe adopted reflationary policies to revive economic growth. However, these interventionist policies failed to work. Faced with persistent inflation, currency instability and a rapid rise in unemployment, many politicians and industrialists began to believe that Fordism had reached its inherent social, organisational and technological limits (Lipietz 1984: 41–4; Gauron 1988: 15–16).

Yet, ironically, the inability of the governments of the industrialised countries to co-ordinate their own economies was caused by the spread of Fordism across the world. At the end of the Second World War, the US had forced its allies in western Europe and east Asia to abolish their tariffs against imported goods. With the end of protectionism, American, European and Japanese companies started to form multinational corporations to obtain economies of scale on a global scale. In the 1960s, faced with the revolt of young workers in the industrialised countries, investment from these multinationals flowed into those southern European and Third World economies with anti-union laws, low wages and minimal welfare provisions. As Fordism became globalised, national governments were no longer able to control the activities of their multinationals. Instead, by the early 1970s, the world trading system was increasingly regulated by the international financial system. As fixed exchange rates collapsed, competition between different currencies encouraged the equalisation of social, industrial and other conditions across the major industrialised nations. Above all, reflation in a single country was prevented by balance-of-payments crises and currency speculation. After the devaluation of the dollar in 1971, it was obvious that even the world's most powerful economy was unable to resist the power of the global financial system (Lipietz 1984: 46–8; 1987: 149; Wallerstein 1984: 60–5).

Giscard's Liberalism

In France, the crisis of Fordism precipitated the end of the Gaullist party-state. In the late 1950s and early 1960s, de Gaulle had united all classes behind the modernisation of the country. After the May 1968 Revolution, however, the Gaullists rapidly lost their working-class supporters to the parties of the Left (Johnson 1981: 98–9). Under Chaban-Delmas, the left-wing Gaullists tried to win back these voters through social reforms, such as the revival of the public service model within the electronic media. Bitterly opposed to Chaban-Delmas' concessions to the Left, conservative Gaullists first had him sacked as prime minister and then sabotaged his subsequent bid to become president by supporting the candidacy of his right-wing rival: Valery Giscard d'Estaing. Although he was the first non-Gaullist president of the Fifth Republic, Giscard's election was not a complete break with the past. Lacking a majority in the National Assembly, the new president had to appoint Jacques Chirac, the leader of the conservative Gaullists, as his first prime minister (Portelli 1989: 132–5).

Yet Giscard's election did demonstrate the waning of Gaullism as a political project. As support for the Left had risen, the Gaullist party had split into conservative and reform factions. More seriously, these political divisions anticipated the demise of the party's economic strategy. Under the General, the Gaullists had successfully used the interventionist state to deliver higher living standards for their voters. By the early 1970s, however, the crisis of Fordism had exposed the limits of state planning. As interventionist policies faltered, Giscard was able to win support from the conservative Gaullists for a return to the liberal economic policies of the Third Republic (Gauron 1988: 272). According to Giscard, the revival of liberalism was necessary to overcome the crisis of Fordism. For example, the Gaullists' moral and cultural conservatism had sparked off the revolt of the New Left. In contrast, as a neo-liberal, Giscard was able to defuse some of the appeal of radical social ideas by removing restrictions on individuals' personal lives, such as the laws against abortion, contraception and divorce (Giscard d'Estaing 1977: 117). Crucially, the new president believed that the relaxation of

controls over morality and culture justified the demise of interventionist economic policies. Alongside the New Left, the crisis of
Fordism had created a New Right as well.

For 30 years, French politicians had believed that the Jacobin
state was needed to create the economic conditions whereby all
citizens could exercise their political rights. By contrast, Giscard
claimed that 'the fusion of political and economic power ... leads
away from democracy, not towards it'. Hence he asserted that 'to
be able to enjoy his freedom in security, a man should possess private
property' (Giscard d'Estaing 1977: 87, 91). For the neo-liberals,
the revival of individual property-ownership was the solution to the
danger of social revolution. After the modernisation of the economy,
the peasants and petit-bourgeoisie had been turned into propertyless wage-workers. Fearful of the appeal of left-wing ideas to
these people, Giscard advocated the extension of private property-
ownership to all workers. As under the Third Republic, self-reliant
individuals would not support collective solutions to their problems,
such as the public service state or workers' councils. Instead, these
property-owning wage-earners would be more interested in
expressing their individual autonomy, especially within their private
lives. For Giscard, the extension of the individual ownership of
private property underpinned the new personal moral freedoms.
In the name of liberty, the New Right advocated the replacement
of the Jacobin state with market competition.

With the globalisation of production and finance, the internal
French economy was already partly regulated by external market
competition. However, contrary to the predictions of the neo-
liberals, the dominance of the world market further diminished the
individual ownership of property. When compared to their overseas
rivals, most French companies were still too small and too dependent
on self-financing. In order to prevent the domestic market from
being taken over by imports, the French state had to help companies
to become 'national champions'. While centralised planning for the
whole national economy was abandoned, the Giscard government
still encouraged mergers, directed investments and gave subsidies
to favoured companies in certain key sectors, such as the computer,
electronics, nuclear power and media industries. In many sectors,
these 'national champions' were established as *sociétés d'économie
mixte*, with shares owned by both state and private capital. For
Giscard, these parastatal corporations combined the advantages of
state intervention with the disciplines of market competition. Yet,
as joint-stock companies, these 'national champions' did not aid
the revival of individual property ownership within France. Despite
its neo-liberal rhetoric, the Giscard government's economic policies
further concentrated the control over production into the hands

of a small minority of shareholders and bureaucrats. As a return to the liberal past was impossible, the French government instead hoped to find a technological fix for the crisis of Fordism (Gauron 1983: 180–201).

The Hi-tech Neo-liberals

By the mid-1970s, most French politicians believed that the introduction of new information technologies was the only solution to the global economic depression. In both France and the US, futurologists were predicting that the convergence of computer, media and telecommunications technologies would create a new form of society to replace Fordism. Back in the early 1960s, Marshall McLuhan had been the first prophet of the post-industrial age. According to this guru, the development of human societies was determined by their technologies. Above all, McLuhan stressed the impact of different forms of media, which supposedly shaped human consciousness. For example, industrial society had been created by the invention of printing, which brought about discipline, individuality and rationality. With the introduction of radio and television broadcasting, however, this industrial society had begun to break down. Because the electronic media encouraged participation and involvement, the younger generation would no longer accept the hierarchical disciplines of Fordism (McLuhan 1964: 7–21, 35–6, 69–70, 320–1).

For McLuhan, the student revolts and hippie counter-culture were simply symptoms of a clash between two rival forms of media. In his view, the challenge of the New Left could only be overcome by the final triumph of the new information technologies. With the spread of computer automation, oppressive and boring assembly-line work would be transformed into participatory and enjoyable 'paid learning' (McLuhan 1964: 137–8, 346–59). Similarly, the spread of the electronic media would overcome national and social divisions between people. As a devout Catholic, McLuhan hoped that the whole world would be united in a mystical version of the electronic agora: the 'global village' (McLuhan 1964: 61, 93, 255). Wishing to emulate this guru's media stardom, American and French academics and journalists also began to predict the imminent advent of the information age (Bell 1974; Toffler 1971; Touraine 1974). Soon after he was elected president, Giscard followed this intellectual fashion by commissioning Nora and Minc, two top civil servants, to investigate the social and economic impact of the new information technologies within France. Inspired by McLuhan, these two nomenklaturists claimed that the growing convergence of the computer, media and telecommunications technologies was radically changing all aspects of contemporary society. Above all, they believed that there would soon be a rapid shift in employment from the Fordist manufacturing industries towards the service sector, especially its media and computer companies. As a consequence, semi-skilled manual workers would be transformed into white-collar professionals. After epochs of agricultural and industrial civilisations, a new post-industrial society was being born (Nora and Minc 1980: 2–3, 13, 126, 134–40).

Like McLuhan, Nora and Minc believed that the media were at the centre of this social transformation. In the post-industrial society, the existing models of media freedom would become obsolete. On the one hand, the various Jacobin models could only create a one-way flow of communications from the centre towards the people. On the other, the Girondin model could only provide a limited form of two-way communications between individuals (Nora and Minc 1980: 139). Instead, Nora and Minc called for the creation of an interactive cable television and computer network to provide two-way communications for all members of society. Once they were connected to this system, 'the recipients ... [would] also [be] the transmitters' (Nora and Minc 1980: 138). Once everyone was connected to the cable network, the contradiction between participation and democracy within the media would finally be resolved. Crucially, as in the self-management model, this development meant that every individual would then be able to participate directly in decisions about social and political policies. Echoing the New Left, Nora and Minc's name for their hi-tech media utopia was the 'informational agora' (Nora and Minc 1980: 140).

Despite these radical predictions, Nora and Minc's prophecies were used by the Giscard government to justify its economic policies. By forecasting the replacement of large corporations with a myriad small firms and artisans, Nora and Minc's report could be used to support policies favouring the individual ownership of private property. Similarly, by warning against the domination of the French computer and communications markets by American multinationals, the two nomenklaturists' findings could be used to defend the creation of 'national champions' in the computer and media industries. Named after Nora and Minc's neologism for the new information technologies, the Programme Télématique was set up by Giscard to direct state subsidies towards the development of information technologies, such as videotext, electronic telephone directories, telecommunications satellites and fibre-optic cables. While terrestrial frequencies remained vacant, the French government subsidised the development of high-technology methods of distributing television programmes to French viewers (Gauron 1983: 180–93; Marchand 1988: 25–65).

In the US, the work of the futurologists had already been appropriated by neo-liberal economists. As international competition
intensified, some American multinational corporations had accepted
the need for more competition within their domestic markets.
According to neo-liberal economists, the prophecies of the futurologists demonstrated that most state regulations of industries
should be eliminated as soon as possible. In the past, the American
state had introduced regulations controlling the activities of private
corporations to prevent the abuse of 'natural monopolies', such as
public utilities or the electronic media. However, the neo-liberal
economists argued that the new information technologies would
abolish any remaining monopolies within the American economy.
For example, the shortage of frequencies had been used to justify
the regulation of broadcasting. But with the construction of cable
networks, free-market competition between different commercial
television stations would inevitably replace the state regulation of
broadcasting.

According to Nora and Minc, the new media technologies would
transform society into an electronic agora. In contrast, American
neo-liberal economists argued that this technological convergence
would create an electronic marketplace. In their view, the imposition
of state regulations had inhibited the competition between capitalists for 'profit opportunities' within the electronic media. With
the emergence of new information technologies, however, these
restrictions could soon be removed. As there could be unlimited
cable channels, any commercial company would be able to set up
its own television station. These channels would compete on quality
and price for viewers by offering a wide range of television services.
By creating this electronic marketplace, the new technologies would
have removed the need for state ownership or regulation of the
electronic media. As a consequence, the Girondin model could now
be successfully extended from newspaper publishing to the electronic
media (Coase 1970: 96–8; de Sola Pool 1983: 151–251).

By advocating this free-market media utopia, the American neo-
liberal economists tried to counter the revolutionary demands of
the New Left. On the one hand, they accepted the opposition of
the hippie counter-culture to moral and cultural restrictions, such
as media censorship. But on the other hand, these economists
rejected workers' and students' demands for the self-management
of social and economic institutions, especially within the electronic
media. In the eyes of the New Left, individual freedom was only
possible through the collective ownership of property by co-
operatives or voluntary organisations, as in the electronic agora. By
contrast, the New Right saw individual freedom as the absence of
state regulations within the marketplace, such as free competition
between different cable television stations. For them, post-industrial

society could only be organised as an electronic marketplace. However, the American neo-liberal economists carefully obscured the consequences of market competition within the electronic media. Although individuals could produce their own media, the electronic marketplace would be dominated by the output of large corporations.

The Underdevelopment of the French Commercial Media

After the Second World War, Fordist methods of production were successfully adopted by French firms under pressure from American competition. In the early 1970s, however, many French politicians believed that their country faced a new 'American challenge'. With the emergence of the new information technologies, French companies were once again in danger of being left behind by their American rivals, such as the IBM computer corporation. Agreeing with this neo-liberal analysis, the Giscard government subsidised 'national champions' within the computer and telecommunications sectors. However, it was more difficult to apply this economic strategy to the French media. Within the world market, American multinationals completely dominated the cinema, popular music and television industries (Tunstall 1977: 278–303).

Within France, certain sections of media were already controlled by large corporations. After the failure of the post-war reforms, most local and national newspapers were run by joint-stock companies. During the 1960s, Groupe Hersant started buying up local newspapers to create a monopoly over advertising in certain regions. In 1975 this corporation became the largest French press company by taking over *Le Figaro*, the leading right-wing newspaper. During the same period, Hachette restored its pre-war monopoly over newspaper distribution and Havas regained its leading position within the French advertising industry. By the mid-1970s, newspaper publishing in France was dominated by the three Hs: Hersant, Hachette and Havas. Alongside newspaper publishing, commercial companies also owned the *périphériques*. In the early 1970s, Radio Luxembourg was Europe's only multinational media corporation, with operations in France, Belgium and West Germany. However, unlike the firms in neo-liberal economics textbooks, the French commercial media corporations were either subsidised or indirectly owned by the interventionist state (Bellenger et al. 1975: 239–46, 318–20, 364–5).

Above all, the ORTF's monopoly over the electronic media hampered the development of commercial media corporations. Prevented from owning radio and television stations within their home market, French firms could not develop the same synergy of different media as their American rivals. As a neo-liberal, Giscard believed that this obstacle to the development of commercial media companies in France had to be removed. In 1977 some members of his party in Montpellier decided to turn this commitment into reality by starting their own pirate station: Radio Fil Bleu. In contrast with the free radio stations, this Giscardian station mainly transmitted entertainment programmes and was funded by advertising. While the New Left wanted to build the electronic agora, Radio Fil Bleu's owners advocated the introduction of an American-style commercial broadcasting system in France (Cojean and Eskenazi 1986: 25–32). After lobbying from this pirate, Giscard's party promised to license local radio stations after the 1978 legislative elections. The Gaullists, however, vigorously opposed any relaxation of the state's monopoly over radio broadcasting (Bombled 1981: 93–5). Looking at the Italian situation, they believed that the end of the state's broadcasting monopoly would allow revolutionary groups to incite unrest over the airwaves. As one prominent Gaullist put it: 'In France, Radio Fil Bleu risks, innocently, opening up the way for Radio Red Brigades [an Italian extreme Left terrorist group]' (Defrance 1979: 22).

The Break-up of the ORTF

Because he was dependent on the Gaullists for a majority in the National Assembly, Giscard was unable to license local radio stations and was forced to increase the penalties for pirate radio broadcasting (Giscard d'Estaing 1978). However, although the Gaullists were determined to preserve the state's monopoly over the electronic media, the ORTF was nearly bankrupt by the end of Pompidou's rule in 1974. During the late 1960s and early 1970s, the ORTF had set up a third regional television station and begun broadcasting in colour on all its channels. But as the market in receivers was almost saturated, the rise in revenue from increased ownership of television sets was coming to an end. According to its critics, the ORTF's financial crisis was exacerbated by its management's incompetence. The early 1970s saw a series of scandals at the nationalised broadcasting corporation, such as the bribery of camera operators to pan across certain advertising posters at sports events (Ledos et al. 1986: 71–3, 182–3).

After he was elected to the presidency, Giscard seized the opportunity of this financial crisis to restructure the ORTF. Prevented by the Gaullists from introducing commercial television broadcasting, the new president decided to break up the corporation into seven different companies covering the transmission, production and broadcasting of the electronic media. Crucially, the television stations were transformed into three separate companies: Télévision Française 1, or TF1; Antenne 2; and France Régions 3, or FR3 (Giscard d'Estaing 1974a: 8,355–8). For Giscard, the break-up of the ORTF was the first step towards the privatisation of radio and television broadcasting in France. In particular, although they remained nationalised, the former ORTF television stations were placed in direct competition with one another for the same audiences and advertising revenue. In Giscard's view, the introduction of competition within television broadcasting would solve the financial problems of the ex-ORTF companies by containing the rising costs of production.

However, the 1974 law was not simply designed to solve the temporary financial crisis of the state-owned electronic media. Inspired by the Girondin model, the president asserted that private ownership was the only means of guaranteeing media freedom (Giscard d'Estaing 1977: 84). But because he could not privatise the electronic media, Giscard instead created a simulation of commercial broadcasting by introducing competition between the three state-owned television stations. He claimed that now they were competing against each other, these TV stations would be more interested in achieving high ratings by presenting a diversity of opinions in their news and current affairs programmes, rather than producing propaganda for the ruling party. According to Giscard, market competition within the electronic media automatically created political pluralism over the airwaves. Under the public service and Gaullist models, individuals had exercised their right of media freedom through their elected representatives. By contrast, in this neo-liberal version of the Girondin model, the individual citizen's political right of media freedom was equated with consumer choice between competing television stations.

In the traditional Girondin model, individuals had exercised their right of media freedom by owning their own printing presses as private property. In 1970s France, however, it was impossible for every individual citizen to own their own radio or television station. Because of the technical and economic limitations on individual ownership of the electronic media, Giscard replaced this Girondin ideal with consumer choice between competing channels. In his view, the battle for ratings between the independent stations would ensure the representation of the full diversity of political opinions over the airwaves. Instead of being producers engaged in two-way communications, individual citizens could now only exercise their right of media freedom by choosing between the competing one-way flows of communications from the corporate radio and television stations. Because it was developed by the New Right, this definition is called *the neo-liberal model of media freedom*.

Yet, in reality, the implementation of the neo-liberal model was hampered by the continuation of state ownership and controls within the electronic media. Under the 1974 law, the level of the licence fee and the appointment of managers were still decided by the government (Giscard d'Estaing 1974: 8,355–7). Although he had promised full economic and political autonomy to the electronic media, Giscard was unable to abandon the Gaullist model. Despite competing for audiences, the news and current affairs programmes of the ex-ORTF television stations were still biased towards the ruling party. On its own, market competition between nationalised television channels was unable to end the dominance of the Gaullist model over the French electronic media.

The Arrival of Commercial Television

During the late 1970s, the rise of the free radio movement gradually weakened support for the Jacobin models within the French Left. By 1981, the victory of the parties of the Left signalled the end of the state's monopoly over the airwaves. At first, the new Socialist government only granted licences to non-commercial free radio stations. However, although they were committed to the public service and self-management models, many Socialist politicians also believed in Nora and Minc's prophecies of a post-industrial future centred on the new information technologies. Like its predecessor, the Socialist government intervened to help 'national champions' within the computer and telecommunications industries, including nationalising the Thomson electronics group. According to this company's management, a rapid expansion in the number of television stations was the best way of expanding the internal demand for its television receivers (Miège et al. 1986: 104–7).

After strong lobbying, the Socialist government decided to license the first non-state-owned television station in France: Canal Plus. Although it was commercial, this new station was owned by the parastatal Havas corporation and its boss was a close friend of the president (Missika 1986: 8). However, in practice, political controls over Canal Plus were not really necessary. Unlike its foreign equivalents, the new station was funded by subscriptions. By encrypting its most popular programmes, Canal Plus was able to impose a price on the consumption of television programmes. In order to attract subscribers, the station mainly transmitted new films, soft porn and live sports events. Within two years of operation, Canal Plus had become a great success, with over 1 million subscribers to its service (Canal Plus 1987: 6). For the Socialist government, the licensing of Canal Plus was never really part of its media policies. Instead, the new station was primarily designed to stimulate the development of the latest media technologies, such as decoders. In order to create post-industrial 'national champions', the Socialist government had permitted the commercial ownership of television stations for the first time.

In other high-technology sectors, post-industrial economic policies also provided further opportunities for the expansion of commercial media corporations. Under Giscard, the French and German governments had agreed to create satellite television services for the two countries. After the Socialists were elected in France, this project was continued as part of their interventionist industrial strategy. Although it was state-funded, the satellite television service depended on commercial media corporations to provide its new channels. Because of technical difficulties, however, these new satellite television stations were never launched (Cluzel 1988: 168–72). In parallel, the Socialists also decided that the building of the interactive cable network was a national priority. Inspired by Nora and Minc's report, they believed this fibre-optic cable grid would provide not only extra television stations, but also interactive information services for industrial and domestic users (Cluzel 1988: 160–1). Although the infrastructure for the cable network was to be built by the nationalised telephone corporation, each local cable franchise was to be run by a Société Locale d'Exploitation Commerciale (SLEC), whose shares were owned by both municipal authorities and commercial corporations (Mitterrand 1984b).

By the end of 1985, the first local cable television networks were operational. Despite massive state subsidies, these local cable networks never fulfilled Nora and Minc's prophecies. When the scheme was started in 1983, it was predicted that there would be over a million subscribers to the networks within three years. But by 1986 they had hardly any subscribers. Because Canal Plus was already providing a film and sports service, there was little demand for extra television stations (Cluzel 1988: 163). Although they were popular with the few subscribers to the networks, the local community television channels were also too expensive to fund out of the SLEC's limited revenues (Goyet 1987: 60–2). Under financial pressure, the local authorities abdicated responsibility for running their cable networks to three large commercial utility companies: Lyonnaise des Eaux, Générale des Eaux and Caisse des Dépôts (Charon 1987: 11–13, 54–8, 71–4).

As their financial difficulties grew, many SLECs began to lower the technical quality of their local cable television systems. Although copper wires were much cheaper, the early cable systems had used fibre optics to create two-way communications for access channels and videotext services. However, the new commercial cable operators were only interested in providing specialist television channels, which could be distributed over cheaper copper-wire networks (Cluzel 1988: 63, 160–1). Instead of creating the electronic agora, the SLECs had become a highly subsidised distribution system for the channels of the commercial media corporations. Yet, while terrestrial frequencies remained vacant, even copper-wire cable networks were an expensive means of distributing television signals.

The Commercialisation of Local Radio Broadcasting

In the early 1980s, the Socialist government restricted the expansion of commercial ownership to the post-industrial sectors of the electronic media. Yet by the mid-1980s, the most commercialised sector of the electronic media was the old technology of radio broadcasting. Under the 1981 and 1982 laws, the ownership of local radio stations had been confined to co-operatives and the selling of advertising had been banned. In practice, however, these new regulations were unenforceable. With limited staff and resources, the regulatory body was unable to prevent the commercial takeover of the airwaves. With the exception of the FNRL's members, most local radio stations were soon owned by joint-stock companies and were funded by advertising (Cojean and Eskenazi 1986: 171–3, 207, 226–8).

By 1984, the Mitterrand government finally accepted that the FNRL's purist version of the self-management model had failed. The Socialists had already been forced to abandon their expansionary industrial policies and their traditional hostility to private enterprise. Instead, they now wanted to create the post-industrial society through increased market competition between commercial companies. During a visit to Silicon Valley in California, a reporter questioned Mitterrand on the role of private enterprise in another service industry: radio broadcasting. Impressed by the pioneering role of small companies in the computer industry, the president announced an imminent change in the laws on local radio broadcasting. Abandoning the self-management model, the Socialist government decided to create an electronic marketplace of competing local commercial radio stations. Under its new law, local radio stations could now be owned by private shareholders and be funded by advertising (Mitterrand 1984a).

From 1981 onwards, commercial radio broadcasting had existed in semi-legality. In Paris, the most successful commercial local radio station was NRJ (Energy). By playing top 40 pop hits, NRJ soon obtained a large audience of teenagers and young adults in the capital. Because it attracted these listeners, the radio station was able to sell advertising slots to the producers of commodities aimed at the youth market, such as record companies or clothes manufacturers. In order to attract a large audience for these advertisers, the owners of NRJ invested heavily in transmission technology. Ignoring the law, the radio station used a transmitter 40 times more powerful than the legal limit (Cojean and Eskenazi 1986: 293–4). In 1984 the Haute Autorité suspended NRJ's licence for blatantly flouting the conditions of its licence agreement (Haute Autorité 1985: 38–40). Adopting the slogan of 'Don't Kill Freedom', the radio station quickly organised a demonstration of over 100,000 teenagers against the suspension. Inspired by the neo-liberal model, the owners of NRJ claimed that media freedom was based on the absence of state controls over commercial media companies.

Yet despite this neo-liberal rhetoric, the Gaullist model had also been secretly adopted by NRJ. Although owned by a private entrepreneur, three of the nine directors of this top 40 radio station were connected with the Socialist party. By broadcasting news bulletins favourable to the government, NRJ was assured of the support of leading Socialists. Under both popular and political pressure, the Haute Autorité soon found it impossible to enforce the laws on local radio broadcasting on the station (Eskenazi, 1984; Cojean and Eskenazi 1986: 275–305). With the support of leading Socialists, NRJ successfully undermined the self-management model. In its place, the pop music station had won 'the right of loud broadcasts' for its young listeners (July 1984). In the neo-liberal model, the media freedom of individuals could only be realised by unregulated competition between commercial companies.

Even before it was passed, the 1984 law was already obsolete. Inspired by Silicon Valley, the Socialists wanted to restrict the ownership of local radio stations to small businesses. While the new law was being debated, however, local radio stations were being combined into national networks. The concentration of ownership in radio broadcasting was encouraged by the economies of scale within the electronic media. By renting a satellite link, the first-copy costs of programme production for a national service were not much larger than they were for a professional local radio station. Yet, with many more listeners, a radio station could charge advertisers much higher prices for the commercials it broadcast. The development of national networks was encouraged by the successful introduction of the American-style radio formats to France. As different formats were developed, the commercial radio stations provided programmes for listeners from distinct age and class groups. Because these audiences were not limited to a specific local community, the same programme formats were popular among listeners across the whole country. For example, wherever they lived, large numbers of teenagers would tune into NRJ's top 40 hit format. By the end of 1984, NRJ had created a network of 23 pop music stations across the country (Cojean and Eskenazi 1986: 311).

Once they were established, these national channels soon marginalised their local radio competitors. As they gained larger and larger audiences, the national networks attracted an increasing proportion of radio advertising revenue. Soon, many local commercial radio stations followed the radical free radio stations into bankruptcy. As they failed, these small business radio stations were bought up by the new national networks. For example, Groupe Hersant decided to construct its own national top 40 music network to compete with NRJ. After the collapse of the law against the multiple ownership of licences, the largest newspaper publishing company was rapidly transformed into a multimedia corporation with radio stations in almost every major French city (Charon 1991: 218–20, 312–21). In parallel, the *périphériques* also bought up many bankrupt local radio stations. When local radio broadcasting was legalised, these stations had lost nearly a third of their listeners to the new local radio services. In response, the *périphériques* revitalised their programming and bought up FM franchises to overcome the technical problems of their traditional medium- or long-wave frequencies (Prot 1985: 62–3; Gavi 1984).

By the end of its term of office in 1986, the Socialist government had accepted the failure of its attempts to control the development of radio broadcasting in France. From now on, market competition between different commercial radio stations would determine the future of this sector of the electronic media. But despite the adoption of the neo-liberal model, the new commercial radio broadcasting system had not become the decentralised electronic marketplace predicted by the New Right. Just as the self-management model had failed, a competitive market of small business radio stations was also unsustainable in the long term. Although radio broadcasting was regulated through the competition for audiences and advertisers, the development of this sector of the electronic media was dominated by the national networks of a few media corporations.

The Commercialisation of Terrestrial Television Broadcasting

In the early 1980s, the Socialist government had only tolerated the emergence of commercial television stations within the post-industrial sectors of satellite and cable broadcasting. By the mid-1980s, the ambitious plans for the high-technology industries had been scaled down to a defence of the nationalised Thomson corporation. In order to stimulate the internal market for receivers, the Socialists were once again asked to overcome their hostility to commercial television stations in order to help this electronics company (Cluzel 1988: 184). At the same time, the advertising agencies were also calling for an expansion in commercial television broadcasting to increase their business. Faced with these powerful lobbies, the Socialist government agreed to license more commercial television stations in France (Le Diberder 1987: 67–9).

With the legislative elections approaching, the Socialists tried to win votes by awarding the licences to the new commercial contractors as soon as possible. But this abandonment of state regulation hid a continuation of the Gaullist model. For example, the fifth television channel was awarded to a consortium led by Jérôme Seydoux of the Chargeurs group, a personal friend of Mitterrand, and by Silvio Berlusconi, a television magnate closely connected with the corrupt Italian Socialist party (who was to become Italy's prime minister in 1994). According to the parties of the Right, this blatant example of political favouritism completely discredited the Socialist government's media policies. After the Left lost power, the Right immediately cancelled the licences granted by the Socialist government and awarded them to their political allies instead (Cotta 1986: 238–50). However, this struggle over which commercial companies should own the national television franchises obscured the real consensus between the parties of the Left and Right. By the mid-1980s, both Socialists and Gaullists had abandoned their traditional loyalty to Jacobin models of media freedom. Instead, during the 1986 legislative elections both government and opposition parties competed to show which side was most committed to implementing the neo-liberal model within the electronic media. The major difficulty for the incoming right-wing government was that it was more in favour of commercial broadcasting than its left-wing predecessor had been.

'Savage Liberalism'

In March 1986 the Gaullists and Giscardians won the legislative elections. Although Mitterrand remained president, Chirac, the leader of the Gaullists, became the new prime minister. Despite this 'cohabitation', the parties of the Right were determined to introduce radical changes. In their election manifesto, the Gaullists and Giscardians promised to abandon the interventionist economic policies of the previous 40 years in favour of neo-liberalism (RPR/UDF 1986). In the US and Great Britain, the Reagan and Thatcher governments were already privatising and deregulating the financial and industrial sectors of their nations' economies. By abandoning interventionist policies, the American and British gov-

ernments hoped to revitalise their economies through the rapid integration of their financial institutions and manufacturing corporations
within the world marketplace. Ironically, both Reagan and Thatcher
believed that the success of their neo-liberal economic policies
was proved by the overexpansion of the service sector and the
decline of manufacturing industries in their countries.

During the 1970s, the Giscard government had already adopted
some neo-liberal economic policies. After the Socialists' victory in
1981, the Gaullists rapidly reversed their previous opposition to
the abandonment of interventionism. Crucially, both parties were
now convinced that the revival of private property-ownership was
the only way of reversing the decline in their electoral support. As
more people became wage-workers, the parties of the Right had
slowly lost their 'sociological majority' among the electorate, which
culminated in their defeat in the 1981 presidential elections.
Inspired by Giscard, the new right-wing administration was
determined to re-create the republic of property-owners (Bourlanges
1988: 47–57).

In their 1986 election manifesto, the Gaullists and Giscardians
advocated deregulation, privatisations and tax cuts to liberate individuals from the oppressive controls imposed by the state (RPR/UDF
1986: 7). According to the parties of the Right, individual freedoms
had to be protected against the 'hyper-regulation' of civil society
by the state. Breaking with interventionism, the parties of the Right
wanted to restrict the role of the state to the preservation of civil
and public law. After this 'rolling back' of the state was completed,
the French economy would be regulated solely through market competition between private companies (Club 89 1985: 43–9, 92–3).
Following the British example, the new government hoped to win
popular support for these neo-liberal policies by creating a nation
of shareholders through its privatisation policies. In parallel with
financial deregulation, eleven industrial companies and three banks
were floated on the Paris Stock Exchange. Along with measures
to encourage small businesses, these privatisations temporarily
reversed the concentration of property-ownership in France (Bauer
1988: 49–57).

Building the Electronic Marketplace

After the Right's loss of political power, the Gaullists were also rapidly
converted to the virtues of neo-liberal policies in the electronic media.
Soon they were advocating the deregulation and privatisation of
radio and television broadcasting. In his speeches, Chirac used the
continuation of state controls over the electronic media as the
primary example of the inefficiency of the Socialist government's

interventionist economic policies (Club 89 1985: 25–7). In their electoral programme, the parties of the Right promised 'the disengagement of the state' from all forms of broadcasting (RPR/UDF 1986: 9). This neo-liberal media policy did not simply involve the removal of controls over the existing commercial radio and television stations. At the same time, the parties of the Right wanted to privatise the majority of the nationalised television and radio stations. Under their proposals, the remaining public service channels would only broadcast those programmes not provided by the commercial radio and television stations, such as education, culture or current affairs documentaries (Club 89 1985: 151–3; Léotard 1987: 189).

Influenced by American economists, the French neo-liberals also claimed that the deregulation and privatisation of the media was the only effective way of introducing the new information technologies. Successful transition to the post-industrial society depended upon the rapid introduction of a new media technology: the interactive fibre-optic network. Using this network, individuals would be able to participate in two-way communications by producing their own television programmes or other forms of media. At this point, the contradiction between participation and democracy within the media would have been finally resolved. Above all, the French neo-liberals wanted to use the new information technologies to create the electronic marketplace. By introducing encryption technology, a direct cost could be imposed on the consumption of the electronic media.

With the establishment of prices, market competition was possible between different electronic media producers. In place of printing presses, individuals would use cameras, computers and recording equipment to express their opinions through the interactive cable networks. In this hi-tech version of the Girondin model, individuals would no longer be only 'passive communicators' watching programmes provided by others. Instead, they would also become 'active communicators' producing their own television programmes or other forms of media. Because the cable network could be regulated by market competition, the French neo-liberals believed that state intervention in the electronic media would soon become obsolete. Using the new information technologies, the creation of the electronic marketplace would inevitably revive the Girondin model (Frèches 1986: 9–15, 46–58, 65–7).

By hyping this vision of the post-industrial future, the parties of the Right were able to promise access to the electronic media for both individuals and commercial media corporations. However, the creation of an interactive electronic marketplace was a long-term project. Instead, the media corporations were the principal beneficiaries of the deregulation and privatisation of the electronic media in the short term. According to the Right, the growth of the commercial media corporations was also caused by the spread of new information technologies. Using satellite dishes, French viewers could already receive television channels produced by foreign media corporations. Although they were mostly in English and German, the right-wing parties believed that these satellite television services heralded the collapse of the various Jacobin models of media freedom, which were centred around national cultural autonomy. Instead, in order to compete with their American and European rivals, the parties of the Right advocated that the French radio and television stations should become 'national champions' in their sector of the economy. While proclaiming their devotion to the right of media freedom for individual citizens, the Chirac government quietly accepted that the introduction of the new information technologies would principally benefit commercial media corporations (Frèches 1986: 67–130, 147–8; Léotard 1987: 188).

Media Freedom for Commercial Corporations

Within the French courts, the precedent of the Girondin model had already been used to argue for the adoption of the neo-liberal model in the electronic media. In 1977, inspired by the Italian example, Radio Fil Bleu decided to challenge the constitutionality of the French broadcasting laws in the courts. In their submission, the owners of the Giscardian pirate radio station argued that media freedom was an 'unalienable right' protected by article 11 of the 1789 Declaration. As the founding text of the democratic republic, this guarantee of media freedom had to take precedence over any laws banning unlicensed radio broadcasting. Using the original interpretation of the 1789 Declaration, the station's owners argued that their political right of media freedom was based on the natural right to own a radio transmitter as private property (Lapergue 1977a; 1977b; C.H. 1977). However, even though the 1789 Declaration formally guaranteed the Girondin model, the Bill of Rights only had weak juridical status within the French constitution. Therefore, anticipating its failure under article 11, Radio Fil Bleu also appealed for protection under the promise of media freedom found in article 10 of the European Convention for the Protection of Human Rights and Fundamental Freedoms, which had been recently ratified by the Giscard government (Giscard d'Estaing 1974b). Even here, however, the pirate radio station was unsuccessful in its arguments. As a cold war compromise between conservative and socialist parties, the European Convention had been specifically drafted to protect the activities of the public service state, especially within the electronic media. In its decisions, the European Court of Human Rights had always recognised the public service model as a legitimate interpretation of media freedom (Jacobs 1975: 155).

Despite the failure of its court case, Radio Fil Bleu's submission did anticipate the future role of the protection of political and natural rights within western Europe. As the globalisation of production weakened national governments, individual citizens were unable to control the development of civil society by electing members of parliament. Instead, these individual citizens were given legal guarantees of their independence from state controls. While Jacobin rights were founded on participation in decision-making by the nation-people, this revival of Girondin rights was based on the protection of the individual autonomy of each citizen, especially against the abuses of state power. With the globalisation of production, corporations also wanted protection against the arbitrary actions of national governments. As legal persons, joint-stock companies demanded the same juridical guarantees as individual citizens. By reinterpreting article 10 in neo-liberal terms, Radio Fil Bleu anticipated the impact of increased market competition within western European broadcasting. As a consequence, individual citizens would not be able to control radio and television broadcasting through their elected representatives. Instead, the political right of media freedom for individual citizens would have to be based on the natural right of legal persons to own transmitters. In the age of media corporations, the particular interests of private capital were protected by the universal rights of citizens.

After the election of the Socialist government, the two parties of the Right united on a programme of neo-liberal policies, including a commitment to implement the promises of the 1789 Declaration of the Rights of Man and the Citizen. In Chirac's view, the principles of this Declaration outlawed the interventionist state's control over the economic activities of individuals. Instead, the role of government had to be confined to the provision of a framework of civil and public law for market competition between private companies (Club 89 1985: 24). Within the electronic media, this neo-liberal analysis was used to reject state regulation and ownership of radio or television stations. According to the parties of the Right, the deregulation and privatisation of radio and television broadcasting were needed to extend the protection of article 11 of the 1789 Declaration from newspaper publishing to the electronic media (Club 89 1985: 145, 151–2).

When the 1982 law was passed, the right-wing parties decided to challenge the constitutionality of the new broadcasting legislation. Repeating the arguments of Radio Fil Bleu, the two parties claimed that the state regulation of the airwaves contravened article 11 of the 1789 Declaration. In their view, individual citizens' political right of media freedom could only be exercised through the natural right of private property-ownership within the mass media (A. Ch. 1982; L.Z. and P.J. 1982). However, for technical and economic reasons it was impossible for most individual citizens to own radio or television stations. According to the parties of the Right, this contradiction between political and natural rights could only be overcome through the recognition of legal persons as possessing political and civil rights. Thus, even if most citizens could not exercise their right of media freedom, the commercial radio and television stations should be protected by the provisions of article 11 of the Declaration. Although it had a right-wing majority, however, the Conseil Constitutionnel refused to accept these arguments. Unlike the parties of the Right, the judges recognised the constitutional validity of the Jacobin models of media freedom (Conseil Constitutionnel 1982: 2,423). Despite this judicial defeat, the Gaullists and Giscardians were still determined to introduce the neo-liberal model to France's electronic media. In their 1986 election manifesto, the parties proclaimed that 'the freedom of communications is indivisible, it applies as much to radio and television broadcasting ... as to newspapers' (RPR/UDF 1986: 8).

The 1986 Broadcasting Law

After their victory in the 1986 legislative elections, the parties of the Right were determined to fulfil their manifesto promises on the mass media. Within newspaper publishing, the Chirac government repealed the remaining interventionist legislation to restore the 1881 press law to its pristine form. According to the Gaullists and Giscardians, all citizens now had the right to set up their own newspapers with minimal restrictions. In reality, however, the disappearance of any controls over ownership removed the final legal obstacles to the monopolisation of local and national newspaper-ownership by the Hersant and Hachette groups. Using the rhetoric of the Girondin model, the parties of the Right had consolidated the dominance of the neo-liberal model over newspaper publishing (Périer-Daville 1989: 108–9).

Within the electronic media, there was a similar divergence between the promise of individual freedoms and the reality of corporate hegemony. Soon after it was elected, the Chirac government introduced a new law to implement a radical version of the neo-liberal model within radio and television broadcasting in France. Instead of being controlled by nationalised media corporations, the new administration claimed that information and entertainment programmes would now be provided by individual citizens through the electronic marketplace. Echoing the 1881 press legislation, the first article of the 1986 law claimed that radio and television broadcasting was 'free' of state control (Delcros and Vodan 1987: 11). Until the interactive fibre-optic cable network was built, however, the deregulation and privatisation of the electronic media could only introduce more competition between different corporate radio and television stations. Using Girondin rhetoric, the Chirac government had protected the particular interests of the commercial media companies in the name of all citizens' right to media freedom. Crucially, the promise of two-way communications for everyone had been turned into the reality of greater choice of one-way flows of communications from a few commercial radio and television channels.

According to the new minister of culture, 'broadcasting is above all else a business enterprise' (Léotard 1987: 188). In order to realise this neo-liberal vision, the 1986 act abolished the Haute Autorité and transferred its functions to the Commission Nationale de la Communication et des Libertés (CNCL) (Delcros and Vodan 1987: 13–34, 212). By including 'freedom' in the name of the CNCL, the new government signalled its commitment to the removal of most state controls over the electronic media. Within radio broadcasting, the new regulatory body implemented the neo-liberal model by recognising the hegemony of the commercial radio networks over the airwaves (Delcros and Vodan 1987: 66–8). As the original franchises expired, the CNCL reinforced corporate control over the airwaves by reallocating the best frequencies with the most powerful transmitters to NRJ and the *périphériques*. In contrast, the regulatory body deliberately either marginalised the remaining local community and commercial stations to the worst frequencies with low-power transmitters, or did not renew their licences at all. When the reallocation process was finished, many of the original free radio pioneers were once again excluded from the airwaves (P.K. 1987). But the commercial media corporations were not content with owning a single radio network. Alongside their traditional generalist channels, NRJ and the *périphériques* bought up more radio stations to offer top 40 or 'oldies' services to their listeners. Instead of a diversity of different services, market competition within radio broadcasting had reduced the choice of listeners to three basic formats: top 40, 'oldies' and news/speech (Cojean 1988, 1989; Soula 1989).

Despite this monopolisation, the Chirac government wanted the other sectors of the electronic media to imitate the triumph of the neo-liberal model within radio broadcasting. Because of its belief in the prophecies about a post-industrial future, the new administration was determined to transfer control of cable and satellite television broadcasting to the media corporations. Under the 1986 act, commercial companies became major shareholders in the French satellite television project. However, despite continued state subsidies and an infusion of private capital, technical difficulties again delayed the launching of this new method of television broadcasting (Cluzel 1988: 170–3). Within cable television, the implementation of the neo-liberal model was easier. Most local authorities had already passed responsibility for their local cable networks to Lyonnaise des Eaux, Générale des Eaux and the Caisse des Dépôts. Under the 1986 law, this take-over of the SLECs by these commercial utility companies was legally recognised. But, as with the satellite services, privatisation was unable to solve the severe financial problems of the cable networks (Delcros and Vodan 1987: 79–82; Charon 1987: 10–11).

Because of their technical and financial problems, the post-industrial sectors of the media were unable to implement the neo-liberal model within television broadcasting. As a consequence, the Chirac government decided that terrestrial television broadcasting would have to lead the commercialisation of this sector of the electronic media. Cancelling the scandalous allocation of the fifth and sixth channels to Mitterrand's friends, the government decided to readvertise the licences for the two television stations to new operators. After public hearings, the CNCL awarded the franchise for La Cinq to Groupe Hersant and gave M6 to Compagnie Luxembourgeoise de Télédiffusion (CLT), which owned Radio Luxembourg and was controlled by Havas. In both cases, the new television stations were now subsidiaries of major commercial media corporations (Cojean 1987; Benyahia-Kouider 1992a: 6).

According to the minister of culture, the most important symbol of the Chirac government's determination to extend the neo-liberal model to the electronic media was the decision to privatise one of the nationalised television channels. During the elections, the parties of the Right had promised to reduce state involvement within the electronic media to the provision of a minimum public service of educational, regional and cultural programmes. After much debate, the new administration ordered the sale of the most popular state-owned television station, TF1. Because it was already largely funded by advertising, this channel could easily be transferred to commercial ownership (Léotard 1987: 182–3, 188–9). Despite a bid from Hachette, the CNCL awarded the franchise to the Bouygues construction group, the largest public works and building company in the world. Following the privatisation of TF1, the neo-liberal model had been successfully imposed on terrestrial television broadcasting (Renard 1987).

Concentration of Ownership within the Electronic Media

Before the 1986 elections, French radio and television broadcasting was dominated by the mediaklatura of the public service state. At first, commercial television broadcasting had only been developed as additional services to the public service channels. But after the privatisation of TF1 and the adoption of other neo-liberal policies, French television broadcasting was largely controlled by the commercial media corporations. Under these new owners, the electronic media had been taken over by the 'Bouygues boys' and other managers drawn from mainstream businesses, who were committed to maximising profits (Dagnaud and Mehl 1989: 32). Yet, ironically, this triumph of the neo-liberal model also hid a continuation of the Gaullist model. As soon as it abolished the Haute Autorité, the Chirac government used the CNCL to replace the Socialist-appointed presidents of the nationalised radio and television stations with its own supporters. At the same time, when new television franchises were awarded, the CNCL favoured companies owned by Gaullist sympathisers. For example, the franchise for La Cinq was given to Groupe Hersant, which was owned by a Gaullist member of the National Assembly. Without fear of election defeat, this Gaullist political-financial network could now control the electronic media in its own party's interest (Queyranne 1987; Mamere 1988: 88–95, 121).

Faced with this privatised form of the Gaullist model, the Socialist party strengthened its own links with rival commercial media companies. Soon there was a highly publicised battle between the allies of the government and opposition parties over control of the newly privatised Havas. As well as the highly successful Canal Plus and its subsidiaries, this company ran the leading advertising agency in France and also controlled CLT, which owned Radio Luxembourg, the M6 television station and local channels in French towns. For the rival political parties, the prize of victory in the boardroom was ideological control over these radio and television stations. Yet by the late 1980s this form of political manipulation over the media seemed anachronistic. Havas was now a multimedia corporation with interests in many different sectors. Following privatisation, the company and its subsidiaries had expanded into other countries, such as Belgium, Spain, West Germany and eastern Europe. By diversifying at home and abroad, Havas had achieved the necessary size to compete against the other large international media corporations, such as those of Murdoch, Maxwell, Time-Warner, Berlusconi and Bertelsmann. Facing this international competition, political interference from the rival national parties had become irrelevant. Instead of political control, the policies of

Havas were shaped by competition within the global media markets. Eventually, after years of quarrels, the two political-financial factions compromised on a neutral management board. Under the neo-liberal model, the management board had to concentrate on improving the economic performance of the firm within the world market, rather than pleasing its political allies at home (de Coustin 1989: 141–2; Jourdain and Trocme 1991: 69–77).

Following Havas' example, other French media corporations also tried to become 'national champions' by spreading their operations into several different sectors of the mass media and linking up with similar operations in other countries. For example, Groupe Hersant had rapidly expanded from newspaper publishing into radio and television broadcasting (Musso and Pineau 1989: 82–5). Similarly, after it failed to win the TF1 franchise, Hachette borrowed heavily to finance its growth into the world's fifth largest publishing company. At the same time, the corporation retained control of a leading *périphérique* company with two major networks (Aeschimann 1992). But despite these successes, the corporation was still unable to challenge the major global media empires. As the president of Hachette declared: 'you can't be a large international multimedia group without a television station' (Soula 1990: 20).

By the late 1980s, the French electronic media were dominated by an oligopoly of four large media corporations: Havas, Hachette, Hersant and Bouygues. Using Girondin rhetoric, the neo-liberals had promised to realise the right of individual citizens to express their opinions through the electronic media. However, in practice, the neo-liberal model had placed control over the airwaves into the hands of a small oligarchy of shareholders of these four big media corporations. This monopolisation of the electronic media exposed the contradiction inherent in the neo-liberal model of media freedom. On the one hand, the parties of the Right believed in the freedom of individuals to establish their own radio and television stations, which would create a wide variety of different broadcasters. On the other hand, they also supported the freedom of large corporations to compete within the global media markets, which led to the concentration of production within the domestic radio and television system. With technical and economic pressures for centralisation, the latter interpretation of the neo-liberal model predominated in practice.

Infotainment

When it became obvious that the overwhelming majority of people remained passive consumers, the defenders of the neo-liberal model again began praising the electronic marketplace for creating an increased choice of programmes for listeners and viewers. Under the public service model, individual citizens had only indirectly expressed their views in the electronic media by voting for the political parties. In contrast, market competition between commercial media corporations directly reflected the wishes of the audience. Because the competing stations wanted to maximise their audiences, individual listeners and viewers determined the content of programmes by selecting channels on their radio or television sets. Unlike the representative democracy of its public service rival, the neo-liberal model had created direct democracy within radio and television broadcasting. Although they could not be 'active communicators', individuals were still empowered as citizen-zappers (Le Diberder and Coste-Cerdan 1988: 37–8). According to the director of programmes at TF1: 'television is a perilous undertaking. Each evening, the public vote. And the next morning, the public are right' (Chamard 1989a).

This neo-liberal version of participatory democracy within the electronic media was created through the use of ratings. During the 1950s, the RTF had pioneered studies on viewers' appreciation of its television programmes. After the authorisation of television advertising, the first measurements of audience size were carried out to determine the number of viewers watching the commercials. Because the government used these figures to determine the distribution of licence fees and advertising revenue, the television channels' schedules were gradually reorganised to maximise their share of the audience. By the mid-1980s, the three competing television stations were using measuring devices and audience surveys to construct daily ratings of the popularity of television programmes, with their audiences divided by region, class and age. Using interactive technologies, the changing size of the audiences for each channel could even be measured in 'real time' (Médiamétrie 1988: 3–7, 90; Folléa 1992: 16).

Because of the existence of these daily ratings, the advocates of the neo-liberal model argued that viewers directly influenced the content of programmes on the commercial stations. For example, more entertainment programmes were now provided for viewers. Crucially, the neo-liberals claimed that the intense competition for audiences between channels created a diversity of political opinions over the airwaves. Like the *périphériques*, the commercial television stations could not afford to alienate potential viewers who held left-wing views. For example, Hersant did not impose the Gaullist views of his newspapers on the news programmes of La Cinq (Senamaud 1989). As a consequence, after the imposition of the neo-liberal model on the electronic media, popular confidence in the truthfulness of the television news programmes rapidly increased. By the late 1980s, the producers of the news programmes at TF1 could credibly claim that: 'there is total freedom of expression within the private sector' (Keiffer 1989: 17).

In reality, however, the diversity of opinions expressed over the airwaves was limited by the neo-liberal model. Because they employed the radio and television journalists, the commercial media corporations could censor programmes on their own channels. For example, TF1 journalists were prevented from investigating the other activities of the Bouygues corporation. On all commercial television stations, programmes were censored to avoid embarrassing large advertisers (Mamere 1988: 79–80, 112, 142). More subtly, the owners and journalists of new channels were soon absorbed into the mediaklatura. Although competition for audiences prevented a return to the overt bias of the past, the opinions expressed within news and current affairs programmes were usually confined within the parameters of debate acceptable to the political parties and the state bureaucracy (Documents Observateur 1988: 49).

The rivalry between the commercial radio and television stations also determined the role of news and current affairs programmes within the daily schedule. For most listeners and viewers, the electronic media was primarily a provider of entertainment, such as serials, films, sport, game shows, talk shows, variety and music programmes. In their competition for advertising revenue, the commercial TV stations particularly wanted to maximise their audiences during prime time, which was between 7 p.m. and 11 p.m. (Médiamétrie 1988: 17). Because they only achieved low ratings, current affairs, documentary and cultural programmes were usually only shown at the end of the evening, while prime time was filled with entertainment programmes designed to attract the largest possible audience. As the director of programmes at La Cinq pointed out: 'Commercial television is a spectacle with the aim of promoting advertisements' (Ramonet 1989: 275).

Despite this emphasis on entertainment, news bulletins still played a key role in the schedules of the commercial television stations. On TF1 and La Cinq, the results of the competition between the rival 8 p.m. news bulletins often determined their share of the audience for the rest of the evening. Because watching the evening news programme was a daily habit for most people, the two television stations competed fiercely to win the loyalty of viewers for their own 8 p.m. bulletin (Chamard 1989c). With this intense competition for ratings, the content of the news bulletins was modified to prevent viewers from switching to rival channels. Soon the producers of news bulletins were imitating the entertainment programmes which filled the rest of the schedules. For example, the presenters of the news bulletins were turned into stars, with their personal lives becoming an integral part of the show. Copying the talk shows, news reports started to include more gossip about celebrities and human interest stories alongside their political reports. Above all, the commercial stations relied on compelling visual images to illustrate their news bulletins. Using live broadcasts, these bulletins provided the 'emotional shock' of watching history as it was being made, such as the fall of the Berlin Wall or the bombing of Baghdad. Exclusive pictures of wars, famines and natural disasters were exciting viewing for audiences safe in their own homes (Ramonet 1991: 11–12; Labé and Mamou 1992).

By the late 1980s, this combination of information and entertainment in news programmes was known as infotainment. Because it resulted from competition between the commercial television stations, this style of news coverage was defended as an expression of the direct wishes of viewers. However, at the same time, the dominance of infotainment was attacked for restricting access to the airwaves for the elected representatives of the voters. After an appearance by Mitterrand led to a large fall in La Cinq's ratings, the commercial TV stations became increasingly reluctant to carry in-depth interviews with politicians during prime time (Jarreau and Mamou 1991). From the late 1980s onwards, the range of opinions expressed over the airwaves was determined by the relative popularity of the competing news programmes. If it attracted more viewers, the opinions of a political party were more likely to be reported. Under the neo-liberal model, politicians could now only represent the opinions of their voters in the form of infotainment.

During the 1980s, parties of both Left and Right imitated American and British techniques of political marketing. Under the public service model, individual citizens were supposed to decide how to vote by listening to open debate between the political parties over the airwaves. By contrast, under the neo-liberal model, individual citizens became consumers of different advertising messages produced by the competing political parties. Because they were made as infotainment, these political advertising campaigns were criticised for relying on style rather than reasoned arguments. According to defenders of the public service model, the parties of both Left and Right were using advertising techniques to hide the real consequences of their proposed policies from the voters (Brune 1989: 39–46; Mamere 1988: 176–90).

The advocates of the public service model also criticised the neo-liberal model for breaking down the distinction between truth and fiction within the news bulletins. Trying to win higher ratings, the news producers started to embellish their bulletins with faked pictures or unsubstantiated rumours. For example, on one infamous occasion TF1 inserted questions spoken by the star presenter of their evening news programme into an interview with Fidel Castro (Labé and Mamou 1992). More seriously, the competition for scoops and sensational pictures between the different news programmes was exploited by unscrupulous politicians, especially abroad. During the Romanian revolution, for instance, the French electronic media broadcast horrific coverage of a massacre of civilians, which it was later found had never taken place. When these incidents were discovered, public confidence in the truth of television news programmes began to fall. Although infotainment programmes were made to please their audience, many viewers had realised that the neo-liberal model had created its own restrictions on the free flow of information (Ramonet 1991: 11; Missika 1991: 99–101).

In place of the Jacobin models, the right-wing parties claimed that the neo-liberal model had created direct democracy within the electronic media. For instance, the competition for viewers determined the content of television news reporting, rather than the interests of the political parties. But because they were competing for the same viewers, the commercial channels increasingly adopted similar methods of transforming the news into infotainment. For example, the content and presentation of the 8 p.m. news bulletins of TF1 and La Cinq were almost always exactly the same (Chamard 1989c). Because of this conformity, one star presenter denounced the neo-liberal model for creating a 'totalitarian nightmare' within French broadcasting (Ockrent 1988: 4). Under the pressure for high ratings, the electronic media could not reflect the full diversity of opinions held by individual citizens. Aiming to obtain the majority share of the potential audience, the news bulletins systematically ignored the views of many different political and social minorities, especially if their opinions would offend other viewers. Despite promises of participatory democracy over the airwaves, the implementation of the neo-liberal model had created a one-way flow of almost identical infotainment programmes from the commercial radio and television stations to the viewers.

> We have indeed more channels than we used to, but we seem to have less consumer choice as programming recipes to reach the largest possible audience are of course the same everywhere. Conformity, uniformity settle in with their usual populist justifications. (Ockrent 1988: 8–9).

The Diffuse Monopoly

During the mid-1980s, the neo-liberal policies of the American government created a global economic boom. In France, the success of neo-liberalism in the US won popular support for the programme of deregulation and privatisation advocated by the parties of the Right. However, the rapid expansion of private and public credit in the US led to large balance-of-payments deficits and financial instability. In France, the subsequent down-turn in the global economy quickly discredited the Chirac government. Instead of the promised economic miracle, neo-liberal economic policies had led to low growth and social discontent. As its popularity fell, the government was challenged by massive demonstrations by students and workers against its policies. Although he was able to buy off the protesters, Chirac was beaten by Mitterrand in the 1988 presidential elections. At this point, the neo-liberal economic experiment was over in France (Portelli 1989: 275–83).

The failure of deregulation and privatisation within the wider economy was reflected within the electronic media. In particular, the adoption of the neo-liberal model had not encouraged the spread of advanced information technologies. Instead of developing interactive electronic media, the SLECs were only installing a one-way delivery system for more television stations. Even with this reduction in infrastructure costs, the commercial cable operators could not make any profits from their networks. Despite deregulation and privatisation, these operators had been unable to construct the electronic marketplace within France (CSE 1989: 14–15; Charon and Simon 1988: 14). In satellite broadcasting, the entry of private capital was also unable to save an overambitious post-industrial project from financial difficulties. After many technical difficulties, the satellites were launched and came into service. However, as with the cable networks, the arrival of Canal Plus and the additional terrestrial television stations had removed the potential audience for the new channels (Gavi 1990b: 39–40; Chamard 1989b).

In commercial television broadcasting, the introduction of the neo-liberal model also created an economic crisis. Before the 1986 law was passed, the advocates of neo-liberal media policies had predicted that the deregulation and privatisation of television broadcasting would cut the costs of programme production (Frèches 1986: 121). However, the creation of competition between television production companies pushed up the price of the most popular programmes. During the late 1980s, television stars were able to obtain large pay rises for their appearances and film companies were able to charge much higher prices for their products. Ironically, the adoption of the neo-liberal model had greatly increased the costs of television broadcasting in France (Le Diberder and Coste-Cerdan 1988: 71–86). Because of the increased costs of programme production, La Cinq and M6 were soon only providing 'ersatz' services. Although home-produced material was more popular with the viewers, the schedules of La Cinq and M6 were increasingly filled with cheap American serials and films. In imitation, TF1 and the nationalised television companies also tried to cut costs by buying more programmes from Hollywood producers. By 1989,

French television stations were the largest importers of American programmes within the European Community. Far from stimulating domestic programme production, the introduction of the neo-liberal model had led to the schedules of French TV stations being filled by the serials and films of the Hollywood media corporations (Le Diberder and Coste-Cerdan 1988: 86–90; Gavi 1990b: 40).

Despite the greater use of American imports, the commercial television stations soon entered into a 'scissors crisis'. Although the revenue from advertising was rising, the cost of television programmes was increasing much more rapidly. By the late 1980s, this growing disproportion between rising revenues and costs had plunged some commercial stations into severe financial difficulties (Le Diberder and Coste-Cerdan 1988: 110, 116–17). The economic difficulties of the commercial channels were exacerbated by competition from the remaining nationalised television stations. Despite the privatisation of TF1 and the cut in the licence fee, the state-owned channels still attracted around one-third of the television audience and sold considerable amounts of advertising. Repeating the election manifesto of Gaullists and Giscardians, the commercial stations demanded that Antenne 2 and FR3 should only be allowed to provide current affairs, cultural and educational programmes (Forer 1989: 14, 20–3; Gavi 1990a: 18–19).

Before this lobbying could take effect, the Chirac government was defeated in the 1988 general elections. With no curbs on competition from the nationalised channels, the commercial television stations' financial crisis had to be solved through the centralisation of this sector of the electronic media. Each commercial station knew that its financial difficulties could only be overcome by becoming the most popular channel. Because of their daily routine, most wage-workers could only watch TV in the few hours of evening prime time. In the ratings war, each commercial television station tried to maximise its audience in these few key hours. By attracting the largest audience, the leading channel would not only sell more commercials, it could also charge higher prices for its advertising space. Because they did not want to fragment their spending across several different audiences, advertisers tended to concentrate their spending on the most successful channel (Le Diberder and Coste-Cerdan 1988: 116–25).

During the late 1980s, both TF1 and La Cinq invested heavily in expensive programmes, such as news, serials, films and sports coverage. By offering large salaries, La Cinq even bought many of TF1's leading stars to appear on its own programmes (Lacan 1987). Despite this setback, the newly privatised channel still provided enough high-cost entertainment programmes to increase its share of the audience. Soon TF1 was being watched every day by nearly half the total audience, especially during prime time. Once it was confirmed as the leading channel, TF1 enjoyed a virtuous circle of growth. With high ratings attracting a large advertising income, the television station was able to afford the high-cost programmes needed to attract viewers. In contrast, La Cinq and M6 were caught in a vicious circle of decline. With low ratings cutting advertising income, these two channels were forced to buy cheaper programmes, which were less popular with viewers. Instead of creating diversity, market competition between the commercial television channels had resulted in the concentration of viewers and advertisers on a single channel: TF1 (Coste-Cerdan, Gillou and Le Diberder 1987: 61–4; Cluzel 1988: 117).

Over time, the popularity of TF1 entrenched the channel's dominant position within French television broadcasting. While La Cinq only received 6 per cent of television advertising revenues and M6 was even more unsuccessful, TF1 had over half of this type of advertising in France (Forer 1989: 14). With their low income, the two new commercial channels were permanently in the red. Although CLT could cover its losses at M6 from other profitable enterprises, the long-term survival of Groupe Hersant was threatened by the continuing deficits of La Cinq. After huge losses, Hersant was forced to abandon its plans to become a multimedia corporation and returned to newspaper publishing (Chemin and Mamou 1991; Charon 1991: 219–20, 246). When Hersant gave up La Cinq, the franchise of the fifth television channel was reallocated to Hachette, which already owned a publishing company and a radio network. Ever since its failure to buy TF1, this media corporation had been determined to acquire a French commercial television station. After it took over La Cinq, Hachette tried to relaunch the channel. Although large investments were made, La Cinq continued to obtain low ratings and to lose large amounts of money (Chemin 1991; Sabouret 1992). By the end of 1991, because of disastrous results at its American publishing subsidiaries, Hachette no longer had the resources to meet La Cinq's continuing deficits. Like Hersant, Hachette was eventually forced to relinquish the franchise of the fifth television channel to ensure its own long-term survival (Chemin and Mamou 1991; Aeschimann 1992).

After their failure at La Cinq, both Hersant and Hachette had to renounce their ambitions to become leading multimedia corporations. After fierce competition, Bouygues and Havas had emerged as the only two French 'national champions' in the electronic media. Because of its ownership of TF1, the Bouygues group dominated commercial terrestrial television broadcasting within France. In parallel, Havas monopolised pay-television broadcasting in the country. Through a complex network of shareholdings, this media corporation not only controlled Canal Plus, it also dominated cable and satellite television broadcasting. When the La Cinq franchise was advertised, Bouygues and Havas-CLT decided to make a joint bid for the bankrupt channel. Under their scheme, TF1, Canal Plus and M6 would provide a 24-hour news service along the lines of the American CNN television station. After a few years of fierce competition, commercial TV broadcasting was now controlled by only two corporations: Bouygues and Havas-CLT. Far from resolving the contradiction between participation and democracy in the media, the neo-liberal model had concentrated control over television broadcasting into a single diffuse monopoly. In the event, the Socialist government decided to block this potential corporate cartel and awarded La Cinq's frequency to Arte, a state-owned cultural channel (Y.M. and Y-M. L. 1992a; Bobin 1992).

Across the European Community, the commercial electronic media were being concentrated in the hands of a few large corporations, such as the Berlusconi and Bertelsmann conglomerates (Tessier 1990: 81). During the reallocation of the franchise for France's fifth television channel, the only commercial challenger to the Bouygues–Havas-CLT consortium came from the Italian Berlusconi corporation, which offered to integrate La Cinq with its channels in Italy, Spain and Germany (Y.M. and Y-M. L. 1992b). But on either a French or European level, both bids involved the greater concentration of ownership within the electronic media. According to the advocates of the neo-liberal model, the deregulation and privatisation of the airwaves would guarantee media freedom for every individual citizen. Instead, by the early 1990s the electronic marketplace had confined media freedom to a cartel of a few large corporations. In this model of media freedom, the majority of French citizens remained passive consumers of programmes produced by other people. Following the failure of the neo-liberal model, a new version of media freedom was needed in France.

THE MENTAL MAP OF THE NEO-LIBERAL MODEL

Figure 7.1 shows the psychogeography of the neo-liberal model of media freedom. This is an ahistorical and abstract model of the media policies of the Giscardian and Gaullist governments. Media freedom is exercised in a society of atomised individuals. Both physical and legal individuals are guaranteed freedom of speech in the mass media through the private ownership of printing presses or transmitters. Although some individuals have access to the electronic market-place, most people only influence the content of radio and television programmes by choosing between the different media produced by the competing corporations. Wanting the largest possible audiences, media corporations provide the newspapers or radio and television programmes desired by the individual citizens. *Since legal individuals can own newspapers and radio or television stations as private property, individual citizens can exercise their media freedom by buying a particular newspaper or by zapping between rival channels.*

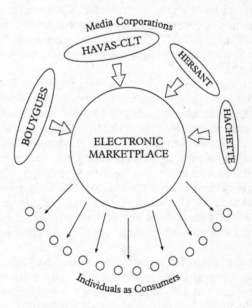

Figure 7.1: The Mental Map of the Neo-liberal Model

→   Information flows

○   Individuals

⇨   Ownership

8

The Liberty of the Regulators

The Victory of the Left

On 10 May 1981 François Mitterrand beat Giscard d'Estaing in the presidential elections. Soon afterwards, the Socialists won an absolute majority of seats in the National Assembly. When he framed the Fifth Republic's constitution, de Gaulle had tried to exclude the parties of the Left permanently from government. Yet, ironically, his constitution provided the institutional framework for the first stable left-wing administration in French history. Alongside its constitutional powers, the authority of the Socialist government was reinforced by the support of left-wing activists across the country. By sharing government posts between the different Socialist factions and appointing Communists as ministers, Mitterrand united the French Left behind his new administration (Portelli 1989: 226–32).

After liberation from the German occupiers, the Communists had been the most popular political party within the French Left. However, the Communist party's dominance of the Left in France was slowly undermined by the industrialisation of the country. With the spread of Fordism, the majority of the population were transformed into wage-workers. In particular, a new intermediary layer of technical and administrative workers was created. During the 1960s, many of the younger members of this 'new working class' were radicalised by the student revolt. Rejecting the Jacobin traditions of the Communist party, these student radicals called for the introduction of self-management into all areas of social life (Mallet 1975).

By the early 1970s, the expected revolution had failed to materialise. As a consequence, many New Left activists abandoned their previous commitment to direct democracy and began contesting elections. Because of their hostility to the Communist party, most of these white-collar radicals joined the Socialist party, which had been created out of a fusion of the SFIO with other left-wing groups. By the late 1970s, the Socialists had successfully supplanted their Communist 'brother-enemy' and become the most popular party within the French Left (Johnson 1981: 155–63). However, unlike the old SFIO, the Socialist party had very few manual working-class members and no institutional links with the trade union movement. Instead, the party was overwhelmingly composed of engineers, teachers, civil servants and other professionals. Lacking a mass membership among the working class as a whole, the Socialist party soon became dominated by a few full-time politicians (Portelli 1983: 57–8).

Competing against the Communists in the early 1970s, the Socialists rhetorically embraced many of the demands of the May 1968 Revolution, especially self-management. But by the time they were elected, the Socialists had decided to rule through the existing republican institutions. Although they removed some officials who were too closely associated with the old regime, the Socialists did not carry out a massive purge of right-wing bureaucrats. Instead, the new government recruited members of its party, other left-wing organisations and the new social movements into the state bureaucracy. Although the social and political composition of the state bureaucracy was widened, public administration remained dominated by the nomenklatura. Despite their extensive powers under the constitution of the Fifth Republic, the radical aspirations of the Socialists were limited by their decision to rule through the existing institutions of the state (Wickham and Coignard 1988: 214, 242–3, 448–9).

This absorption of left-wing activists into the nomenklatura was encouraged by the interventionist economic policies of the Socialist government. After it was elected, the new administration not only improved welfare benefits and employment conditions, it also nationalised almost all private banks and many leading industrial companies (Portelli 1989: 240–3). Despite this increase in state intervention, the new government's economic policies did not represent a complete break with the past. Like Giscard's administration, the main aim of the Socialist government's industrial strategy was to create 'national champions' to preserve the country's economic sovereignty (Attali 1978: 6, 222–4). In particular, the new administration initiated a development strategy for the post-industrial electronics sector, known as the Programme d'Action pour la Filière Electronique (PAFE). Inspired by Nora and Minc's report, PAFE's advocates promoted the vision of social liberation through media and information technologies. Once again, workers were promised the participatory democracy of an electronic agora in the long term through submission to the rule of the nomenklatura in the short term (Moynot 1987: 263–5).

After it was elected, the Socialist government also adopted more interventionist cultural policies. Jack Lang was appointed as a high-profile minister of culture and state expenditure on the arts was nearly doubled. Inspired by the Jacobin tradition, many leading Socialists believed that the state had a duty to educate all sections of the population in the national high culture of literature, painting

and music. The promotion of French culture was designed to
overcome not just the supposed aesthetic poverty of the working
class, but also the perceived threat from the American media corporations. Just as industrial intervention preserved national
sovereignty from foreign economic domination, so the Socialists'
arts policies were designed to prevent the 'coca-colonisation' of
French culture. During the 1982 UNESCO conference, Lang
emphasised this link between the new government's interventionist industrial and cultural policies by declaring: 'economy, culture:
the same struggle' (Niedergang 1982).

At this UNESCO conference, Lang hoped to form an alliance
between the francophone and Third World countries against
cultural imperialism from Hollywood. Yet the francophone countries
were products of France's own cultural and economic imperialism.
At the same time, this Jacobin nationalism also reflected cultural
elitism at home. For some Socialists, the 'banalisation' of French
culture by American media corporations was equated with the
emergence of the consumer society. Ironically, these left-wingers
were dismissive of the popular culture of their own voters: 'the very
movement that packs the discos is emptying the lecture theatres'
(Debray 1981: 244). This enthusiasm for the traditional arts among
these leading Socialists demonstrated the wider rehabilitation of
the Jacobin tradition within the French Left. Despite the rhetorical
support for self-management, the new government looked to the
state bureaucracy for the organisation of economic and cultural
activities in the interests of all citizens.

Just as its arts policies reinforced the role of the state within the
cultural sector, the Socialist government also initially revived the
Jacobin model within the electronic media. When the Communists
and Socialists had formed an electoral alliance in 1972, the two
parties of the Left had agreed to preserve the state's monopoly over
broadcasting. Inspired by Blum, they had interpreted individuals'
'right of information' as the expression of the views of the various
political parties elected to the National Assembly (Parti Communiste
et Parti Socialiste 1972: 163–6). But by 1981 the Socialists' support
for the public service model had been weakened by Giscard's
manipulation of the ex-ORTF broadcasting companies and the rise
of the free radio movement. Soon they were also advocating the
introduction of the self-management model to radio broadcasting.
Complementing the decentralisation of power to local authorities,
the ending of the state's media monopoly became one of the
principal themes of the 1981 election campaign. Among the 110
propositions in his programme, Mitterrand not only promised that
'television and radio will be ... pluralist', but also that 'local radio
stations will be able to establish themselves freely' (MacShane
1982: 271).

Despite this support in their manifesto for the public service and self-management models, the new Socialist government initially continued the Gaullist model of previous conservative administrations. Immediately after the 1981 elections, the director-generals and news producers of the state-owned radio and television stations 'voluntarily' resigned from their jobs, along with the chief managers of the *périphériques*, SOFIRAD and Havas. Excluded from power for over 20 years, the Socialists were determined to replace these people with their own loyal supporters. Despite their commitment to more libertarian models of media freedom, the new government had allowed the nationalised broadcasting companies to be treated once again as part of the spoils of electoral victory (Cotta 1986: 57–9).

The Second Left

Just as the French Socialist government began implementing its interventionist policies, the central bank of the US precipitated the world economy into a deflationary crisis. This global 'monetarist shock' soon derailed the reflationary policies of the Socialist government. By 1983, as the balance-of-payments deficit rose and the franc declined in value, the French Left was faced with a 'terrible choice' between protectionism and austerity (Lipietz 1984: 216). Fearing an international trade war would lead to a complete collapse in their electoral support, the majority of the Socialist party decided to submit to the disciplines of the global financial markets and to impose austerity policies on the French people. By causing a fall in living standards and a rise in unemployment, these neo-liberal measures did end the immediate monetary crisis. However, the forced adoption of austerity policies caused an ideological crisis within the Socialist party. As the traditional Jacobin policies of the French Left had failed, a new political and economic strategy was needed.

Before the 1981 elections, Michel Rocard and the Second Left had predicted that the Socialists' interventionist economic policies would end in failure. Following the 1983 franc crisis, this faction of the Socialist party believed that their prophecies had been vindicated. According to their analysis, the globalisation of production meant that individual governments could no longer insulate their economies from the world market through nationalisations and import controls. Crucially, the end of national economic autonomy had coincided with the introduction of post-industrial technologies. As Fordism was superseded, the rigid and hierarchical structures of the state bureaucracy and large corporations would be replaced by more flexible and spontaneous methods of working (Rocard 1986: 19–31, 99–100). For the Second Left, state control of the economy was not only unrealisable, it was undesirable too.

In this group's view, the rights of individuals and political democracy were threatened by the centralisation of power into the hands of a state bureaucracy claiming to represent the 'general will' (Furet 1988: 58–64). Seeking a replacement for Jacobinism, the Second Left appropriated the slogan of self-management from the New Left. In its interpretation, however, self-management did not just include workers running their own factories and institutions, but also capitalist companies competing in the marketplace. In Rocard's redefinition, the utopia of participatory democracy had been reduced to the need for institutional and regional pluralism within civil society (Rocard 1986: 28–9).

Although the Second Left embraced some neo-liberal positions, Rocard and his followers did not support the complete deregulation and privatisation of the economy. In the US and Great Britain, the financial markets were unable to organise the necessary long-term investments for infrastructure and research (Delmas 1991: 93–102). As a consequence, the Second Left believed that the state had to channel the egoism of private entrepreneurs towards fulfilling the public good. Inspired by Japan, West Germany and northern Italy, the Second Left wanted the public service state to be replaced by the regulator state. By mediating between the conflicting interests of the corporations, small firms and employees, the state could use regulations to accelerate the modernisation of the country (Rocard 1986: 36–49, 138–205). Unlike the public service state, this post-Fordist form of intervention was not to be imposed on enterprises and workers by the government. Instead, the regulator state would win consent for its industrial strategy from the autonomous members of civil society through negotiations and consensus. By creating a new social compromise, the post-Fordist state would act 'at the same time, [as] conciliator, catalyst and arbiter' (Delmas 1991: 204).

As part of its rejection of Jacobinism, the Second Left urged that this social consensus should be extended from the national level into every region. Soon after it was elected, the new Socialist government decentralised power to local councils by removing many central controls over their activities (Portelli 1989: 239). Although this measure was needed to democratise local government, the Second Left also supported decentralisation for economic reasons. In northern Italy, local authorities played a key role in co-ordinating market competition between many small firms by providing collective services, such as research and development (Caroux 1983: 105, 110–13). Similarly, the Second Left supported the introduction of new labour laws requiring limited participation by employees in commercial companies. By creating a social compromise within the workplace, French companies would be able to develop the more participatory management structures of post-Fordism (Albert 1993: 110–13).

The regulator state of the Second Left was a synthesis of public service and neo-liberal ideas, with borrowings from post-industrial and self-management theories. Offering the best of all worlds, this eclectic ideology of social compromise reflected the rapid absorption of left-wing activists into the nomenklatura. By the late 1980s, every institution of the French state had become more or less 'politically transsexual', with officials recruited from both Right and Left parties (Wickham and Coignard 1988: 116–24, 295). In parallel, the compromise between the opposing political parties within the nomenklatura had also been extended into the economy. After its interventionist policies had failed, the Socialist government returned to direct co-operation between the public and private sectors. Furthermore, the ruling party also constructed its own political-financial networks with leading corporations, such as Compagnie Générale des Eaux and Canal Plus. By the end of the 1980s, the main party of the Left had been almost completely absorbed within the major political and economic institutions of France (Wickham and Coignard 1988: 294–5, 339–44).

After the 1986 legislative elections, this search for a political consensus culminated in the 'cohabitation' of a right-wing prime minister with a left-wing president. With the failure of their neo-liberal experiment, the Gaullists and Giscardians were also forced to abandon their ideological illusions. By the late 1980s, all major political parties had accepted the need for the regulator state and a mixed economy. Crucially, these mainstream parties claimed that this social compromise realised the abstract principles of the 1789 Declaration of the Rights of Man and the Citizen. While the political rights of citizens were fulfilled through the democratic republic, the natural rights of individuals were guaranteed by the mixed economy (Furet 1988: 31). By the 1988 elections, Mitterrand was able to take advantage of this growing social compromise to win the presidential and legislative elections. Fulfilling his promise to create a consensus government, Mitterrand appointed Rocard as his prime minister. Under the founder of the Second Left, the second Socialist government became the pragmatic regulator of the social compromise (Portelli 1989: 257–9, 294–7).

Media Pluralism

When the first pirate radio stations started broadcasting, Rocard's faction within the Socialist party had enthusiastically championed their fight against the state's broadcasting monopoly. As it became more involved in the campaign, the Second Left even tried to set up its own *périphérique* to broadcast into France (Cojean and Eskenazi 1986: 67–71). Although the pirate station was a failure, this practical involvement in the free radio movement led to supporters of Rocard taking control of the ALO, the main group lobbying for a change in the broadcasting law. Using Rocard's criticisms of nationalisation, the ALO demanded that the state's monopoly over the airwaves should be ended. Instead, this lobby group wanted the licensing of local radio stations as self-managed enterprises. This advocacy of the self-management model was particularly aimed at the Jacobin inclinations of sections of Left. As shown by the Communist leadership's take-over of LCA (see p. 104), the independence of free radio stations was threatened not only by the central government, but by elements within the opposition parties too (Bombled 1981: 98–9).

However, this convergence between the ALO and the Second Left also expressed the ambiguous strategy of the free radio movement during this period. Before the 1978 legislative elections, the ALO had formed an alliance with Radio Fil Bleu, an unlicensed commercial radio station, to lobby the Giscard government for local radio licences. Because they obscured the disagreements between the two sides, the double meanings of 'pluralism' and 'self-management' were very useful for the ALO leadership. On the one hand, these slogans could mean that the ALO supported the creation of the electronic agora, which was the goal of the radical free radio stations. On the other, these concepts could justify the introduction of commercial broadcasting, which was the aim of Radio Fil Bleu. As in Rocard's own analysis, both positions could be defended as encouraging more pluralism in civil society, which was founded on the autonomy of institutions from state control.

After the passing of the 1978 broadcasting act, the ALO's attempt at creating a social compromise against the state's monopoly over the airwaves had failed. Faced with increased repression, the radical free radio stations left the ALO and formed the FNRL, which rejected any compromise with the commercial radio pirates. In their view, the ALO's use of the slogans of 'pluralism' and 'self-management' hid its tacit support for the private ownership of both radio broadcasting and other enterprises. For the FNRL's supporters, this deception was symbolised by the abandonment of the self-management model by *Libération*. They believed it was no coincidence that this newly commercial publication now supported the modernisation strategy of the Second Left (Cojean and Eskenazi 1986: 49–50).

The Moinot Report

Despite the split within the free radio movement, the Socialists continued to support the licensing of local community radio stations. For many Socialists, the replacement of the state's monopoly over the electronic media with a network of local community radio stations paralleled the decentralisation of political and economic power from the state bureaucracy and large corporations to the regions and small enterprises. The free radio stations were also an expression of radical culture. Because of his experience in the community theatre movement, the new minister of culture not only promoted high art and cultural nationalism, he also aided artists involved in popular culture, such as rock musicians and cartoonists. In a similar fashion, Lang wanted to encourage participation within the electronic media by licensing local community radio stations (Desneux 1990: 17–37, 62–3, 171–2).

After it was elected, the Socialist government set up the Moinot Commission to investigate how its manifesto commitments to reform the media could be rapidly turned into new legislation. Reflecting the iconic significance of the 1789 Declaration, the Commission centred its report on article 11's guarantee of the right of media freedom. For nearly 200 years, there had been a continuous struggle within France to create a society 'where the voice of everyone would be able to be heard' (Moinot 1981: 9). By defining media freedom as a political right of all citizens, the Moinot Commission rejected any version of the Girondin model. In its view, the technical and economic limitations on individual access to the electronic media meant that the major radio and television stations had to be nationalised (Moinot 1981: 9–12, 78–80, 128). As a defender of the public service model, the Commission not only advocated a major expansion of the state-owned electronic media into local broadcasting, but also proposed regulation of the *périphériques* and the cable television stations. Accepting the arguments of the Communist media union, Moinot even suggested that the ORTF should be resurrected to end the direct competition between the television channels (Moinot 1981: 37–9, 53–6, 71–2). According to the Commission, this state intervention within the electronic media would realise the aspirations of article 11 of the 1789 Declaration by creating real pluralism within all radio and television programmes. Inspired by the public service model, the Commission defined this pluralism as: 'the fairest possible expression of the whole [range] of ideological, political and doctrinal tendencies' (Moinot 1981: 13).

By interpreting article 11 of the 1789 Declaration as the creation of a pluralism of viewpoints within the electronic media, the Moinot Commission decisively rejected the Gaullist model. Yet, at the same time, the Commission did not advocate the 'pillarisation' of the nationalised broadcasting system. Instead, inspired by the Second Left, it proposed that the electronic media be supervised by an independent regulatory authority, similar to the IBA in Great Britain.

Seeking independence for its proposed institution, the Commission called for this authority's members to be selected from all political parties, the judiciary and people working within the industry (Moinot 1981: 27–8). According to the Moinot Commission, the creation of a regulatory body for the electronic media was the 'keystone' of its new version of the public service model. By removing direct control from both executive and legislature, the Commission believed that politicians would no longer be able to impose the Gaullist model on radio and television broadcasting. Because it would be 'politically transsexual', the new regulatory body would be able to create a consensus between the parties of Left and Right over the regulation of the electronic media (Moinot 1981: 20, 150).

Crucially, like the Second Left, the Commission no longer believed that state ownership of the electronic media was the only method of guaranteeing pluralism within radio and television broadcasting. Supporting the decentralisation of the electronic media, it recommended that community groups should be allowed to establish their own local radio and cable television stations. Despite this partial denationalisation of broadcasting, Moinot believed that the local electronic media could only adopt the self-management model under the supervision of the regulatory body. According to the Commission, intervention by the regulator state would guarantee 'freedom of communications and equal access for everyone' within the local community radio and television stations (Moinot 1981: 56–60, 67–8). By reinterpreting article 11 of the 1789 Declaration as media pluralism, the Moinot Commission had successfully defused the conflict between the defenders of state broadcasting and the activists of the free radio movement within the French Left. Because it rejected the Girondin and neo-liberal models, supporters of both Jacobin and Second Left positions accepted the Commission's definition of media freedom as a political right of all citizens.

Under this model of media freedom, the two sides could simultaneously realise their contradictory policies for the reconstruction of the ORTF and the licensing of free radio stations. In its report, the Moinot Commission synthesised these opposing media policies by advocating two different forms of pluralism. On the one hand, the Commission called for the creation of an internal pluralism of different political opinions, which would be expressed within the programmes of the state broadcasting corporation. On the other, it supported the establishment of an external pluralism with many different forms of media, which would be achieved by the licensing of local community radio and cable television stations.

By blurring these two contradictory policies, the Commission won support from the Jacobins for the Second Left's key innovation: the creation of consensus through an independent regulatory body. In the Commission's view, this institution had to enforce both types of pluralism within the electronic media. On the one hand, the regulatory authority would guarantee that a variety of political viewpoints were presented within the programmes of the new ORTF and the *périphériques*. On the other, the institution would ensure that a wide variety of political and social groups were granted local radio and cable television licences. Yet the establishment of the new regulatory body was designed not only to unite the different Socialist factions, but also to create a social compromise on state intervention within the electronic media between the parties of both Left and Right. By redefining article 11 as media pluralism, the Moinot Commission had turned a temporary and pragmatic compromise within the electronic media into the realisation of the eternal and abstract principles of the 1789 Declaration of Rights. As this version was inspired by the Second Left, this definition is known as *the regulation model of media freedom*.

The 1982 Broadcasting Law

Soon after the Moinot Commission had reported, the Socialist government turned its recommendations into new broadcasting legislation. Echoing the 1881 press law, the first article of the new law promised that 'radio and television broadcasting are free' (Casile and Drhey 1983: 14). After this promise of 'free' broadcasting, the 110 subsequent clauses of the 1982 law ensured that this right could only be exercised under regulatory supervision. As advocated by the Moinot Commission, this new form of state intervention within French radio and television broadcasting was centred on the creation of internal and external pluralism within the electronic media. Under the 1982 law, these two forms of media pluralism were both enforced by the independent regulatory body: the Haute Autorité de la Communication Audiovisuelle (Casile and Drhey 1983: 19, 30–1, 36). Because the creation of an independent regulatory authority removed any temptation for the government to control the electronic media, Mitterrand described the formation of the Haute Autorité as 'the most visible sign of a break with the past' (Cojean and Eskenazi 1986: 191).

By creating the Haute Autorité, the Socialist government demonstrated the demise of the authoritarian Jacobin models. Instead, the new administration accepted that the electronic media should be regulated by an independent state institution, which was composed of members of all major political parties. Building on the work of the parliamentary broadcasting committees, the government hoped that the Haute Autorité would institutionalise a social compromise between the major political parties on the future of the electronic media in France (Bourdon 1986: 47–8). Like the devolution of various responsibilities to local authorities, the formation of the Haute Autorité reflected the emergence of more flexible and polycentric methods of political control in the post-Fordist era. For example, a single nationalised broadcasting corporation could not produce the diversity of programmes needed for the great variety of ethnic communities in the major French cities. As in other areas, the most effective method of reimposing some political supervision over the expansion and diversification of radio and television broadcasting was the creation of an independent regulatory body (Pisier and Bouretz 1988: 157–60).

Under the 1982 law, the Haute Autorité had nine members: three nominated by the National Assembly, three by the Senate and three by the president, who also appointed one of his nominees as head of the regulatory body. There was a rotating method of nomination to prevent an incoming government from immediately changing the political composition of the authority (Casile and Drhey 1983: 43–4). This system of appointing the members of the Haute Autorité was based on the method used for the Conseil Constitutionnel. As the guarantor of the principles of the 1789 Declaration of Rights, this institution had pioneered the social compromise between the parties of the Left and Right on the existing constitution and the mixed economy (Pisier and Bouretz 1988: 156–7). By adopting this method of appointment, the Socialist government hoped to endow the Haute Autorité with the legitimacy of the Conseil Constitutionnel.

Table 8.1: Composition of the Haute Autorité, 1982

Members appointed by the President of the Republic
Chair: Michelle Cotta (ex-president of Radio France, Left)
Paul Guimard (writer, Left)
Marcel Huart (trade unionist, Left)

Members appointed by the National Assembly
Marc Paillet (AFP journalist, Left)
Danny Karlin (television producer, Left)
Stephane Hessel (ambassador, Centre)

Members appointed by the Senate
Gabriel de Broglie (ex-head of INA, Right)
Jean Autin (ex-head of TDF, Right)
Bernard Gandrey-Rety (television producer, Centre)

Sources: Ridoux 1982: 8; Cojean and Eskenazi 1986: 190–1.

Because of its system of nomination, the make-up of the Haute Autorité resembled a 'mini-parliament', with members drawn from the Communist, Socialist, Centre, Giscardian and Gaullist parties. But although the opposition parties were directly involved in the regulation of radio and television broadcasting for the first time, the 'umbilical cord' between the government and the electronic media was not completely cut (Chevallier 1982: 567). Because it controlled the presidency and the National Assembly, the Socialist party could nominate the majority of the members of the Haute Autorité. In response, the parties of the Right called for methods of appointment to the authority favouring their own side, such as nominations by the conservative judiciary (Casile and Drhey 1983: 43). Despite the pioneering inclusion of the opposition parties in an important state institution, neither Left nor Right could completely abandon Jacobin traditions in favour of a social compromise over the regulation of the electronic media.

Internal Pluralism in State Broadcasting

After the 1982 law was passed, the Haute Autorité took over supervision of the state-owned radio and television stations from the government. Every year, the regulatory body published detailed reports on how far the nationalised radio and television stations had fulfilled their public service obligations, such as by providing a suitable mix of information and entertainment programmes (Casile and Drhey 1983: 42–3). According to the Haute Autorité's president, regulation of the state-owned electronic media was needed to ensure the provision of 'popular quality television' for French viewers (Cotta 1986: 154). In reality, however, the Socialist government was not very interested in improving the range of entertainment programmes on the nationalised television stations. In its view, the primary purpose of the Haute Autorité was to end the dominance of the Gaullist model over the nationalised electronic media. For instance, the new administration rejected the Moinot Commission's proposal to resurrect the ORTF for fear of making it easier for a ruling party to exercise control over radio and television broadcasting. After the 1982 law was passed, the responsibility for appointing the heads of TF1, Antenne 2, FR3, Radio France and the other ex-ORTF companies was transferred to the Haute Autorité. By picking 'neutral' candidates, the regulatory body was supposed to create a consensus between the political parties on the management of the French nationalised electronic media (Casile and Drhey 1983: 35, 72–3).

Despite this search for compromise, the Socialists were still unable to give up completely the habit of asserting political power over the nationalised broadcasting organisations. For example, after a public quarrel with the government, the head of Antenne 2 was quickly retired in 1983. At the same time, although it no longer directly appointed the news teams of the nationalised electronic media, the Socialist government continued to use informal methods to influence radio and television journalists. Because they shared a common leftist culture with Socialist politicians, many journalists were reluctant to embarrass their friends by reporting their mistakes. For instance, the scandal over the French secret police's 1985 bombing of the Greenpeace boat in New Zealand received little coverage on the state-owned radio and television stations (Mamere 1988: 101, 129, 150).

Despite these limitations, the Haute Autorité provided the institutional framework for the implementation of internal pluralism within the nationalised electronic media. As recommended by the Moinot Commission, the regulatory body had a duty to enforce the 'honesty, independence and pluralism of news' on the state-owned radio and television stations (Casile and Drhey 1983: 19–20, 32–3). Under the 1982 law, the Haute Autorité fixed the 'rules of the game' for the transmission of parliamentary debates and the granting of equal airtime to opposing sides in political or economic disputes. Inspired by the public service model, the Socialist government believed that internal pluralism within the electronic media could only be created by granting equal access to the airwaves to the representatives of political parties. While individual citizens and social groups were only allocated minimal access, the Haute Autorité enthusiastically defended the rights of minority political parties. In defence of internal pluralism, the authority ensured that airtime was allocated to election broadcasts by parties that had no National Assembly deputies, such as Trotskyists and fascists (Haute Autorité 1983: 11–12, 50–3; 1985: 378–85; 1986: 289–91).

The Socialist government wanted the Haute Autorité to create a consensus between the main political parties over the rules for the appearances by their spokespeople on the nationalised radio and television stations. Following the 1969 ORTF directive, political airtime was already divided into thirds between the government, the ruling party and the opposition parties. Despite calls for the government and the opposition to be given equal airtime, the Socialists showed no enthusiasm for changing the 'rule of three-thirds', which was now working in the Left's favour (Paillet 1988: 142–4). Instead, they encouraged the Haute Autorité to enforce this ruling in a rigorous manner. By measuring the amount of airtime given to members of the main political parties, the regulatory body was soon able to compile detailed analyses of the length of appearances on the state-owned radio and television stations by representatives of the different parties. For example, in 1984 the

Haute Autorité issued a break-down of the political airtime allocated to the ruling and opposition parties on the nationalised electronic media (see Table 8.2).

Table 8.2: The Division of Political Airtime on French Television, 1984

Government: being 39.8%	47 hours 53 minutes
Parties of the Majority: being 26.3% (Centre Left/Socialists/Communists/extreme Left)	21 hours 36 minutes
Parties of the Opposition: being 33.9% (Giscardians/Gaullists/fascists)	40 hours 46 minutes

Source: Haute Autorité 1985: 58.

The Haute Autorité's statistics on political airtime were compiled to monitor the compliance of the state broadcasting companies with the 'rule of three-thirds'. But the regulatory body had major difficulties in constructing these statistics. For example, it was difficult to distinguish between appearances by Socialist politicians as representatives of the government and as members of the ruling party. These methodological problems soon became a matter of dispute between the parties of the Left and the Right. By producing his own statistics on the allocation of political airtime in 1985, the Gaullist president of the Senate tried to prove discrimination against the opposition parties on the nationalised radio and television stations (Haute Autorité 1986: 31, 259–62).

These disputes demonstrated the problems in constructing a cross-party consensus over the 'rules of the game' for internal pluralism within the nationalised electronic media. But with increased experience, the Haute Autorité showed growing sophistication in the monitoring of political airtime. For example, after analysing the statistics for the first eight months of 1985, the regulatory body required the state-owned radio and television stations to carry out a 'reequilibrium' of political airtime in the remaining four months of the year. During elections, this rigorous enforcement of pluralism and balance was further intensified. By carrying out weekly surveys on politicians' appearances on the state-owned radio and television stations, the regulatory body ensured that equal airtime was granted to the parties of Left and Right (Haute Autorité 1985: 24, 27–9; 1986: 39–41, 267–70). Although disputes between the Left and Right continued, a compromise over the division of political airtime

had been created within the electronic media. As predicted by the
Second Left, the consensus on the constitution and the mixed
economy was being slowly extended to all areas of society.

External Pluralism in Commercial and Community Broadcasting

Alongside the regulation of the nationalised electronic media, the
Haute Autorité was also responsible for the creation of external
pluralism within local community radio and cable television broadcasting. After the 1982 law was passed, the Holleaux Commission
was transformed into the local radio subcommittee of the Haute
Autorité. Following the granting of a licence, each franchise-holder
had to conclude a licence agreement stating the 'principal object'
of its proposed service (Casile and Drhey 1983: 135–6). Under the
1982 law, external pluralism was created by forcing local radio
stations to respect these promises of performance. Within each city
or region, the Haute Autorité licensed a wide variety of local radio
stations, which were affiliated to different organisations. For
example, there were several political local radio stations in Paris,
from a service run by anarchists to a channel funded by the extreme
Right (Cojean and Eskenazi 1986: 181–8). If they could be made
to respect their licence agreements, these different stations would
reflect a diversity of political opinions across their competing
services.

At the same time, the Haute Autorité was also made responsible for the granting of franchises to the SLECs, which wanted to
run local cable television networks. In their contracts, each SLEC
agreed to provide a variety of different cable TV stations on its local
grid, which was designed to create external pluralism. At the same
time, any commercial television channels had to observe the rules
on internal pluralism (Casile and Drhey 1983: 36). Under the
1982 law, the SLECs also had to provide access for community
television channels. Within this limited electronic agora, the Haute
Autorité hoped 'a free and pluralist expression of ideas and currents
of opinion' would be created over the cable television networks
(Haute Autorité 1985: 51, 333, 341). By combining elements of
the public service, neo-liberal and self-management models, the
authority ensured that the development of cable television broadcasting took place within the framework of the regulation model.

The Limitations of the Haute Autorité

When it founded the Haute Autorité, the Socialist government hoped
to create a consensus between the parties of Left and Right over

the regulation of the electronic media. However, the formation of any compromise between the two sides was blocked by the fierce opposition of the Gaullist and Giscardian parties to the 1982 law. In part, this hostility was caused by the popularity of the neo-liberal model among the parties of the Right. But by retaining elements of the Gaullist model, the Socialist government also contributed to this failure to reach a bipartisan consensus. Because of its system of nomination, the opposition parties never accepted that the Haute Autorité was politically autonomous from the government. Although it was a pioneering institution of the regulator state, the Haute Autorité was unable to form a long-term compromise between the political parties on the regulation of radio and television broadcasting.

As well as lacking political and financial autonomy, the Haute Autorité was not given undivided responsibility for regulating the electronic media. For example, the Ministry of Culture retained considerable influence over the state-owned radio and television stations, such as deciding the terms of their licence agreements and the level of the licence fee (Casile and Drhey 1983: 34, 104–11). The powers of the Haute Autorité over independent radio and television broadcasting were also limited. While the authority granted licences to local radio and cable television stations, the franchises for national radio or terrestrial television stations were awarded by the Ministry of Culture without any direct intervention from the Haute Autorité. For instance, Canal Plus received its licence for a national pay-television service directly from the government with no official involvement by the regulatory body. Lacking control over this important sector of the electronic media, the credibility of the Haute Autorité was much reduced (Casile and Drhey 1983: 126–30).

In addition to these limitations on its powers over the nationalised and independent electronic media, the Haute Autorité had no juridical autonomy. Under the 1982 law, the only available penalty for persistent offenders was the complete revocation of their licences, which was unworkable in practice. Without clear and flexible legal powers, the authority was forced to rely on the pressure of publicity to enforce the observance of licence agreements (Casile and Drhey 1983: 42–3, 46–8). However, the regulatory body could only acquire this type of moral authority through support from all political parties. But because it did not have full autonomy from the Socialist government, the Haute Autorité's claims to independence were never accepted by the parties of the Right. Without a compromise between the two sides, the regulation model could not be fully implemented within the French electronic media (Chevallier 1982: 563–4).

The Economic Crisis of Regulation

During the early 1980s, the institutional limitations of the Haute Autorité were exposed by the growing financial problems of French radio and television broadcasting. The successful adoption of the regulation model depended upon the existence of adequate revenues to finance the provision of internal and external pluralism by the electronic media. Within the nationalised electronic media, the failure of rises in the licence fee to keep pace with increases in the costs of programme production led to increasing deficits. Because it did not want to antagonise the voters by raising the cost of television viewing, the Socialist government was forced to cancel its plans for the expansion of state-owned radio and television broadcasting (Cluzel 1988: 200–1).

With the ending of the growth in revenue from the licence fee, the state-owned television companies increasingly relied on the sale of advertising. By the mid-1980s, while Antenne 2 and FR3 received enough advertising revenue to balance their budgets, TF1 raised two-thirds of its income from commercials (Cluzel 1988: 97–107, 185–96). Because they had to sell advertising, these state-owned stations needed high ratings for their programmes. Most documentaries and high-culture programmes were therefore removed from prime time and replaced with soaps, serials and variety shows. Although the Haute Autorité continued to impose internal pluralism and other public service obligations on them, the state-owned TV stations were increasingly controlled by market competition for viewers and advertising revenue. Within these stations, the regulation model was slowly being undermined by the neo-liberal model.

At the same time, the Haute Autorité encountered serious difficulties in enforcing the regulation model within independent radio broadcasting. Because the self-management model was economically unworkable, the authority was unable to prevent the commercialisation of local radio broadcasting. Even when the Socialist government allowed the sale of advertising and private ownership, many urban local radio stations still flouted their licence conditions. Following the failure to punish NRJ, these franchiseholders knew that the Haute Autorité could not force them to respect the terms of their licences (Haute Autorité 1985: 41–5; 1986: 157). Despite its duty to enforce external pluralism, the Haute Autorité could only monitor the changes made by market competition between different commercial radio stations, such as the emergence of national networks.

As in radio broadcasting, the observance of the regulation model by television stations was undermined by the spread of the neo-liberal model. By 1986, three of the six national TV channels were commercial companies directly supervised by the Ministry of

Culture. With such an important sector of the electronic media outside its control, the credibility of the Haute Autorité was severely weakened. In particular, the scandalous allocation of the licences for the fifth and sixth television channels to friends of the Socialist party was seen as a snub to the regulatory body (Cotta 1986: 238). Moreover, under their licence agreements, Canal Plus, La Cinq and the sixth television station were not required to meet the same public service obligations as their state-owned rivals. In the competition for viewers, these television stations overtly ignored their public service obligations to broadcast educational and cultural programmes, which further discredited the Haute Autorité (Prat 1986: 67).

The Conseil Constitutionnel Sanctifies the Regulation Model

According to the Second Left, the social compromise over the democratic republic and the mixed economy was the contemporary realisation of the abstract principles of the 1789 Declaration of the Rights of Man and the Citizen. Before the Socialists were elected, the Conseil Constitutionnel had already begun to turn this document into France's 'de facto Bill of Rights' (Keeler and Stone 1987: 177). After they lost the 1981 elections, the parties of the Right tried to hamper the implementation of the Socialist party's programme by appealing to the Supreme Court over the constitutionality of several new laws, such as the nationalisation programme. Despite its electoral mandate, the Socialist party could only rule through the constitution of the democratic republic, which was policed by the unelected Conseil Constitutionnel (Pisier and Bouretz 1988: 155–7).

Following the successful amendment of earlier legislation, the Giscardians and Gaullists also decided to challenge the constitutionality of the 1982 broadcasting law. In their submission to the court, the parties of the Right argued that the political right of freedom of speech in the electronic media could only be exercised through the natural right to own radio and television stations as private property (L.Z. and P.J. 1982). Despite its conservative majority, the Conseil Constitutionnel rejected this neo-liberal interpretation of article 11 of the 1789 Declaration. Because the shortage of frequencies prevented most people from owning their own radio and television stations, the judges believed that the French state had a constitutional duty to restrict the rights of some property-owners in the interests of the media freedom of all citizens. By defining media freedom as a political right, they wanted to ensure that a variety of political opinions would be given access to the airwaves. With this interpretation of article 11, the Conseil Constitutionnel had incorporated the regulation model of media freedom into the French constitution. The legal enforcement of both internal and external pluralism within the electronic media now became the practical expression of the abstract principles of the 1789 Declaration. After this judgement, the rights of individuals as citizens took priority over the rights of corporations as individuals (Conseil Constitutionnel 1982).

Yet after they won the 1986 legislative elections, the Gaullists and Giscardians introduced new legislation to deregulate and privatise radio and television broadcasting. Inspired by the neo-liberal model, the Chirac government saw no contradiction between the privatisation of the airwaves and the expression of a pluralism of opinions within the electronic media. Because they could not stop the new government from passing its broadcasting bill, the Socialists decided to challenge the constitutionality of the proposed changes. In their submission, they tried to prevent the privatisation of TF1 and the removal of controls over commercial broadcasters. Inspired by the public service model, the Socialists argued that state ownership was the best method of guaranteeing media freedom for all citizens. However, the Conseil Constitutionnel dismissed this public service interpretation by stating that state control of the electronic media was only one form of ownership among others (Conseil Constitutionnel 1986: 11,294–300).

Although they recognised the constitutionality of commercial ownership within the electronic media, nevertheless the judges reaffirmed their opposition to the neo-liberal model. Unlike the parties of the Right, the Conseil Constitutionnel believed that there was no absolute freedom of property for the owners of radio and television stations. Instead, commercial broadcasters could only operate within the constraints of the 1789 Declaration, especially article 11. Repeating its 1982 judgement, the Conseil Constitutionnel declared that the state had a duty to reconcile the technical limitations on broadcasting with a variety of constitutional duties, such as the preservation of public order. Above all, state intervention was needed to guarantee the expression of a diversity of opinions within the electronic media.

> Considering that the pluralism of currents of socio-cultural expression is itself a constitutional objective; that the respect of this pluralism is one of the conditions of democracy; that the free communication of ideas and opinions, guaranteed by article 11 of the 1789 Declaration of the Rights of Man and the Citizen, will not be effective if the public are not able to arrange in radio and television broadcasting, both as a duty for the public sector as well as the private sector, programmes which guarantee the

expression of tendencies of different character and respect the
necessity for honesty of information ... (Conseil Constitutionnel
1986: 11,295)

With this ruling, the Conseil exalted the necessity for the
expression of a 'pluralism of currents of socio-cultural expression'
above all other considerations. Crucially, the judges ruled that the
pragmatic compromise of the regulation model was the only possible
method of implementing the abstract principles of article 11 of the
1789 Declaration within the electronic media. Despite allowing the
privatisation of TF1, the Conseil Constitutionnel had outlawed
the adoption of the neo-liberal model within radio and television
broadcasting. After the ruling, the state could not abdicate its
responsibilities over the electronic media to market competition
between different radio and television stations. In contrast with
newspaper publishing, the owners of radio and television stations
could only exercise their right of media freedom under state supervision. 'Freedom is therefore limited in the name of pluralism and
free choice' (Cluzel 1988: 30).

The Commission Nationale de la Communication et des Libertés

When it was elected, the Chirac government was determined to
impose the neo-liberal model on the French electronic media.
Because it had enforced the regulation model, the Haute Autorité
was condemned as a major obstacle to this proposed reorganisation of radio and television broadcasting. Instead, the parties of the
Right called for the creation of a new regulatory body, which would
promote 'competition and pluralism' within the electronic media
(RPR/UDF 1986: 8–9). After the election of the Reagan administration in the US in 1980, supporters of neo-liberal media policies
had taken control of that country's Federal Communications
Commission (FCC). Far from limiting the effects of market competition, the neo-liberal FCC actively promoted the further
commercialisation of the American electronic media (Tunstall
1986: 248–53). According to the Gaullists and Giscardians, a new
broadcasting regulatory body was needed to implement similar media
policies in France. This was the CNCL.

In their manifesto, the parties of the Right promised that the
members of their new regulatory body would be selected for their
'independence and competence' (RPR/UDF 1986: 9). While politicians would still nominate some representatives, the majority of the
members of the CNCL would be appointed by the judiciary and
lobby groups (Delcros and Vodan 1987: 19–21). In reality, however,
this method of appointment adopted for the new broadcasting

regulatory body was not truly impartial. Because of the right-wing sympathies of most judges and lobby groups, the overwhelming majority of the members of the CNCL were supporters of the Chirac government. In theory, the parties of the Right wanted an independent regulatory body. In practice, the creation of the CNCL was in part a continuation of the Gaullist model.

Table 8.3: Composition of the Commission Nationale de la Communication et des Libertés, 1986

Members appointed by the President of the Republic
Bertrand Labrusse (ex-president of SFP, Centre)
Catherine Tasca (theatre director, Left)

Members appointed by the National Assembly
Daisy de Galard (media bureaucrat, Right)
Jacqueline Baudrier (ex-president of Radio France, Right)

Members appointed by the Senate
Jean Autin (ex-head of TDF, Right)
President: Gabriel de Broglie (ex-lawyer for Conseil d'État, Right)

Member appointed by the Conseil d'Etat
Pierre Huart (ex-lawyer for Conseil d'État, Right)

Member appointed by the Cour de Cassation
Yves Rocca (head of lawyers' association, Right)

Member appointed by the Cour des Comptes
Michel Benoist (ex-civil servant, Right)

Member appointed by the Académie Française
Michel Droit (writer for *Le Figaro*, Right)

Member co-opted to represent the newspapers
Roger Bouzinac (director-general of Fédération Nationale de la Presse Française, Centre)

Member co-opted to represent the telecommunications industry
Jean-Pierre Bouyssonie (ex-president of Thomson electronics, Right)

Member co-opted to represent the radio and television sector
Pierre Sabbagh (ex-president of TF1 and A2, Right)

Sources: Chirac 1986a: 12,770; 1986b: 13,201; Le Monde 1986a; 1986b; 1986c; 1986d.

Because of its right-wing majority, the CNCL was never truly independent of the Chirac government. Yet far from weakening the supervision of the electronic media, the creation of this neo-liberal regulatory body actually enhanced the state supervision of radio and television broadcasting. For example, the CNCL acquired a more flexible range of disciplinary measures. As well as being able to suspend or remove licences of recalcitrant operators, the Commission could also ask a judge to impose large fines or jail sentences on persistent offenders (Delcros and Vodan 1987: 114–16, 183–90). With these new powers, the CNCL was able to carry out a successful campaign against the remaining pirate radio stations and those franchise-holders who were breaking the technical conditions of their licences. Instead of deregulating the electronic media, the increased disciplinary powers of the CNCL strengthened the effectiveness of state regulation over radio and television broadcasting (CNCL 1988: 185–8, 192–4).

Using its increased resources and staff, the CNCL also intensified the supervision of both public and private broadcasters. Within the nationalised electronic media, the new regulatory body stepped up the monitoring of the state-owned radio and television stations' observance of public service obligations. At the same time, the Commission continued the close monitoring of the commercial channels' observance of public service obligations too (CNCL 1987: 144–77; 1988: 85–102). For example, the new regulatory body tried to prevent La Cinq from showing too many imported American serials. Despite the popularity of these programmes with the viewers, this commercial television station was ordered to place the fulfilment of its public service obligations above its desire to maximise its audience (Senamaud 1989).

This paradoxical triumph of the regulation model over the neo-liberal model was caused by the defeat of the Chirac government in the Conseil Constitutionnel. By rejecting the constitutionality of the neo-liberal model, the judges had sanctified the regulation model as the only possible interpretation of article 11 of the 1789 Declaration. For example, after this decision the observance of internal pluralism became an absolute precondition of retaining a commercial television licence. Although they were privately owned, commercial television stations had to present a diversity of political opinions in their news and current affairs programmes. Like its predecessor, the CNCL guaranteed internal pluralism within the news and current affairs programmes of the main radio and television stations through the three-way split of political airtime between the government, the ruling party and the opposition. By computerising its monitoring service, the new regulatory body was soon issuing monthly reports on the different news services' observance of the 'rule of three-thirds' (CNCL 1988: 52, 69, 311–16).

This intensification of supervision was needed to check the effects of increased competition for audiences within the electronic media. Wanting to produce infotainment, the producers of the chief news programmes tried to ignore the 'rule of three-thirds'. For example, the CNCL complained that the exciting news of the formation of a new government had led to excessive coverage of the Socialist party in early 1988. When this and other infractions of the 'rule of three-thirds' were observed, the regulatory body called for a quick reequilibrium of political airtime from the miscreant radio or television stations (CNCL 1988: 34–5, 51). During elections, this supervision of political pluralism was intensified even further. In the 1988 presidential campaign, the Commission issued daily reports on the division of political airtime between the rival candidates in order to facilitate corrections in any cases of imbalance in the coverage of the rival candidates (CNCL 1988: 15–30, 101–2, 351).

Because of the threat to external pluralism, the Conseil Constitutionnel also forced the Chirac government to strengthen the powers of the CNCL over the concentration of ownership within the mass media (Conseil Constitutionnel 1986: 11,297). Under the 1986 act, the regulatory body could prevent any single corporation from obtaining a dominant position within national or local television broadcasting. These anti-monopoly rules covered not just the cumulative ownership of television stations and radio networks, but national and local newspapers too (Delcros and Vodan 1987: 90–2, 103–7). For instance, the regulatory body used these powers to prevent the fusion of two national radio networks, which would have allowed Hachette too much influence in this sector of the electronic media (CNCL 1988: 133–4). As with internal pluralism, the constitutional duty to guarantee external pluralism within the electronic media enhanced the influence of the regulation model over French radio and television broadcasting.

Despite its increased resources and authority, the CNCL encountered several major problems. From its foundation, the new regulatory body was overloaded with work. In one year, the Commission had to supervise the privatisation of TF1, allocate the franchises for two other television channels and relicense the local radio stations. Not surprisingly, the authority was unable to carry out all these tasks adequately. For instance, the CNCL encountered greater difficulties in controlling errant commercial television operators. Although they respected internal pluralism in their news bulletins, these commercial stations tried to evade their other public service obligations, such as the production of French-made films and serials. In particular, La Cinq openly flouted the conditions of its licence agreements through its excessive use of imported American programmes (CNCL 1987: 162–77; 1988: 92–5). However, the administrative courts were very reluctant to impose fines on the commercial TV stations for infractions of the conditions of licence agreements. Lacking support from the courts, the CNCL was increasingly seen as a 'toothless tiger' which was as incapable of policing the airwaves as its predecessor had been (Alderman 1988: 40, 66).

The continuing legal weakness of the regulatory body was compounded by its lack of all-party support. Because of the dominance of right-wing members, the CNCL took some very dubious decisions on political grounds. For example, when local radio stations were relicensed in Paris, the regulatory body openly favoured candidates from commercial operations or right-wing parties over those from community organisations or left-wing organisations (Fornari 1987). The final collapse of the CNCL's reputation was caused by the arrest of Michel Droit for corruption. According to his accusers, this Commission member had taken money in return for using his influence to secure a local radio licence for the pro-Gaullist Hersant corporation (Portelli 1989: 284). Shortly afterwards, following their victory at the 1988 elections, the Socialists seized this opportunity to abolish the CNCL and set up yet another regulatory body. The victory of the regulation model was about to be completed.

The Triumph of the Regulation Model

In 1981 and 1986, incoming governments had promised a funda-mental transformation of French society. However, in practice these radical socialist and neo-liberal experiments had ended in failure. According to Rocard, this experience proved that 'the time of sudden huge reforms or revolutions is ... behind us' (Rocard 1987: 121). For the Second Left, the dramatic struggles of the past were now irrelevant. With the creation of a consensus over the democratic republic and the mixed economy, the parties of Left and Right were no longer divided by any issues of substance. With its goals finally realised, 'the [French] Revolution is over' (Furet 1981: 1–79). Because there was no need for a social revolution, Rocard's government was only committed to the pragmatic administration of the existing order. Under the guidance of the regulator state, market competition within a mixed economy would be directed towards furthering the modernisation of the French economy.

When they fought the 1988 elections, the Socialists made very few promises in their manifestos, especially on economic and social issues. However, the reform of broadcasting legislation was the one notable exception to this overall lack of policies. According to Rocard, the failure of neo-liberalism in practice had been dra-matically proved by the Chirac government's broadcasting policies, such as the privatisation of TF1 (Rocard 1987: 111, 149). By

1988, the French electronic media were suffering from growing economic difficulties and the regulatory body was discredited by the Droit corruption scandal. In his presidential campaign, Mitterrand took advantage of this crisis by openly deriding the CNCL as the 'national commission for non-communication and has-beens' (AFP 1988). In its place, he called for the creation of a new supervisory body to consolidate the regulation model within French radio and television broadcasting. Unlike its discredited predecessor, this new regulatory body would be politically neutral (Mitterrand 1988: 7).

In a new broadcasting law, the new Socialist government abolished the CNCL and set up the Conseil Supérieur de l'Audiovisuel (CSA). As with previous legislation, the parties of the Right and Left quarrelled over the method for nominating members of the new regulatory body. Although they claimed to want a consensual regulatory body, both sides advocated the system of appointment favouring their own interests. Once again, the Socialist government decided that the members of the CSA would be nominated in the same way as the Conseil Constitutionnel, which resulted in six out of the nine members being left-wing sympathisers (Mitterrand 1989a: 2). Faced with vigorous opposition to this method of appointment, the Socialist government was finally forced to use its executive powers to pass the new broadcasting bill through the legislature. Despite being a key institution of the social compromise, the establishment of the CSA had failed to win all-party support (Portelli 1989: 297).

During the debates on the new broadcasting legislation, the Socialists had promised that 'the CSA will not be composed of retired people [like the CNCL], but of active personalities' (Queyranne 1988: 7). However, although they were not committed Socialists, the CSA members were not independent personalities who could resist pressures from the government. For example, Boutet, the chair of the new regulatory body, was a well-known government functionary (Chamard and Keiffer 1989: 10). Although not as politicised as its predecessors, the CSA's composition still favoured the ruling party.

Despite this dispute over the method of appointing members of the CSA, the 1989 law did improve the implementation of the regulation model within radio and television broadcasting. For instance, new legislation increased the legal powers of the CSA through the introduction of contracts laying down the specific public service conditions of each franchise (Mitterrand 1989a: 12). Building on the work of its predecessors, the new regulatory body now possessed enough flexible and substantial legal powers to discipline any miscreant radio or television stations.

Table 8.4: Composition of the Conseil Supérieur de l'Audiovisuel, 1989

Members appointed by the President of the Republic
President: Jacques Boutet (ex-president of TF1, Centre-Left)
Roger Burnel (president of l'Union National des
  Associations Familiales, Centre)
Geneviève Guicheney (Radio Luxembourg journalist, Left)

Members appointed by the National Assembly
Igor Barrère (television producer, Left)
Bertrand Labrusse (ex-CNCL, ex-president of SFP, Centre)
Monique Augé-Lafon (academic scientist, Left)

Members appointed by the Senate
Francis Balle (media academic, Right)
Daisy de Galard (ex-CNCL, media bureaucrat, Right)
Roland Faure (ex-head of Radio France, Centre-Right)

Sources: Mitterrand 1989b; Les Echos 1989.

The Regulation of Commercial Broadcasting

Under the 1989 law, the contracts of the commercial franchise-holders laid down their specific public service obligations. As well as fulfilling their constitutional duty to present a pluralism of political opinions, the commercial radio and television stations also had to accept other limits on their managerial independence, such as quotas and restrictions on the showing of American serials and films. As part of its cultural policies, the Socialist government was determined to protect the French television and cinema industries from competition by American media corporations. Like its predecessors, the CSA produced annual reports on the commercial television stations' compliance with their public service obligations, especially their observance of the rules on internal pluralism. Inheriting the monitoring service of the CNCL, the new regulatory body was even able to break down the political airtime given to the competing parties into hours, minutes and seconds (CSA 1990: 21). Although internal pluralism was respected on order to attract viewers of all political persuasions, the commercial stations took much less notice of the CSA's criticisms of infotainment in their news and current affairs programmes, such as the voyeuristic reporting of violent incidents and the unattributed use of archive film to illustrate current events (CSA 1989a: 11; 1990: 25–6, 33–4).

This need for higher ratings also encouraged the commercial TV channels to flout the quotas on imported material, restrictions on the transmission of films, obligations to provide educational or cultural broadcasts and commitments to commission new programmes. Because they were cheap and popular with viewers, American serials and films filled the schedules of the commercial television channels, especially in prime time. In contrast, cultural and educational programmes were transmitted in off-peak slots, such as TF1's classical music concerts in the middle of the night. After many complaints, the regulatory body did finally force TF1 to broadcast mainly French and European programmes in its schedules (CSA 1988: 14, 11–30, 36–46; 1989a: 10; 1990: 10). However, the CSA encountered more difficulties in persuading the other two commercial television channels to comply with the conditions of their contracts. After years of disputes, the new regulatory body finally decided to impose heavy fines on the fifth television channel for various breaches of its licence agreement, including showing violent and pornographic films in prime time (CSA 1989b: 19, 33, 41–2; 1990b: 10–11, 28–32; 1990c: 11–12, 33–4).

This conflict between the CSA and La Cinq exposed the contradiction between the interests of shareholders and the observance of public service obligations in commercial television broadcasting. Not surprisingly, the commercial TV stations tried to avoid any public service obligations, which raised their costs and restricted their potential revenue from advertisers. In response, the regulatory body had to increase the scope and detail of its monitoring of the observance of the contracts' conditions. Despite the growing financial crisis within commercial television broadcasting, there was to be no relaxation in the enforcement of public service obligations on the commercial franchise-holders. Unlike its conservative predecessor, the Socialist government was not afraid of forcing one of the commercial franchise-holders into bankruptcy. Blaming the neo-liberal policies of her conservative predecessor, the minister of communications bluntly commented: 'there is one generalist television channel too many' (Tasca 1990).

The Regulation of Nationalised and Community Broadcasting

Under the law of 17 January 1989, the CSA also produced annual reports on the nationalised television stations and Radio France. As with the commercial operators, the regulatory body checked the state-owned channels' observance of public service obligations. Above all, the Council ensured that the news and current affairs programmes respected the 'rule of three-thirds' in everyday reporting and gave balanced coverage in elections (Mitterrand 1989a: 34).

Yet the schedules of the nationalised television stations were still shaped by the need for high ratings. Like their commercial competitors, the nationalised channels had to provide popular programmes in peak viewing hours in order to win large audiences for their advertisers. However, this attempt by Antenne 2 and FR3 to beat their commercial rivals was doomed to failure. Even in news and current affairs, Antenne 2 lacked the resources to compete effectively with TF1, which spent heavily to maintain its 8 p.m. bulletin's dominance in the ratings war. More seriously, the aping of the style of the commercial television channels led to a crisis of identity within Antenne 2 and FR3, whose public service traditions had apparently been discarded in the competition for more viewers (Deymard 1990: 46–8; Martin 1989: 26).

In its annual reports on the nationalised television stations, the CSA regularly called for the licence fee to be increased to the level in other European Community countries and for compensation for licence-exemptions granted to pensioners (CSA 1990d: 11; 1990e: 9–11). Some commentators also believed that more state funding was needed to solve the economic crisis within television broadcasting as a whole. In their view, because neo-liberal media policies had failed, the British system of reserving licence-fee income for the nationalised television stations and advertising revenue for the commercial channels ought to be introduced in France. As in the mid-1980s, this campaign was supported by the commercial television channels, which wanted a monopoly over this form of advertising. By the late 1980s, the proposal to remove advertising from the state-owned television stations was also being promoted by ardent defenders of public service broadcasting. By reducing the need to maximise their ratings, Antenne 2 and FR3 would be able to compete on quality of programmes with their commercial rivals.

> A country which spends 200 billion francs on national education is able to devote a derisory 2 billion francs to its television service. Public service broadcasting plays a crucial role in creating our national identity. Everything else is secondary. (Deymard 1990: 48)

Despite this campaign, the Socialist government refused to remove advertising from the nationalised television stations. According to the minister of communications, this proposal would lead to the ghettoisation of culture on Antenne 2 and FR3. Instead, the minister proposed a long-term plan to rebuild the nationalised sector of the electronic media, especially Antenne 2 and FR3 (Tasca 1990). By reversing Chirac's cut in the licence fee and giving direct funding from the central budget, the Socialist government did end the immediate financial crisis within the two state-owned television stations. By rescinding a proposed increase in the tax on television commercials, Rocard's administration won support from the parties of the Right for increased funding for the nationalised electronic media. After years of neo-liberal hostility to the state-owned channels, a social compromise had finally been created between the rival political parties on the future of the nationalised radio and television stations (Grundmann 1989; Gay 1991).

As well as increasing their revenue, the Socialist government also introduced a joint presidency for the two state-owned television channels, which were renamed France 2 and France 3. Finally implementing the recommendation of the Moinot Commission, the Ministry of Culture recognised the need for close co-ordination of the two state-owned television channels, especially in providing complementary programmes for viewers (Tasca 1990). In addition, the administration was determined to create a new state-owned television station. Originally, this channel was founded to provide an arts and cultural service for the ailing satellite and cable television systems. After it was merged with a similar German television station, this station was appropriately named Arte. In 1992, La Cinq's bankruptcy finally freed a terrestrial frequency for the arts channel. By allocating the franchise of the fifth television station to Arte, the Socialist government created parity between the number of channels of the public and private sectors of television broadcasting (Nassib 1990; Bobin 1992). Moreover, Arte unashamedly revived the traditions of the *télé des profs* which had been pioneered by the RTF and ORTF (see pp. 70–1, 78). Despite its designer graphics and rock programmes, the majority of its output consisted of high culture and documentaries. As an official symbol of unity between French and German ruling classes, Arte's 'conception of culture is a nostalgic reification of bourgeois art' (Emanuel 1992: 296).

Within radio broadcasting, the Socialist government also intervened to help the remaining community stations. Like the nationalised television stations, the original free radio pioneers had suffered from intense commercial competition. By 1990, there were only 350 community projects left out of a total of 1,800 local radio stations (Groupe de Travail 1990: 1–2). Because of the decline of the self-management model, the remaining community radio stations urgently needed more state financial aid to stave off bankruptcy. Therefore both central government and local authority funding were made available to help the community radio stations with money, training and institutional support (Groupe de Travail 1990: 3–4, 9–10; SJTI 1990: 3). As with the nationalised television stations, active state intervention was needed to preserve the remnants of the self-management model within radio broadcasting.

The long-term consolidation of the regulation model depended upon the authority of the CSA. As the next legislative elections were not due until 1993, the regulatory body also had time to win more autonomy from central government. When the Socialists did lose these elections, the incoming right-wing government made very few changes to the regulation of broadcasting. By slowly gaining the respect of all political parties, the CSA institutionalised a social compromise over the implementation of the regulation model within French radio and television broadcasting. Because of the ending of the state monopoly over the airwaves, the public service model could no longer be applied within the electronic media. Because of the financial crisis in commercial broadcasting, the neo-liberal model could not be implemented. Because of the collapse of the alternative media, the self-management model had also failed. By the early 1990s, the parties of both Right and Left agreed that the French electronic media had to be organised as a mixed economy of private, public and community broadcasters. Reflecting the wider social compromise, the regulation model had become the only possible form of media freedom in France.

The Europeanisation of the Regulation Model

As predicted by the Second Left, the autonomous Jacobin state had been made obsolete by the internationalisation of production and finance. In its place, many French Socialists now advocated the rapid integration of the member states of the European Community into a single economic and political union. Faced with fierce competition from Japan and the US, they believed that the European countries needed federal institutions to co-ordinate their economic development and protect their social institutions (Albert 1993: 211–29). The development of this European regulator state was founded on a social compromise between the Socialist and Christian Democratic parties. The determination of the main continental parties to lay the foundations for this federal regulator state was demonstrated by the 1985 appointment of Jacques Delors, a leading advocate of consensus politics within the French Socialist party, to be president of the European Community

For the French Socialist government, the emerging federal regulator state was particularly needed to supervise television broadcasting in western Europe. During the early 1970s, the European Community had initially become involved in the regulation of the electronic media through the introduction of satellite television broadcasting, whose signals spilled across the boundaries of the member states. At the same time, the legalisation of commercial radio and television stations in several member states had created the conditions for the emergence of European media corporations. By the late 1980s, French, Italian, British and West German commercial media companies were extending their activities across national borders. For example, Canal Plus established new pay-

television stations in Belgium, Switzerland, Spain and West
Germany. Because of the emergence of these European media
corporations, the French Socialist government called for the introduction of federal laws on the regulation of radio and television
broadcasting (Conso 1990: 121–2; Tessier 1990: 76–8).

Yet the initial impact of European legislation was to weaken the
state regulation of the electronic media across the continent.
Funded by advertising agencies and media corporations, advocates
of the neo-liberal model successfully argued that the public service
and regulation models contravened the political and natural rights
of commercial radio and television station owners. In the late
1980s and early 1990s, the European Court upheld the neo-liberal
interpretation of article 10 of the European Convention on Human
Rights by outlawing some national restrictions imposed on
commercial broadcasters (Benyahia-Kouider 1992b: 11; Porter
1992: 8–9, 11). Despite these rulings, the French government was
still determined to impose the regulation model throughout the
European Community.

Within the EC, the programmes of the American media corporations already dominated the output of television stations in some
smaller member states. The European programme producers with
their fractured national markets in differing languages could not
compete with companies enjoying economies of scale in a continental market mainly speaking one language. After some lobbying,
the EC member states adopted the French proposals for the Eureka
initiative to channel EC subsidies and other aid towards the
production of television programmes (CEC 1990: 7–9, 12, 21). In
parallel, the French and German governments launched Arte,
which was supposed to break down cultural barriers between the
two countries (see p.176) (Emanuel 1992: 286–94). This state intervention in television broadcasting was complemented by the
introduction of European Community regulation of this sector of
the electronic media. Already members of the Council of Europe
were negotiating the European Convention on Transfrontier
Television Broadcasting, which imposed minimal public service
obligations on satellite television stations (Council of Europe 1989:
337–8). Although neo-liberal British politicians were opposed to
further controls, the French Socialist government was determined
to toughen the regulation of these services by promoting EC legislation on cross-border broadcasting. By invoking its duty to create
a common market in services and to encourage economic development, the European Community could be given powers to
regulate the integration of television broadcasting across member
states (CEC 1989: 12, 21–3).

Crucially, this imposition of the regulation model at a European
level was based on the rejection of the neo-liberal interpretation of

article 10. By claiming the EC's right to protect the political rights of all its citizens, the European Commission was able to restrict the natural rights of the media corporations. The need to guarantee political pluralism within the electronic media justified the imposition of other public service obligations on satellite television channels, such as import quotas and restrictions on showing films (CEC 1989: 21, 24–7; 1990: 12). Within France, many people still denounced the European Community directive as a 'cultural Munich' for diluting import quotas on the sales of programmes from the American media corporations (Desneux 1990: 94–5, 106–7). Yet although its contents were still weak, this directive protected the application of the regulation model within France from any dilution by the neo-liberal interpretation of article 10. Although pan-European broadcasting remained hampered by language barriers, the European Community had now laid the basis for the implementation of the regulation model at a federal level when necessary.

'Media Democracy'

The triumph of the regulation model was consolidated by the economic weakness of the electronic media. According to the predictions of the futurologists, workers in the declining manufacturing industries were supposed to find new jobs in the post-industrial sectors, such as computers and the media. Yet radio and television broadcasting never developed into an important employer within the French economy. By the early 1990s, the turnover of all television stations in France was still less than that of the local subsidiaries of some foreign multinationals, such as the Nestlé food-processing corporation (Colonna d'Astria 1992). Because of the dramatic economies of scale in information production, a few thousand media workers were able to provide a wide range of radio and television channels to millions of listeners and viewers. Despite this economic weakness, radio and television broadcasting played a very important role in French society. By the late 1980s, the French population was spending more time watching television than working. Although its economic importance remained marginal, the social impact of the electronic media was immense (Le Diberder and Coste-Cerdan 1988: 14–15, 29–36).

For Rocard, this contradiction between economic weakness and social influence fatally discredited the neo-liberal model. If their economic importance was limited, the electronic media needed regulation to protect their role as political and cultural institutions (Rocard 1987: 147). From the early 1970s onwards, the Socialist party had relied heavily upon the electronic media to win support from voters. At the same time, leading left-wing activists found employment in the mass media. After the 1981 election victories, both Socialist politicians and media workers were rapidly absorbed into the mediaklatura of top television stars, newspaper editors and managers of broadcasting organisations. Not surprisingly, with their political life centred on the media, most left-wing activists championed state intervention to protect the extra-economic role of radio and television stations from short-term commercial considerations (Debray 1981: 89; Wickham and Coignard 1988: 234–5).

Reflecting these views, Rocard claimed that the primacy of the political role of radio and television broadcasting could only be assured through the implementation of the regulation model. Crucially, both the self-management and neo-liberal models had failed to create access to the electronic media for all individuals. Because the political right of media freedom could not be guaranteed by the natural right of co-operative or private property, the regulator state was justified in imposing internal and external pluralism within radio and television broadcasting. Inspired by Blum, Rocard believed that the voters could only make an informed choice between the competing parties in elections by hearing or watching politicians debating on impartial news programmes. Moreover, the electronic media had completely transformed the relationship between citizens and their representatives. Borrowing the rhetoric of the New Left, Rocard claimed that a limited form of the electronic agora had already been built within radio and television broadcasting.

According to Rocard, the combination of media pluralism and the regular sampling of public opinion by polls had created a form of two-way communications between citizens and their representatives. Although representative democracy remained in place, a restricted form of participatory democracy could be created by the electronic media. For the Second Left, this limited version of the electronic agora facilitated the formation of the social compromise within the country. Instead of imposing its views on the voters through propaganda, Rocard's government wanted an 'intelligent relationship' between citizens and their representatives. By explaining government policies and listening to the views of voters, the Socialist party hoped to win public support for the long-term policies needed for modernisation. For the Second Left, the widespread social consensus over the future development of France was underpinned by the imposition of the regulation model within radio and television broadcasting (Rocard 1987: 148–50, 178–82, 188–90; Julliard 1988: 117). 'No democracy without the freedom of communications, no freedom of communications without democracy' (Rocard 1987: 148).

The Minitel Explosion

The Second Left believed that the regulation model combined the best features of the public service, neo-liberal and self-management models. Although it was not supervised by the CSA, the Minitel videotext system provided the best example of how these different models of media freedom were synthesised into the regulation model. After Nora and Minc's report was published, France Telecom, the nationalised telephone monopoly, had begun intensive research into the convergence of computer, media and telecommunications technologies (Giraud 1991: 68–71). As part of the Programme Télématique and PAFE initiatives, this corporation decided to introduce a videotext service, which would be distributed over the telephone network. Unlike cable or satellite television broadcasting, this post-industrial experiment did not become a high-technology media without an audience. Determined to create a large base of videotext users, France Telecom distributed free terminals to its subscribers. In return, the recipients of these terminals had to agree to use an electronic telephone directory in place of the traditional paper version (Marchand 1988: 72–8). Over a decade before the American Internet system took off, an enthusiastic minority of the French public were using the wide range of videotext services available to Minitel subscribers. Soon businesses were selling their products over Minitel, from railway tickets to the latest stock market results. Above all, the success of the Minitel system was assured by the popularity of bulletin boards, especially the erotic message services (Marchand 1988: 101–14, 134–41).

For individual subscribers, the Minitel bulletin boards offered a limited form of two-way communications. As a combination of telephone and broadcasting technologies, the videotext system could simultaneously allow an intimate conversation between two subscribers and arrange the widespread dissemination of information to many different users (Marchand 1988: 88–91). Influenced by Nora and Minc's vision of the electronic agora, leading newspapers, radio and television stations established their own Minitel services, which were designed to develop two-way communications with their audiences (Charon 1991: 292–311; Marchand 1988: 133, 142–9). Similarly, some local authorities tried to create a form of direct democracy by offering Minitel services to their voters. Using their terminals, individuals were able to communicate their views to their representatives through the municipal bulletin boards (Loiseau 1991). Inspired by these examples, in 1986 student protesters used the Minitel system to co-ordinate their campaign against the Chirac government's university reforms. In conjunction with *Libération*, they set up their own bulletin board service, which relayed arguments against the proposed educational bill, information about future demonstrations and a satirical video game. Crucially, this Minitel system created a space for two-way communications between student protesters across the country. As in Guattari's version of the self-management model, individuals used

the electronic agora to create their own autonomous organisations, without being represented by political parties or trade unions
(Marchand 1988: 151–5).

Yet although videotext was used for radical politics, the Minitel
system never fulfilled the utopian dreams of the New Left. The contradiction between participation and democracy within the media
was not finally resolved through the introduction of new information technologies. Despite the free distribution of terminals, the
majority of the French population did not want to be connected
to Minitel. Instead, the main users of videotext services were young
people and professionals, especially men (Arnal and Jouët 1991:
24–7). Without mass participation, the electronic agora could not
be built through the Minitel system. Moreover, this videotext
network was never designed to implement the self-management
model. On the contrary, the success of the Minitel system was a
triumph of the regulator state. While the nationalised telephone
corporation had built the infrastructure and distributed free
terminals, a wide variety of commercial and community enterprises
provided the different videotext services to subscribers. The Minitel
system had been constructed through co-operation between state,
private and self-managed initiatives. As a practical example of the
social compromise, Minitel realised the regulation model of the
Second Left.

Telethon-Politics

Despite the success of the Minitel system, no post-industrial
experiment in 'media democracy' could remove the exclusion from
society felt by many voters. During the 1980s, the economic policies
of successive governments had created a two-tier society in France.
Following Japanese and Third World examples, the French labour
force had been slowly polarised into a core of full-time workers and
a periphery of temporary or part-time employees (Lipietz 1984: 93).
While traditional supporters of the parties of the Left suffered
from economic insecurity, many Socialist activists had been co-opted
by the nomenklatura. With the abandonment of radical policies,
these left-wingers were now more interested in enjoying the perks
of power than in changing society (Guillebaud and Joffrin 1990).
Betrayed by their representatives, young people in the most deprived
suburbs started riots to protest against police brutality and their
social conditions. Inspired by American rappers, a new generation
of musicians soon gained a large following by denouncing the false
promises of the social consensus in their songs (Muller 1991;
Loupias 1991).

The alienation of young people in the suburbs exposed the limitations of the social compromise of the Second Left. Without full employment, 'media democracy' could not create support for consensus politics on its own. Among right-wing voters, opposition to the social compromise was expressed through the growth in support for the fascist National Front. According to Rocard, the adoption of the regulation model by the electronic media should have created an 'intelligent relationship' between citizens and their representatives. Yet the National Front skilfully used the electronic media to win support for racism and other forms of bigotry. Despite being demonised by left-wing journalists, the fascists won the support of those right-wing voters disillusioned by the mainstream parties (Mamere 1988: 190–4). Ironically, the revival of fascism was aided by the imposition of the regulation model on the electronic media. Despite its hostility to the democratic republic, the regulatory body ensured that the National Front received its allotted quota of political airtime on the radio and television stations to promote its fascist policies (Haute Autorité 1986: 263–4).

As support for the National Front grew, racial attacks on the ethnic communities increased as well. In response, a left-wing faction of the Socialist party launched SOS-Racisme, a broad-based anti-fascist campaign. Using the latest media techniques, this movement hoped to isolate the supporters of the National Front through the mobilisation of popular disapproval against their racist views. For example, the first great success of SOS-Racisme was the mass distribution of an anti-racist badge. Building on this triumph, the movement won increasing support through the electronic media, pop concerts and the recruitment of media stars (Malik 1990: 45–51, 77). By appealing directly to young people through radio and television broadcasting, SOS-Racisme demonstrated the power of 'media democracy' in practice. However, the anti-fascist movement was compromised by its close association with the Socialist government, which did little to protect the ethnic communities against racist attacks. By concentrating on its coverage in the electronic media, SOS-Racisme was accused of engaging in 'Telethon-politics'. In a 'media democracy', the appearance of concern was given greater importance than practical help for those in danger (Malik 1990: 70, 152–6, 165, 172–3).

The media war between the National Front and SOS-Racisme reflected the dominance of infotainment in French politics. As most people learnt about political developments from the electronic media, rival political groupings conducted their struggle for power through the news and current affairs programmes of the radio and television stations. For the producers of the major television news programmes, the struggle between fascists and anti-fascists was a good sensationalist story, which helped to boost the ratings. Because

they were both skilled in media techniques, the leaders of the
National Front and SOS-Racisme even performed well in front of
the cameras. Despite the creation of 'media democracy', the
violence caused by the rise of racial intolerance had just become
more vicarious infotainment for audiences watching safely in their
own homes.

In mutual complicity, the politicians and the electronic media
had transformed political debate into infotainment for listeners and
viewers. However, the competing political marketing campaigns
of the mainstream parties hid the growing 'crisis of representation'
within France. Because there was no credible radical opposition,
many citizens felt that elections could no longer change anything.
Although they had perfected their media skills, the political parties
encountered increasing difficulties in arousing the interest of the
voters. For example, many inhabitants of the deprived suburbs did
not want to participate in any dialogue with politicians without the
promise of social change (Rosanvallon 1988: 137–46; Jarreau and
Mamou 1991). By the early 1990s, this discontent with 'media
democracy' had spread to wider sections of the French population.
After the scandals over the reporting of the Romanian revolution
(see p. 142), the credibility of the infotainment news programmes
among their audiences rapidly declined. Following the lead of the
alienated youth of the ghettos, the wider population had become
very wary of politicians and their media techniques (Missika 1991:
99–101, 112–14). As a consequence, the socialists were badly
defeated in the 1993 legislative elections.

The Implosion into Hyper-reality

During the late 1970s, many French intellectuals were attracted
by the analyses of the Second Left. Losing their faith in revolutionary
solutions, they rejected the need for radical social change. Instead,
they championed the defence of political democracy and social
pluralism. Jean-François Lyotard and other intellectuals turned the
Second Left's political and economic positions into a new social
theory: post-modernism. Echoing the New Left and the futurologists, the post-modernists claimed that the development of industrial
capitalism had been completed. In their view, the next stage of
economic development was the emergence of a post-industrial
society. With the replacement of Fordism, civil society would be
increasingly organised around autonomous work groups and communities. In parallel, the globalisation of the economy would create
international links between these decentralised producers. Above
all, the triumph of these autonomous and pluralist forms of social
organisation was based on the adoption of the new information tech-

nologies, which would create two-way communications between the members of civil society (Lyotard 1984: 3–6, 14–15, 60–7).

Like the Second Left, the post-modernists promiscuously combined the media theories of the New Right and New Left. On the one hand, they advocated the creation of the electronic marketplace. Rejecting the state control of radio and television broadcasting, the post-modernists accepted that market competition between 'active communicators' would create direct access to the electronic media. But on the other hand, they also called for the construction of the electronic agora. Inspired by the community media activists, the post-modernists demanded 'free access' to the interactive cable television grids and computer networks (Lyotard 1984: 67). Like Nora and Minc, they believed that the introduction of information technologies would eventually realise the New Left's hopes for participatory democracy in all social institutions. '[P]ost-modernism is the substitute for the sixties and the compensation for their failure' (Jameson 1991: xvi).

By the mid-1980s, many post-modernists had even abandoned the limited radicalism of the Second Left. Disillusioned by the failings of the Socialist government, they uncritically celebrated the diversity of commodities and identities of the post-Fordist world, especially within the electronic media. However, embracing cynicism and nihilism, Jean Baudrillard developed a much more pessimistic version of post-modernism to explain the final collapse of the hopes of the French Left. Renouncing his own left-wing past, Baudrillard explained that the failure of both revolutionary and reformist policies had been actually caused by the implementation of the various models of media freedom. Far from being champions of liberty, all sections of the French Left were implicated in the development of the latest stage of capitalist oppression: post-modernism (Baudrillard 1983b: 60–1, 95).

Like earlier post-modernists, Baudrillard claimed that a post-industrial society had already been created in the advanced capitalist countries through the widespread ownership of computers and television sets (Baudrillard 1983a: 38–48). However, in the 1970s and early 1980s both New Left and New Right had predicted that the advent of the post-industrial society would liberate individuals from the social hierarchies of Fordism. By contrast, Baudrillard asserted that the spread of information technologies was creating a new form of domination. In the post-modern era, individuals had been reduced to passive viewers of computer and television screens. According to Baudrillard, the electronic media did not simply spread incorrect ideas among the population. More importantly, they were pioneering an entirely simulated world of information: hyper-reality. As interactive computer and cable television networks became widely available, all aspects of social life would be eventually subsumed within the synthetic world of information technologies (Baudrillard 1983a: 25, 55, 99; 1983a: 83). 'In the image of television, the beautiful prototypical object of this new era, the surrounding universe and our very bodies are becoming monitoring screens' (Baudrillard 1987: 12).

Because the information technologies had replaced the production of things with the simulation of images, all aspects of social life had been transferred from the real world into hyper-reality. Far from creating a 'media democracy' or the electronic agora, radio and television broadcasting had transformed politics into show business. Dependent on the electronic media to communicate with voters, politicians had already adopted the techniques of infotainment to maximise their appeal to voters. For example, the Gulf war had not been waged by the US and its allies for the oil resources of the Middle East, but as a thrilling diversion for the television audiences back home (Baudrillard 1991). Similarly, French politics had been reduced to a 'gigantic special effect' simulating a false rivalry between the Left and Right. Explaining the advent of 'Telethon-politics', Baudrillard claimed that the media image of politicians was now more important than their social or economic policies (Baudrillard 1985: 69–71, 107–12; 1990: 87–8).

With the advent of 'political hyper-reality', Baudrillard attacked both the regulation model of the Socialist party and the self-management model of the New Left. According to this philosopher, Rocard's 'media democracy' was simply a 'feedback' mechanism for the social compromise between the parties of the Left and the Right. Because the advent of consensus politics had ruled out any major social change, the politicians had to simulate political controversy through the electronic media. According to this analysis, the constant use of opinion polls actually demonstrated the end of political democracy. Instead of being represented by elected politicians, the views of citizens were now perpetually sampled by polling organisations. Like sports commentators, television news presenters assessed the latest position of the rival parties through their most recent poll ratings (Baudrillard 1985: 112–16, 124). '[Y]ou participate in socialism like a video game or a drama on the television' (Baudrillard 1985: 90).

Breaking with his own past, Baudrillard also attacked the New Left advocates of the electronic agora. When they pioneered cable television and free radio broadcasting, the community media activists had hoped to create the electronic agora. Yet instead of creating a self-managed society, the introduction of the new information technologies had ended all opportunities for political and economic participation. While they were watching television or using computers, individuals could not act as citizens or members of civil society. By encouraging the use of information technologies, the advent of two-way communications extended the dominance of hyper-reality over social life. Far from overthrowing the spectacle, the construction of the electronic agora had created a 'new, involuntary servitude' oppressing the entire population (Baudrillard 1983b: 25–6, 95–102; 1985: 97, 141–3).

Because both political representation and direct access intensified the dominance of hyper-reality, the failure of the regulation and self-management models demonstrated that the creation of media freedom was not only impossible, but undesirable. In the post-modern world, individuals were 'seduced' into the servitude of hyper-reality by infotainment programmes and two-way communications. For Baudrillard, the only form of resistance was the refusal to participate in either 'media democracy' or the electronic agora. In his view, people should demonstrate their hostility to the 'cold seduction' of hyper-reality by switching off their television sets and computers (Baudrillard 1983b: 37–8; 1985: 135–6; 1990: 96). 'Banality, inertia, apoliticism used to be fascist; they are in the process of becoming revolutionary – without changing their meaning' (Baudrillard 1983b: 40).

In the late 1980s and early 1990s, the popularity of Baudrillard's theory of hyper-reality reflected not only the failure of the promises of participatory democracy made by the advocates of the self-management and neo-liberal models, but also the limitations of the Socialist government's regulation model. For pessimistic post-modernists, the theory of hyper-reality appeared to explain the contradiction between the extraordinary potential of the electronic media and their limited uses in contemporary society. As the 'crisis of representation' intensified, there was increasing scepticism about the social consensus underpinning the regulation model. But, by rejecting the possibility of any other form of media freedom, Baudrillard's theory of hyper-reality offered no practical solution to the alienation of the audience other than ironic detachment and political nihilism. Instead, by advocating 'inertia', this philosopher was implicitly encouraging acceptance of the dominance of the regulation model. With implementation of the New Left's and New Right's dreams of the electronic agora or the electronic marketplace also having stalled, the social compromise within the electronic media was still secure. Despite its manifest failings, the regulation model remained the only possible form of media freedom in contemporary France.

THE MENTAL MAP OF THE REGULATION MODEL

Figure 8.1 shows the psychogeography of the regulation model of media freedom. This is an ahistorical and abstract model of the 'media democracy' of the Rocard government. Media freedom was exercised in a society based on the social compromise between the parties of the Left and the Right over the democratic republic and the mixed economy. Within this society, citizens expressed their opinions by voting in general elections and participating in opinion poll surveys. In the electronic media, the democratic republic acted as a regulator state, which created the social and economic conditions for the exercise of the political rights of citizens. By licensing state, commercial and community radio and television stations, the regulator state created external pluralism within the electronic media. By regulating all radio and television stations, the regulator state guaranteed internal pluralism within the electronic media. The opinions of the citizens were expressed in the electronic media by their elected representatives from the competing parties. *Since there was internal and external pluralism within radio and television broadcasting, citizens exercised their media freedom by electing candidates from the competing political parties, responding to opinion polls and choosing between channels.*

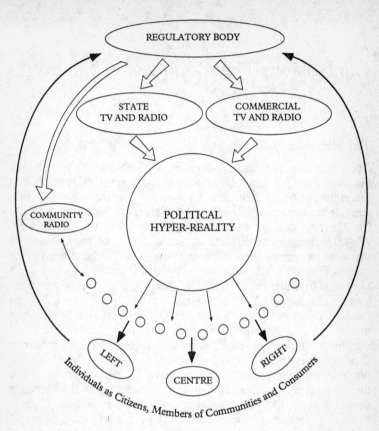

Figure 8.1: The Mental Map of the Regulation Model

→   Information flows   ➤   Elections and opinion polls

⇨   Regulation and legal controls   ○   Individuals

Conclusion: The Conquest of Liberty

The Republic of the Spectacle

According to Hegel and Kojève, the 1789–99 French Revolution discovered the fundamental principles of modern society, including the right to media freedom. Ever since, there has been a long struggle to realise this 'end of history' in practice. For instance, media freedom was defined as a form of participatory democracy in the 1789 Declaration of Rights. In principle, all citizens possessed the right to express their own opinions to each other through the media. For 200 years, successive models of this basic human right have tried to realise this combination of participation and democracy within the media. Yet in practice, it has been impossible to implement one side of this contradiction without negating the other half. For example, under the Girondin model, a limited number of individuals could express their opinions by producing their own newspapers. But by making the media available to the majority of the population, any individual participation within their production became impossible. As was shown by the television coverage of the 1989 bicentenary parade, even the latest definition of media freedom assumes that most people will only passively consume the opinions of others. Despite claims of the advent of post-modernity, the basic contradiction between participation and democracy within the media has not yet been resolved. But without the transcendence of this contradiction, the principle of media freedom cannot be fully realised in practice.

The development of the successive models of media freedom pioneered the emergence of France as a modern state and economy. There can be no modernity without the media; there can be no media without modernity. In traditional society, the overwhelming majority of the population lived in autarchic rural communities. These peasants were divided from one another not just by the mutual incomprehensibility of different local dialects, but also by mass illiteracy. Over time, this traditional society was destroyed by the advent of modernity. As village communities were absorbed within the money economy and the state, the peasants were transformed into members of civil society and citizens of the republic. The media played a key role in breaking down the isolation of individuals from one another. For example, the creation of the mass-circulation newspapers demonstrated how the formation of a unified national market would eventually lead to the Fordist industrialisation of the economy. However, the centralisation of the traditional communities into a single nation was not just an economic process, but a political endeavour too. Under the absolute monarchy, politics had been the private affair of the king. Following the 1789–99 Revolution, political decision-making slowly became the interest of all citizens. Crucially, the involvement of the people within politics was impossible without the creation of media freedom.

The contradiction between participation and democracy in media freedom was derived from the political nature of this basic human right. Under the Girondin model, the physical limits to direct democracy were partly overcome through the participation of citizens in political debate by publishing their own newspapers and books. Yet the ability of the journalist-printers to express their own views in print depended upon the ownership of printing presses as private property. In this model of media freedom, the universal rights of all citizens were derived from the particular interests of the bourgeoisie. Because media freedom was restricted to a minority of private property-owners, the various Jacobin models were developed. The development of the Jacobin models paralleled the introduction of Fordism. In the era of the journalist-printers or broadcaster-engineers, individuals could gain access to the media by using artisanal methods of production. But with the evolution of Fordism, mass-circulation newspapers and radio or television channels had to be produced on expensive machines, using collective labour. Journalists, printers, broadcasters and engineers were therefore transformed into wage-labourers in nationalised and commercial media corporations. Despite the wider availability of different types of media, the increased productivity of collective labour only intensified the separation between a minority exercising media freedom and a majority restricted to being an audience.

Because most individuals could no longer participate in the media, the views of all citizens now had to be represented by politicians. For their advocates, the relative merits of the Jacobin, totalitarian, public service and Gaullist models depended upon how far each version effectively represented the interests of the majority of the population. As France industrialised, internal and external crises created the conditions for successive experiments with the various forms of the Jacobin model. Yet, despite their democratic claims, these Jacobin models were limited by the economic and technical capacities of Fordism. For instance, there was always an imminent danger of the separation of the interests of politicians and the citizenry. As the 'general will' of all citizens, the state could assert its autonomy from the particular interests of any group of individuals. In its authoritarian variants, the Jacobin model even implied the

abandonment of democratic accountability in the short term in
favour of the supposed long-term interests of the people. Above
all, the various interpretations of the Jacobin model could not
resolve the contradiction between participation and democracy
within the media. Although everybody could now read, hear or see
their political leaders, citizens could not engage in two-way communications within the Fordist media. Instead, there was only a
one-way flow of communications from the politicians and the
mediaklatura to the citizens.

In the May 1968 Revolution, a new generation of radicals rejected
the need for their opinions to be represented through political
parties. With modernisation completed, they demanded the
immediate adoption of participatory democracy in all social institutions, including the media. Crucially, the New Left believed
that the implementation of its new model of media freedom would
provide a technical solution to the physical limits of direct democracy.
By creating horizontal links between workers' councils or new
social movements, the electronic agora would allow everybody to
take part in political and social decision-making for the first time.
According to advocates of the self-management model, the co-
operative ownership of the media had resolved the contradiction
between participation and democracy. In reaction, the New Right
developed its own version of participatory democracy within the
media. In the electronic marketplace, individuals became 'active
communicators' selling each other their own media products.
According to advocates of the neo-liberal model, the individual
ownership of the media had resolved the contradiction between participation and democracy. Yet in both models, the contradictions
of media freedom were not really resolved. In the self-management
model, the electronic agora was dominated by a handful of
committed activists. In the neo-liberal model, the electronic
marketplace came under the control of a few media corporations.
'In all that has happened in the last twenty years, the most important
change lies in the very continuity of the spectacle' (Debord 1990: 7).

The Revival of the Media Utopias

The failure of both New Left and New Right to create two-way
communications within the media opened the way for the triumph
of the regulation model. For the Second Left, this interpretation
eclectically combined the best elements of all previous models of
media freedom. By enforcing internal and external pluralism, the
regulation model implemented both the political diversity of the
public service model and the economic competition of the neo-liberal
model. With state funding, even remnants of the self-management

model were preserved. At the same time, the adoption of this inter-pretation signalled the abandonment of any radical solutions to the contradiction between participation and democracy in the media. With the New Left and New Right discredited, the political and economic debates in France were now restricted within the parameters of the social consensus on the democratic republic and mixed economy. Because most people had gained their political rights and enjoyed the benefits of the consumer society, the 'end of history' had almost been achieved in contemporary society (Fukuyama 1992). As a consequence, the regulation model was accepted as the only possible interpretation of media freedom.

Despite often being described as post-modernist, this political and economic compromise demonstrated the inability to proceed beyond the contradictions of modernisation. Although the Socialists lost power in the 1993 elections, the parties of the Right had no intention of repeating the neo-liberal experiments of the 1980s. By abandoning their previous utopianism, both Left and Right now accepted the inevitability of political representation within the media. Although the political rights of citizens were constitution-ally privileged above the natural rights of private property-owners, most citizens could never engage in two-way communications in this contemporary 'media democracy'. As a consequence, the regulation model was only an ersatz solution to the contradiction of participation and democracy in the media.

According to the Conseil Constitutionnel, the regulation model realised the abstract and ahistorical principles of article 11 of the 1789 Declaration. Yet the exercise of media freedom could only take place in a specific society at a particular time. As shown by French history, media freedom has been interpreted in very different ways as political and economic circumstances have changed. Over the past 200 years, the rise and fall of the various models demon-strate the transitory nature of each version of this basic human right. Moreover, rival interpretations of the same model were adopted in other industrialised countries. For example, while in Britain the BBC was set up outside direct party control, Blum's public service model was centred upon the 'pillarisation' of the nationalised broadcasting monopoly. Thus, although the advocates of rival models believed their favoured version was universal and eternal, each interpretation reflected the circumstances of the media in one country at a particular time.

Despite the sanctification of the regulation model by the Supreme Court, the instability of history ensured that this version of media freedom in France can have no real permanence. As the 'crisis of representation' deepens, the social compromise between the different political parties could come apart. With the continuous rise in unemployment and the competitive pressures unleashed by the single

European market, the consensus on the regulator state and the mixed economy will also be threatened. At the same time, technological innovation has not ceased. As in the past, the introduction of new information technologies will create opportunities for co-operative and individual access to the media. For example, many elements of the proposed 'information super-highway' have already been pioneered by the Minitel system, such as videotext and bulletin boards. Because of the inevitability of continuous political, economic and technological changes, the triumph of the regulation model can only be temporary. Crucially, without resolving the contradiction between participation and democracy, the 'end of history' for media freedom has not yet been reached in France.

Under the regulation model, state intervention mitigated the centralisation of the media into the hands of a few public and private corporations. Because the self-management and neo-liberal models had failed to create direct democracy in practice, the regulation model imposed internal and external pluralism on radio and television broadcasting. Yet, like the previous experiments of the New Left and New Right, mass participation in the media will once again be attempted. By trying to go beyond the social compromise of the regulation model, any new or revived model of media freedom will try to overcome the contradiction between the rhetoric of the active right of every citizen to express their viewpoints in the media and the reality of most people's passive consumption of the opinions of others. In new circumstances, the critical question will be once again posed: whether media freedom will be 'the privilege of particular individuals or whether it is a privilege of the human mind' (Marx 1975: 155). The answer to this fundamental question can only be discovered in future struggles to realise the principle of media freedom in practice. The electronic agora has yet to be built.

Bibliography

A. Ch. (1982) 'La Loi sur la communication audiovisuelle pourra être promulguée malgré l'annulation de certains dispositions par le Conseil Constitutionnel', *Le Monde*, 30 July: 16.

Aeschimann, E. (1992) 'Hachette a mal à la dette', *Libération*, 1 January: 4.

AFP (1988) 'A Lyon, Mitterrand veut mobiliser pour "créer la dynamique de l'union"', *Libération*, 16–17 January: 24.

Aglietta, M. (1979) *A Theory of Capitalist Regulation: The US Experience*, London: New Left Books.

Agulhon, M. (1981) *Marianne into Battle: Republican Imagery and Symbolism in France: 1789–1880*, Cambridge: Cambridge University Press.

Albert, M. (1993) *Capitalism vs. Capitalism*, New York: Four Walls, Eight Windows.

Alderman, B. (1988) 'French Watchdog "Dead"', *Variety*, 13 January: 40, 66.

Althusser, L. (1971) 'Ideology and Ideological State Apparatuses (Notes towards an Investigation)' in *Lenin and Philosophy and Other Essays*, London: New Left Books.

Amann, P. (1975) 'The Paris Club Movement in 1848' in R. Price (ed.) *Revolution and Reaction: 1848 and the Second French Republic*, New York: Barnes & Noble.

Arendt, H. (1968) *Totalitarianism*, New York: Harcourt Brace Jovanovich.

Armstrong, D. (1981) *A Trumpet to Arms: Alternative Media in America*, Boston, Massachusetts: South End Press.

Arnal, N. and Jouët, J. (1991) 'Teletel: Images of Residential Users' in J. Jouët, P. Flichy and P. Beaud (eds) *European Telematics: The Emerging Economy of Words*, Amsterdam: North Holland.

Attali, J. (1978) *La Nouvelle economie française*, Paris: Flammarion.

Aulard, A. (1926) *Révolution française: origines et développement de la démocratie et de la république (1789–1804)*, Paris: Librairie Armand Colin.

Avril, P. (1987) *La Ve république: histoire politique et constitutionnelle*, Paris: Presses Universitaires de France.

Azéma, J.P. (1984) *From Munich to the Liberation 1938–1944*, Cambridge: Cambridge University Press.

Baker, K.M. (1990) *Inventing the French Revolution: Essays on French Political Culture in the Eighteenth Century*, Cambridge: Cambridge University Press.

Barral, P. (1968) *Les Fondateurs de la troisième république*, Paris: Armand Colin.

Baudrillard, J. (1975) *The Mirror of Production*, St Louis, Illinois: Telos Press.

Baudrillard, J. (1983a) *Simulations*, New York: Semiotext(e).

Baudrillard, J. (1983b) *In the Shadow of the Silent Majorities*, New York: Semiotext(e).

Baudrillard, J. (1985) *La Gauche divine*, Paris: Editions Grasset & Fasquelle.

Baudrillard, J. (1987) *The Ecstasy of Communication*, New York: Semiotext(e).

Baudrillard, J. (1990) *Fatal Strategies*, New York: Semiotext(e).

Baudrillard, J. (1991) *La Guerre du Golfe n'a pas eu lieu*, Paris: Editions Galilée.

Bauer, M. (1988) 'The Politics of State-directed Privatisation: The Case of France, 1986–88', *West European Politics*, October: 49–60.

Bell, D. (1974) *The Coming of Post-Industrial Society: A Venture in Social Forecasting*, Harmondsworth: Penguin.

Bellenger, C., Godechot, J., Guiral, P. and Terrou, F. (1969) *Histoire générale de la presse française*. Tome 1: *Des origines à 1814*, Paris: Presses Universitaires de France.

Bellenger, C., Godechot, J., Guiral, P. and Terrou, F. (1972) *Histoire générale de la presse française*. Tome 3: *De 1871 à 1940*, Paris: Presses Universitaires de France.

Bellenger, C., Godechot, J., Guiral, P. and Terrou, F. (1975) *Histoire générale de la presse française*. Tome 4: *De 1940 à 1958*, Paris: Presses Universitaires de France.

Bellenger, C., Godechot, J., Guiral, P. and Terrou, F. (1976) *Histoire générale de la presse française*. Tome 5: *De 1958 à nos jours*, Paris: Presses Universitaires de France.

Benyahia-Kouider, O. (1992a) 'De Silvio Berlusconi à Jean-Luc Lagardére', *Libération*, 1 January: 6–7.

Benyahia-Kouider, O. (1992b) 'Frontières sismiques pour l'Europe audiovisuelle', *Libération*, 26 March: 10–11.

Bernard, P. and Dubief, H. (1985) *The Decline of the Third Republic: 1914–1938*, Cambridge: Cambridge University Press.

Bettelheim, C. (1977) *Class Struggles in the USSR: First Period 1917–23*, Brighton: Harvester Press.

Blum, L. (1958) 'Exercise et conquête du pouvoir' in *L'Oeuvre de Léon Blum*. Volume 6: *1945–7*, Paris: Editions Albin Michel.

Blum, L. (1965) 'La Déclaration des Droits de l'Homme' in *L'Oeuvre de Léon Blum*. Volume 4, part 2: *1937–40*, Paris: Editions Albin Michel.

Blum, L. (1972a) 'La Liberté de la presse' in *L'Oeuvre de Léon Blum*. Volume 3, part 1: *1914–28*, Paris: Editions Albin Michel.

Blum, L. (1972b) 'Bolschevisme et socialisme' in *L'Oeuvre de Léon Blum*. Volume 3, part 1: *1914–28*, Paris: Editions Albin Michel.

Bobin, F. (1992) 'Le Réseau de La Cinq est attribué en soirée à la chaîne culturelle européenne', *Le Monde*, 25 April: 7.

Bombled, T. (1981) *'Devine qui va parler ce soir': petite histoire des radios libres*, Paris: Editions Syros.

Boris, C. (1975) *Les Tigres de papier: crise de presse et autocritique du journalisme*, Paris: Editions du Seuil.

Bourdé, G. (1977) *La Défaite du Front Populaire*, Paris: François Maspero.

Bourdieu, P. (1984) *Distinction: A Social Critique of the Judgement of Taste*, London: Routledge & Kegan Paul.

Bourdon, J. (1986) 'Le Statut de la télévision en France: un consensus inavouable?', *Intervention* 15: 44–51.

Bourdon, J. (ed.) (1988) *L'Esprit des lois ou comment reformer l'audiovisuel*, Paris: Institut National de l'Audiovisuel/Documentation Française.

Bourdon, J. (1990) *Histoire de la télévision sous de Gaulle*, Paris: Anthropos/INA.

Bourlanges, J-L. (1988) *Droite année zéro*, Paris: Flammarion.

Bramsted, E. (1965) *Goebbels and National Socialist Propaganda 1925–45*, Ann Arbor, Michigan: University of Michigan Press.

Braverman, H. (1974) *Labor and Monopoly Capital: The Degradation of Work in the Twentieth Century*, New York: Monthly Review Press.

Briggs, A. (1961) *The History of Broadcasting in the United Kingdom*. Volume 1: *The Birth of Broadcasting*, Oxford: Oxford University Press.

Brinton, C. (1961) *The Jacobins: An Essay in the New History*, New York: Russell & Russell.

Brune, F. (1989) 'Les Elections à l'heure de marketing' in *Le Monde Diplomatique* (ed.) *La Communication victime des marchands: affairisme*, Information et Culture de Masse, Paris: La Découverte/*Le Monde*.

Brunet, J.P. (1986) *Jacques Doriot: du communisme au fascisme*, Paris: Balland.

Buonarroti, P. (1836) *Babeuf's Conspiracy for Equality*, London: H. Hetherington.

Burgelman, J.C. (1989) 'Political Parties and their Impact on Public Service Broadcasting in Belgium', *Media, Culture & Society*, April: 167–93.

Burrin, P. (1986) *La Dérive fasciste: Doriot, Déat, Bergery 1933–1945*, Paris: Editions du Seuil.

Canal Plus (1987) *Rapport annuel*, Paris: Canal Plus.

Candar, G. (1988) 'Jean Longuet et l'unité socialiste de 1905' in M. Agulhorn (ed.) *Jean Longuet, la conscience et l'action*, Paris: Editions de la RPP.

Caroux, J. (1983) 'The End of Administrative Centralization?', *Telos*, 55: 105–14.

Casile, N. and Drhey, A. (1983) *Loi sur la communication audiovisuelle (loi du 29 Juillet 1982)*, Paris: La Documentation Française.

Cazenave, F. (1984) *Les Radios libres*, Paris: Presses Universitaires de France.

CEC (1989) 'Council Directive of 3 October 1989 on the Coordination of Certain Provisions Laid down by Law, Regulation or Administrative Action in Member States Concerning the Pursuit of Television Broadcasting Activities', *Official Journal of the European Communities*, 17 October: L 298/23–30.

CEC (1990) *Communication from the Commission to the Council and Parliament on Audiovisual Policy*, Brussels: Commission of the European Communities.

Censer, J.R. (1976) *Prelude to Power: The Parisian Radical Press 1789–1791*, Baltimore, Maryland: Johns Hopkins University Press.

CH (1977) 'Le Droit constitutionnel, est-il legal?', *Libération*, 3–4 December: 3.

Chamard, M-E. (1989a) 'TF1 croise les doigts pour que ça dure', *Libération*, 29 April: 11.

Chamard, M-E. (1989b) 'TDF-1: avaries geostationnaires', *Libération*, 31 August: 10.

Chamard, M-E. (1989c) 'Etienne Mougeotte: "la grande-messe de 20h souffre de sautes d'audience"', *Libération*, 16 November: 12.

Chamard, M-E. and Keiffer, P. (1989) 'Accueil tiède pour le Conseil Supérieur de l'Audiovisuel', *Libération*, 26 January: 10.

Charon, J-M. (1987) 'Les Exploitants du câble', *Reseaux*, 26: 8–78.

Charon, J-M. (1991) *La Presse en France: de 1945 à nos jours*, Paris: Editions du Seuil.

Charon, J-M. and Simon, J-P. (1988) 'Cable's Infancy (1982–1986): The Development of Cable Networks in France', paper given at the 7th International Telecommunications Society, Massachusetts Institute of Technology, Boston, June–July.

Chartier, R. (1990) *Les Origines culturelles de la révolution française*, Paris: Editions du Seuil.

Chemin, A. (1991) 'Celle qui voulait copier la Une ...', *Le Monde (Radio-télévision)*, 29–30 December: 16–17.

Chemin, A. and Mamou, Y. (1991) 'Hachette prêt à abandonner la 5', *Le Monde*, 29–30 December: 13.

Chevallier, J. (1982) 'Le Statut de la communication audio-visuelle', *L'Actualité juridique, droit administratif*, 20 October 1982: 555–76.

Chirac, J. (1986a) 'Décret du 21 octobre 1986 portant nomination de membres de la Commission Nationale de la Communication et des Libertés', *Journal officiel de la république française*, 23 October: 12,770.

Chirac, J. (1986b) 'Décret du 1er novembre 1986 portant nomination de membres de la Commission Nationale de la Communication et des Libertés', *Journal officiel de la république française*, 4 November: 13,201.

Choisel, F. (1987) *Bonapartisme et gaullisme*, Paris: Editions Albatros.

Club 89 (1985) *Une stratégie de gouvernement*, Paris: Editions Albatros.

Cluzel, J. (1988) *La Télévision après six réformes*, Paris: JC Lattès et Licet.

CNCL (1987) *Rapport annuel de la Commission Nationale de la Communication et des Libertés*, Paris: CNCL.

CNCL (1988) *2e Rapport annuel de la Commission Nationale de la Communication et des Libertés*, Paris: CNCL.

Coase, R. (1970) 'The Economics of Broadcasting and Public Policy' in P.W. MacAvoy (ed.) *The Crisis of the Regulatory Commissions*, New York: W.W. Norton & Company.

Cobban, A. (1963) *A History of Modern France*. Volume 1: *1715–1799*, Harmondsworth: Penguin.

Cobban, A. (1965) *A History of Modern France*. Volume 3: *1871–1962*, Harmondsworth: Penguin.

Cohn-Bendit, G. and Cohn-Bendit, D. (1969) *Obselete Communism: The Left-Wing Alternative*, Harmondsworth: Penguin.

Cojean, A. (1987) 'TV6: la télé de la "tribu jeunesse"', *Le Monde*, 3 March: 12.

Cojean, A. (1988) 'Les Temps des réseaux', *Le Monde*, 4 February: 25.

Cojean, A. (1989) '1989 sera l'année de la concentration dans le monde de la FM', *Le Monde*, 10 February: 23.

Cojean, A. and Eskenazi, F. (1986) *FM: La Folle histoire des radios libres*, Paris: Bernard Grasset.

Collectif a/traverso (1977) *Radio Alice, Radio Libre*, Paris: J.P. Delarge.

Collectif Radios Libres Populaires (1978) *Les Radios libres* Paris: Maspero.

Collin, C. (1982) *Ondes de choc*, Paris: Editions l'Hartmann.

Colombani, J-M. (1989) 'Le Bicentenaire s'ouvre sous le signe d'une contestation de gauche', *Le Monde*, 9–10 July: 1, 8.

Colonna d'Astria, M. (1992) 'La Décennie télévisuelle II: le totem de la vidéosphère', *Le Monde*, 8 January: 18.

Comintern (1980) *Theses, Resolutions and Manifestos of the First Four Congresses of the Third International*, London: Pluto.

Conseil Constitutionnel (1982) 'Décision no. 82–141 DC du 27 juillet 1982', *Journal officiel de la république française*, 29 July: 2,422–4.

Conseil Constitutionnel (1986) 'Décision no. 86–217 DC du 18 septembre 1986 loi relative à la liberté de communication', *Journal officiel de la république française*, 19 September: 11,294–301.

Conso, C. (1990) 'Les Stratégies des opérateurs privés en Europe', *Médiaspouvoirs*, October–December: 121–8.

Cornand, B. and Villetard, X. (1982) 'La FNRL refuse toujours toute publicité sur les radio libres', *Libération*, 3 June: 13.

Coste-Cerdan, N., Guillou, B. and Le Diberder, A. (1987) 'La Rentabilité de TF1', *Médiaspouvoirs*, March: 59–65.

Cotta, M. (1986) *Les Miroirs de Jupiter*, Paris: Fayard.

Coty, R. (1954) 'Loi no. 54–782 du 2 août 1954 modifiant certaines dispositions de la loi no. 46–994 du 11 mai 1946 portant transfert et dévolution de biens et d'éléments d'actif d'enterprises de presse et d'information', *Journal officiel de la république française*, 5 August: 7,555–9.

Coty, R. (1957) 'Loi no. 57–32 du 10 janvier 1957 portant statut de l'Agence France-Presse', *Journal officiel de la république française*, 11 January: 582–4.

Council of Europe (1989) 'European Convention on Transfrontier Television', *Rundfunk und Fernsehen*, 2–3: 335–45.

de Coustin, F. (1989) 'Le Dénoyautage en doceur du capital d'Havas', *Médiaspouvoirs*, January–March: 140–2.

Earl of Crawford (1926) *Report of the Broadcasting Committee*, London: HMSO.

CSA (1988) *Deuxième bilan de la société privée 'TF1'*, Paris: Conseil Supérieure de l'Audiovisuel.

CSA (1989a) *Troisième bilan de la société privée 'TF1'*, Paris: Conseil Supérieure de l'Audiovisuel.

CSA (1989b) *Bilan du deuxième exercise de la société 'La Cinq'*, Paris: Conseil Supérieure de l'Audiovisuel.

CSA (1990a) *Bilan de la société privée 'TF1'*, Paris: Conseil Supérieure de l'Audiovisuel.

CSA (1990b) *Bilan du troisième exercise de la société 'La Cinq'*, Paris: Conseil Supérieure de l'Audiovisuel.

CSA (1990c) *Bilan de la société 'La Cinq'*, Paris: Conseil Supérieure de l'Audiovisuel.

CSA (1990d) *Bilan de la société nationale de programme Antenne 2*, Paris: Conseil Supérieure de l'Audiovisuel.

CSA (1990e) *Bilan de la société nationale de programme France Régions 3*, Paris: Conseil Supérieure de l'Audiovisuel.

CSE (1989) 'Digging their Own Graves?', *Cable and Satellite Europe*, 1: 14–15.

Dagnaud, M. and Mehl, D. (1989) 'La Hiérachie cathodique', *Pouvoir*, 51: 25–36.

Dalton, H. (1935) *Practical Socialism for Britain*, London: George Routledge & Sons.

Danos, J. and Gibelin, M. (1986) *Juin 1936*, Paris: Editions de la Découverte.

Debord, G. (1983) *Society of the Spectacle*, Detroit: Black & Red.

Debord, G. (1990) *Comments on the Society of the Spectacle*, London: Verso.

Debray, R. (1981) *Teachers, Writers and Celebrities: The Intellectuals of Modern France*, London: Verso.

Defrance, P. (ed.) (1979) *De la necessité socio-culturelle de l'existence de radios libres independentes*, Lille: IUT Carriéres Sociales Animateurs Socio-culturels Université de Lille.

Delcros, B. and Vodan, B. (1987) *La Liberté de communication (loi du 30 septembre 1986: Analyse et commentaire)*, Paris: CNCL.

Deleuze, G. and Guattari, F. (1984) *Anti-Oedipus: Capitalism and Schizophrenia*, London: Athlone Press.

Delmas, P. (1991) *Le Maître des horloges*, Paris: Editions Odile Jacob.

Delors, J. and Clisthène (1992) *Our Europe*, London: Verso.

Desneux, R. (1990) *Jack Lang: la culture en mouvement*, Paris: Favre.

Deymard, C. (1990) 'A2: A l'eau, la passion', *Le Nouvel observateur*, 19–25 April: 46–9.

Le Diberder, A. (1987) 'Les Lois de l'abondance publicitaire', *Médiaspouvoirs*, June: 64–74.

Le Diberder, A. and Coste-Cerdan, N. (1988) *Briser les chaînes: une introduction à l'après télévision*, Paris: La Découverte.

Dimitrov, G. (1938) *The United Front: The Struggle against Fascism and War*, London: Lawrence & Wishart.

Documents Observateur (1988) *La Mediaklatura*, Paris: *Le Nouvel observateur*.

Doumergue (1934) 'Décret du 12 octobre 1934', *Journal officiel de la république française*, 17 October: 10,492–3.

Downing, J. (1984) *Radical Media*, Boston, Massachusetts: South End Press.

Dreyfus, F. (1983) 'Aux sources de la pensée Gaullienne: nationalisme populaire et non conformisme des années trente' in Institut Charles de Gaulle (ed.) *Approches de la philosophie politique du Général de Gaulle*, Paris: Editions Cujas.

Duclos, J. (1962) 'Liberté et intelligence Française' in L. Figuères (ed.) *Le Parti communiste française, la culture et les intellectuels*, Paris: Editions Sociales.

Dupin, E. (1989) 'Mitterrand ou le consensus appliqué à la Révolution', *Libération*, 14 July: 4.

Duval, R. (1979) *Histoire de la radio en France*, Paris: Editions Alain Moreau.

Les Echos (1989) 'Les Nouveaux sages', *Les Echos*, 25 January: 4–5.

Eck, H. (ed.) (1985) *La Guerre des ondes*, Paris: Armand Colin.

Emanuel, S. (1992) 'Culture in Space: The European Cultural Channel', *Media, Culture & Society*, April: 281–99.

Eskenazi, F. (1984) 'Les Radios associatives s'inquiètent', *Libération*, 15–16 December: 17.

Faure, C. (1989) *Le Projet culturel de Vichy: folklore et révolution nationale 1940–1944*, Lyon: Presses Universitaires de Lyon.

Febvre, L. and Martin, H-J. (1984) *The Coming of the Book: The Impact of Printing 1450–1800*, London: Verso.

Ferry, J. (1881) 'Loi sur la libérte de la presse du 29 juillet 1881', *Journal officiel de la république française*, 30 July: 4,201–5.

Fisera, V. (1978) *Writing on the Wall*, London: Allison & Busby.

Flichy, P. and Pineau, G. (1983) *Images pour le câble: programmes et services des réseaux de vidéocommunication*, Paris: La Documentation française.

Folléa, L. (1992) 'De la boîte noire au bouton-poussier', *Le Monde (Radio-télévision)*, 19–20 January: 16–17.

Forbes, J. (1987) 'Cultural Policy: The Soul of Man under Socialism' in S. Mazey and M. Newman (eds) *Mitterrand's France*, London: Croom Helm.

Forer, C.V. (1989) 'Le Financement de la télévision par la publicité', *Médiaspouvoirs*, July–September: 9–24.

Fornari, R. (1985) *Interview with the Author*, Radio Mouvance Internationale, May.

Fornari, R. (1987) *Interview with the Author*, Frequence-Alizes, June.

Frèches, J. (1986) *La Guerre des images*, Paris: Editions Denoël.

FR-L (1978) 'CFDT et CGT réaffirment leur opposition aux radios libres', *Libération*, 9 June: 3.

FR-L (1979) 'Ici l'onde, un François parle aux français', *Libération*, 25–6 August: 1.

Fukuyama, F. (1992) *The End of History and the Last Man*, Harmondsworth: Penguin.

Furet, F. (1981) *Interpreting the French Revolution*, Cambridge: Cambridge University Press.

Furet, F. (1988) 'La France unie' in F. Furet, J. Julliard and P. Rosanvallon (eds) *La République du centre*, Paris: Calmann-Lévy.

Ganne, V. (1991) 'Le Mélange des genres: la fiction et l'information, *Médiaspouvoirs*, July–September: 19–26.

de Gaulle (1944) 'Ordonnance du 30 septembre 1944 portant création à titre provisoire de l'Agence France-Presse', *Journal officiel de la république française*, 2–3 October: 857–8.

de Gaulle (1964) 'Loi no. 64–621 du 27 juin 1964 portant statut de l'Office de radiodiffusion-télévision française', *Journal officiel de la république française*, 28 June: 5,636–7.

de Gaulle, C. (1970) *Mémoires d'espoir*, Paris: Plon.

de Gaulle, C. (1987) *Lettres, notes et carnets: janvier 1964–juin 1966*, Paris: Plon.

Gauron, A. (1983) *Histoire économique et sociale de la cinquième république*. Tome 1: *Le Temps des modernistes*, Paris: La Découverte/Maspero.

Gauron, A. (1988) *Histoire économique et sociale de la cinquième république*. Tome 2: *Années de rêves, années de crises (1970–1981)*, Paris: Cahiers Libres/Editions La Découverte.

Gavi, P. (1981) 'Les Radios libres sont désormais légales', *Libération*, 22 January: 7.

Gavi, P. (1984) 'RMC offre ses services à la bande FM', *Libération*, 25 January: 7.

Gavi, P. (1990a) 'Télévision: le grand déficit', *Le Nouvel observateur*, 17–23 May: 17–20.

Gavi, P. (1990b) 'Télé: la roue de l'infortune', *Le Nouvel observateur*, 23–9 August: 39–43.

Gavi, P. and Villetard, X. (1982) 'La Premier hit-parade de la FM Parisienne', *Libération*, 26 February: 9.

Gay, P-A. (1991) 'Le Budget de l'état viendra au secours de la télévision publique en 1992', *Le Monde*, 20 September: 36.

Giraud, A. (1991) 'The Technical Genesis' in J. Jouët, P. Flichy and P. Beaud (eds) *European Telematics: The Emerging Economy of Words*, Amsterdam: North Holland.

Giscard d'Estaing, V. (1974a) 'Loi no. 74–696 du 7 août 1974 relative à la radiodiffusion et à la télévision', *Journal officiel de la république française*, 8 August: 8,355–8.

Giscard d'Estaing, V. (1974b) 'Décret no. 74–360 du 3 mai 1974 portant publication de la convention européenne de sauvegarde des droits de l'homme et des libertés fondamentales, signée le 4 novembre 1950, de ses protocoles additionnels no. 1, 3, 4, et 5, signés les 20 mars 1952, 6 mai 1963 et 20 janvier 1966, ainsi que des déclarations et réserves qui ont été formulées par la Gouvernement de la République française lors de la ratification', *Journal officiel de la république française*, 4 May: 4750–61.

Giscard d'Estaing, V. (1977) *Towards a New Democracy*, London: Collins.

Giscard d'Estaing, V. (1978) 'Loi no. 78–787 du 28 juillet 1978 complémant la loi no. 74–696 du 7 août 1974 relative de la radiodiffusion et la télévision', *Journal officiel de la république française*, 29 July: 2,935–6.

Gorz, A. (1970) 'What are the Lessons of the May Events?' in C. Posner (ed.) *Reflections on the Revolution in France: 1968*, Harmondsworth: Penguin.

Gouin, F. (1946) 'Loi no. 46–997 du 11 mai 1946 portant transfert et dévolution de biens et d'éléments d'actif d'enterprises de presse et d'information', *Journal officiel de la république française*, 12 May: 4095–8.

Goyet, H. (1987) 'Télévisions locales en France: tout reste à faire', *Correspondance municipale*, 280–1: 58–64.

Gramsci, A. (1971) 'Americanism and Fordism' in Q. Hoare and G.N. Smith (eds) *Selections from Prison Notebooks*, London: Lawrence & Wishart.

Grimshaw, M. and Gardner, C. (1977) ' "Free Radio" in Italy', *Wedge*, 1: 14–17.

Groupe de Travail (1990) *Rapport du groupe de travail sur le financement des radios associatives*, Paris: Ministère de la Culture, de la Communication, des Grands Travaux et du Bicentenaire.

Grundmann, P. (1989) 'Budget audiovisuel: indice de satisfaction mitigé', *Libération*, 26 October: 6.

Guattari, F. (1979) 'Les Radios libres populaires' in P. Defrance (ed.) *De la necessité socio-culturelle de l'existence de radios libres independentes*, Lille: IUT Carriéres Sociales Animateurs Socio-culturels Université de Lille.

Guattari, F. (1984) *Molecular Revolution: Psychiatry and Politics*, Harmondsworth: Penguin.

Guichard, J-P. (1985) *De Gaulle et les mass media*, Paris: Editions France-Empire.

Guillebaud, J-C. and Joffrin, L. (1990) 'Le Pouvoir rose', *Le Nouvel observateur*, 6–11 September: 4–9.

Hampson, N. (1988) *The Life and Opinions of Maximilien Robespierre*, Oxford: Basil Blackwell.

Haupais, T. (1977) 'Des mini-radios de quartiers à Paris', *Libération*, 19–20 March: 1.

Haute Autorité (1983) *Rapport annuel de la Haute Autorité de la Communication Audiovisuelle septembre 1982–septembre 1983*, Paris: Haute Autorité.

Haute Autorité (1985) *Rapport Annuel de la Haute Autorité de la Communication Audiovisuelle septembre 1984–septembre 1985*, Paris: Haute Autorité.

Haute Autorité (1986) *Rapport annuel de la Haute Autorité de la Communication Audiovisuelle septembre 1985–juillet 1986*, Paris: Haute Autorité.

de la Haye, Y. and Miège, B. (1982) 'Les Socialistes français aux prises avec la question des médias', *Raison présente*, 61: 5–25.

Hegel, G.W.F. (1975) *Lectures in the Philosophy of World History: Introduction*, Cambridge: Cambridge University Press.

Heiber, H. (1972) *Goebbels*, New York: Da Capo.

Institut Hoover (1957) *La Vie de la France sous l'occupation (1940–1944)*, Stanford, California: Stanford University Press.

Jackson, J. (1990) *The Popular Front in France: Defending Democracy, 1934–38*, Cambridge: Cambridge University Press.

Jacobs, F. (1975) *The European Convention on Human Rights*, Oxford: Clarendon Press.

Jameson, F. (1991) *Postmodernism or the Cultural Logic of Late Capitalism*, London: Verso.

Jarreau, P. and Mamou, Y. (1991) 'La Médias-république', *Le Monde*, 10 December: 27.

Jaume, L. (ed.) (1989) *Les Déclarations des droits de l'homme: 1789–1793–1848–1946*, Paris: GF-Flammarion.

Jaurès, J. (1968) *Histoire socialiste de la révolution française.* Volume 1: *La Constituante*, Paris: Editions Sociales.

Jeanneney, J-N. (1988) 'Célébrer la révolution' (interview by François Ewald), *Magazine littéraire*, October: 27–9.

Joffrin, L. (1988) *Mai 68: histoire des evénements*, Paris: Editions du Seuil.

Johnson, R. (1981) *The Long March of the French Left*, London: Macmillan.

Jourdain, A. and Trocme, A. (1991) 'Havas: de la publicité au multimédia', *Médiaspouvoirs*, January–March: 65–78.

Julliard, J. (1988) 'La Course au centre' in F. Furet, J. Julliard and P. Rosanvallon (eds) *La République du centre*, Paris: Calmann-Lévy.

July, S. (1984) 'La Débauche d'énergies', *Libération*, 10 December: 3.

Katsiaficas, G. (1987) *The Imagination of the New Left: A Global Analysis of 1968*, Boston, Massachusetts: South End Press.

Keeler, J. and Stone, A. (1987) 'Juridical-political Confrontation in Mitterrand's France' in G. Ross, S. Hoffman and S. Malzacher (eds) *The Mitterrand Experiment: Continuity and Change in Modern France*, Cambridge: Polity Press.

Keiffer, P. (1989) 'TF1: un nouveau tandem pour piloter l'info', *Libération*, 27 November: 16–17.

Kenez, P. (1985) *The Birth of the Propaganda State: Soviet Methods of Mass Mobilisation 1917–1929*, Cambridge: Cambridge University Press.

Kojève, A. (1969) *Introduction to the Reading of Hegel: Lectures on the Phenomenology of the Spirit*, Ithaca, New York: Cornell University Press.

Kondratieva, T. (1989) *Bolcheviks et jacobins*, Paris: Editions Payot.

Kriegel, A. (1985) *Les Communistes français*, Paris: Editions du Seuil.

Kuisel, R. (1981) *Capitalism and the State in Modern France: Renovation and Economic Management in the Twentieth Century*, Cambridge: Cambridge University Press.

Kuisel, R. (1987) 'French Post-war Economic Growth' in G. Ross, S. Hoffman and S. Malzacher (eds) *The Mitterrand Experiment*, Cambridge: Polity Press.

Labé, Y-M. and Mamou, Y. (1992) 'Côte d'alerte pour les médias', *Le Monde*, 30 January: 1, 14.

Lacan, J-F. (1987) 'Transfert des stars et tensions publicitaires', *Le Monde*, 24 April: 22.

Lacouture, J. (1977) *Léon Blum*, Paris: Editions du Seuil.

Lapergue, M. (1977a) 'Radio pirate Giscardienne', *Libération*, 7 July: 1.

Lapergue, M. (1977b) 'Radio-libre: la phase juridique', *Libération*, 22 July: 1.

Ledos, J-J., Jézéquel, J-P. and Régnier, P. (1986) *Le Gâchis audiovisuel: histoire mouvementée d'un service publique*, Paris: Les Editions Ouvrières.

Lenin, V.I. (1933) *State and Revolution*, London: Martin Lawrence.

Lenin, V.I. (1965) 'Letter to G. Myasnikov, 5th August, 1921' in *Collected Works*. Volume 32, Moscow: Progress.

Lenin, V.I. (1970) *State and Revolution*, Peking: Foreign Languages Press.

Lenin, V.I. (1973) *What is to be Done?*, Peking: Foreign Languages Press.

Lenin, V.I. (1976) *One Step Forwards, Two Steps Back*, Peking: Foreign Languages Press.

Lenin, V.I. (1978) *Imperialism: The Highest Stage of Capitalism*, Moscow: Progress.

Lenin, V.I. (1979) 'Party Organisation and Party Literature' in M. Solomon (ed.) *Marxism and Art*, Brighton: Harvester.

Léotard, F. (1987) *A mots découverts*, Paris: Editions Grasset.

Lipietz, A. (1984) *L'Audace ou l'enlisement*, Editions la Découverte: Paris.

Lipietz, A. (1987) *Mirages and Miracles*, London: Verso.

Loiseau, G. (1991) 'Municipal Telematics in France' in J. Jouët, P. Flichy and P. Beaud (eds) *European Telematics: The Emerging Economy of Words*, Amsterdam: North Holland.

Loupias, B. (1991) 'Le Raps pour le dire', *Le Nouvel observateur*, 20-6 June: 48-9.

Lyotard, J-F. (1984) *The Post-modern Condition: A Report on Knowledge*, Manchester: Manchester University Press.

L.Z. and P.J. (1982) 'M. Filloud: que ceux qui avait épuré l'O.R.T.F. ne viennent pas nous des leçons', *Le Monde*, 29 April: 9.

MacShane, D. (1982) *Francois Mitterrand: A Political Odyssey*, London: Quartet.

Malik, S. (1990) *La Histoire secrète de SOS-Racisme*, Paris: Editions Albin Michel.

Mallet, S. (1975) *The New Working Class*, Nottingham: Spokesman Books.

Mamere, N. (1988) *La Dictature de l'audimat*, Paris: La Découverte.

Marand-Fouquet, C. (1989) *La Femme au temps de la révolution*, Paris: Editions Stock/Laurence Pernoud.

Marchand, M. (1988) *The Minitel Saga: A French Success Story*, Paris: Larousse.

Martin, J. (1989) 'La Télévision sans publicité: une nécessité', *Médiaspouvoirs*, July–September: 25–9.

Marx, K. (1933) *The Civil War in France*, London: Martin Lawrence.

Marx, K. (1965) *The Communist Manifesto*, Peking: Foreign Languages Press.

Marx, K. (1970) *Critique of Hegel's 'Philosophy of Right'*, Cambridge: Cambridge University Press.

Marx, K. (1973) *Grundrisse*, Harmondsworth: Penguin.

Marx, K. (1975) 'Debates on Freedom of the Press' in K. Marx and F. Engels *Collected Works*. Volume 1: *1835–43*, London: Lawrence & Wishart.

Mayeur, J-M. (1984) *La Vie politique sous la troisième république: 1870–1940*, Paris: Editions du Seuil.

Mayeur, J-M. and Rebérioux, M. (1987) *The Third Republic from its Origins to the Great War, 1871–1914*, Cambridge: Cambridge University Press.

McLuhan, M. (1964) *Understanding Media: The Extensions of Man*, London: Routledge & Kegan Paul.

Médiamétrie (1988) *Presentation – Department Audimetrie*, Paris: Médiamétrie.

Mendras, H. and Cole, A. (1991) *Social Change in Modern France: Towards a Cultural Anthropology of the Fifth Republic*, Cambridge: Cambridge University Press.

Mésa (1984) *Mai 68 – les affiches de l'atelier populaire de l'ex-École des Beaux-Arts*, Paris: SPM Edition.

Middlemas, K. (1979) *Politics in Industrial Society*, London: Andre Deutsch.

Miège, B., Pajon, P. and Salaün, J-M. (1986) *L'Industrialisation de l'audiovisuel*, Paris: Editions Aubier.

Millerand, A. (1923) 'Loi portant fixation du budget général de l'exercise 1923', *Journal officiel de la république française*, 1 July: 6,166–83.

Milza, P. (1987) *Fascisme français: passé et présent*, Paris: Flammarion.

Missika, J-L. (1986) 'La Déréglementation de l'audiovisuel en France' in J-L. Missika and T. Videl *La Déréglementation des télécommunications et de l'audiovisuel*, Paris: CNRS.

Missika, J-L. (1991) 'Les Français et leurs médias: le désen-
    chantment', *Médiaspouvoirs*, January–March: 97–114.

Mitterrand, F. (1981) 'Loi no. 81–994 du 9 novembre 1981
    pourtant dérogation au monopole d'Etat de la radiodiffusion',
    Journal officiel de la république française, 10 November: 3,070–1.

Mitterrand, F. (1984a) 'Loi no. 84–742 du 1er août modifant la
    loi du 29 Juillet 1982 sur la communication audiovisuelle et relative
    à certain dispositions applicables aux services de communica-
    tion audiovisuelle soumis à authorisation', *Journal officiel de la
    république française*, 2 August: 2,548–9.

Mitterrand, F. (1984b) 'Loi no. 84–743 du 1er août 1984 relative
    à l'exploitation des services radio-télévision mis à la disposition
    du public sur un réseau câblé', *Journal officiel de la république
    française*, 2 August: 2,549.

Mitterrand, F. (1988) 'Lettre à tous les français', *Le Monde*, 8 April:
    6–9.

Mitterrand, F. (1989a) *Loi no. 86–1067 du 30 septembre 1986 relative
    à la liberté de communication modifée et complétée [loi no. 89–25 du
    17 Janvier 1989]*, Paris: Conseil Supérieure de l'Audiovisuel.

Mitterrand, F. (1989b) 'Décret du 24 janvier portant nomination
    du président et des membres du Conseil supérieur de l'audio-
    visuel', *Journal officiel de la république française de la république
    française*, 25 January: 1,098.

Moinot, P. (1981) *Rapport de la Commission de Réflexion et
    d'Orientation sur l'Audio-visuel*, Paris: La Commission Moinot.

Le Monde (1969) 'Le Conseil de l'ORTF approuve la création des
    "unités d'information" à la télévision', *Le Monde*, 28–9
    September: 19.

Le Monde (1986a) 'Les Grandes corps de l'état designé leurs rép-
    resentants', *Le Monde*, 19–20 October: 6.

Le Monde (1986b) 'Quatre nouveaux membres pour la CNCL',
    Le Monde, 22 October: 24.

Le Monde (1986c) 'Le Président de la république désigne deux
    nouveaux membres', *Le Monde*, 23 October: 24.

Le Monde (1986d) 'La Composition de la commission', *Le Monde*,
    6 November: 20.

Le Monde (1987) 'La Guerre des radios commerciales', *Le Monde*,
    19 November: 16.

Moynot, J-L. (1987) 'The Left, Industrial Policy and the Filière
    Electronique' in G. Ross, S. Hoffman and S. Malzacher (eds)
    The Mitterrand Experiment, Cambridge: Polity Press.

Muller, M. (1991) 'Banlieus: avant l'incendie …', *Le Nouvel obser-
    vateur*, 20–6 June: 4–11.

Musso, P. and Pineau, G. (1989) 'La Stratégie de Berlusconi du
    micro au méga', *Médiaspouvoirs*, July–September: 82–93.

Najman, M. (1980a) 'La Pologne, camarade', *Libération*, 27–8 September: 8.

Najman, M. (1980b) 'Longwy: la fin d'une radio populaire', *Libération*, 31 October: 9.

Nassib, S. (1990) 'La Sept cinq sur cinq sur la Trois', *Libération*, 3–4 February: 42–3.

Negri, T. (1988) *Revolution Retreived: Selected Writings on Marx, Keynes, Capitalist Crisis & New Social Subjects 1967–83*, London: Red Notes.

Nicolaievsky, B. and Maenchen-Helfen, O. (1976) *Karl Marx: Man and Fighter*, Harmondsworth: Penguin.

Niedergang, M. (1982) 'Les Délégués du Tiers-Monde soutiennent la "croisade" de M. Lang contre les Etats-Unis', *Le Monde*, 30 July: 5

Nolte, E. (1969) *Three Faces of Fascism: Action Française, Italian Fascism, National Socialism*, New York: Mentor.

Nora, S. and Minc, A. (1980) *The Computerisation of Society*, Cambridge, Massachusetts: MIT Press.

Ockrent, C. (1988) 'The MacTaggart Lecture', speech given at the Edinburgh International Television Festival, 26 August.

Ory, P. (1983) *L'Entre-deux-mai: histoire culturelle de la France, mai 1968–mai 1981*, Paris: Editions du Seuil.

Ozouf, M. (1988) *Festivals and the French Revolution*, Cambridge, Massachusetts: Harvard University Press.

Paillet, M. (1988) *Télé-gâchis*, Paris: Deneöl.

Paine, T. (1984) *Rights of Man*, Harmondsworth: Penguin.

Paris Match (1989) 'Paris, reine du monde', *Paris Match*, 27 July: 22–35.

Parti Communiste et Parti Socialiste (1972) *Le Programme commun de gouvernment du Parti Communiste Française et Parti Socialiste*, Paris: Editions Sociales.

Pashukanis, E. (1978) *Law and Marxism: A General Theory*, London: Ink Links.

Périer-Daville (1989) 'Menaces sur le pluralisme de presse' in *Le Monde diplomatique* (ed.) *La Communication victime des marchands: affairisme, information et culture de masse*, Paris: La Découverte/*Le Monde*.

van der Pijl, K. (1984) *The Making of an Atlantic Ruling Class*, London: Verso.

Pisier, E. and Bouretz, P. (1988) 'Le Retour des sages' in B. Manin (ed.) *La France en politique 1988*, Paris: Esprit Fayard Seuil.

P.K. (1987) 'La CNCL autorise les grandes radios musicales et fait de spectaculaires exclusions, *Libération*, 25 July: 2.

Poincaré, R. (1926) 'Rapport au Président de la république et décret-loi du 28 decembre 1926', *Journal officiel de la république française*, 31 December: 13,794–801.

Poirier, A. and Serres, J. (1980) *Lorraine Coeur d'Acier: 'une radio dans la ville'*, Paris: Les Films du Rhinocéros.

Pompidou, G. (1972) 'Loi no. 72–553 du 3 juillet 1972 portant statut de la radiodiffusion-télévision française', *Journal officiel de la république française*, 4 July: 6,851–2.

Portelli, H. (1983) 'The New French Socialist Party and Left Unity', *Telos*, 55: 51–60.

Portelli, H. (1989) *La Politique en France sous la Ve république*, Paris: Grasset.

Porter, V. (1992) 'Broadcasting Impartiality, the Freedom of Expression and Democracy', paper given at Conference of Socialist Economists, London, July.

Prat, D. (1986) 'Médias et pouvoirs: la régulation politique en crise', *Intervention* 15: 58–73.

Prot, R. (1985) *Des radios pour se parler: les radios locales en France*, Paris: La Documentation Française.

Queuille, H. (1944) 'Ordonnance du 26 août sur l'organisation de la presse française', *Journal officiel de la république française*, 30 August: 779–80.

Queyranne, J-J. (1987) 'Il n'en reste qu'Une', *Le Monde*, 10 March: 12.

Queyranne, J-J. (1988) 'Queyranne recherche une "large approbation"' (interview with Edouard Mir), *Libération*, 5 December: 7–8.

Ragache, G. and Ragache, J.R. (1988) *Des ecrivains et des artistes sous l'occupation 1940–1944*, Paris: Hachette.

Ramonet, I. (1989) 'Conclusion: confusions' in Le Monde diplomatique (ed.) *La Communication victime des marchands: affairisme, information et culture de masse*, Paris: La Découverte/Le Monde.

Ramonet, I. (1991) 'L'Ere du soupçon: médias, sociétés et démocratie', *Le Monde diplomatique*, May: 11, 18.

Rassemblement Populaire (1964) 'Le Programme du Rassemblement Populaire' in L. Blum *L'Oeuvre de Léon Blum*. Volume 4, part 1: *1934–7*, Paris: Editions Albin Michel.

Raynaud, P. (1988) 'La déclaration des droits de l'homme' in C. Lucas (ed.) *The French Revolution and the Creation of Modern Political Culture*. Volume 2: *The Political Culture of the French Revolution*, Oxford: Pergamon Press.

Rebérioux, M. (1963) 'Babeuf et les tendances du Socialisme français (1884–1914)' in A. Soboul (ed.) *Babeuf et les problèmes du babouvisme*, Paris: Editions Sociales.

Renard, F. (1987) 'Bouygues imperator', *Le Monde*, 7 April: 17.

Reisel, R. (1981) 'Preliminaries on the Councils and Councilist Organisations' in K. Knabb (ed.) *Situationist International Anthology*, Berkeley, California: Bureau of Public Secrets.

Reith, J. (1924) *Broadcast over Britain*, London: Hodder & Stoughton.

Rials, S. (1988) *La Déclaration des Droits de l'Homme et du Citoyen*, Paris: Pluriel.

Ridoux, G. (1982) 'Audiovisual Communications in France, Stage Two: The Act of 29 July 1982', *EBU Review*, November: 6–13.

Rioux, J-P. (1989) *The Fourth Republic: 1944–1958*, Cambridge: Cambridge University Press.

Robespierre, M. (1967) 'On Revolutionary Government (December 25, 1793)' in G. Rudé (ed.) *Robespierre*, Englewood Cliffs, New Jersey: Prentice-Hall.

Rocard, M. (1986) *A l'épreuve des faits*, Paris: Editions du Seuil.

Rocard, M. (1987) *Le Coeur à l'ouvrage*, Paris: Editions Odile Jacob.

Rosanvallon, P. (1988) 'Malaise dans la réprésentation' in F. Furet, J. Julliard and P. Rosanvallon (eds.) *La République du centre*, Paris: Calmann-Lévy.

Rossignol, D. (1991) *Histoire de la propagande en France de 1940 à 1944*, Paris: Presses Universitaires de France.

Rousseau, J-J. (1968) *The Social Contract*, Harmondsworth: Penguin.

RPR/UDF (1986) ' "Pour gouverner ensemble": la plate-forme du RPR et de l'UDF', *Le Monde*, 19–20 January: 7–9.

Sabouret, Y. (1992) 'Non-assistance à télévision en danger', *Le Monde*, 5–6 January: 19.

Salvadori, M. (1990) *Karl Kautsky and the Socialist Revolution: 1880–1938*, London: Verso.

Senamaud, M. (1989) *Interview with Author*, La Cinq, April.

Servan-Schreiber, J-J. (1968) *The American Challenge*, New York: Atheneum.

Sewell, W. (1980) *Work and Revolution in France: The Language of Labour from the Old Regime to 1848*, Cambridge: Cambridge University Press.

Sewell, W. (1988) 'Le Citoyen/la Citoyenne: Activity, Passivity and the Revolutionary Concept of Citizenship' in C. Lucas (ed.) *The French Revolution and the Creation of Modern Political Culture*. Volume 2: *The Political Culture of the French Revolution*, Oxford: Pergamon Press.

SI (1981) 'The Beginning of an Era' in K. Knabb (ed.) *Situationist International Anthology*, Berkeley, California: Bureau of Public Secrets.

Sieyès, E. (1982) *Qu'est-ce que le tiers état?*, Paris: Quadrige/Presses Universitaires de France.

Simard, J-P. (1985) *Interview with the Author*, Fréquence Libre, April.

Simon, J-P. (1987) 'Le Développement des télévisions locales en France', *Correspondance municipale*, 280–1: 65–72.

SJTI (1990) *Étude sur les radios locales associatives-financement*, Paris: Service Juridique et Technique de l'Information.

Soboul, A. (1974) *The French Revolution 1787–99*, London: New Left Books.

de Sola Pool, I. (1983) *Technologies of Freedom*, Cambridge, Massachusetts: Belknap Press.

Soula, C. (1989) 'NRJ: la premiere privée, se place sur le second marche', *Libération*, 4 December: 14.

Soula, C. (1990) 'Hachette: la pieuvre par Cinq', *Le Nouvel observateur*, 15–21 November: 19–22.

de Tarlé, A. (1979) 'The Monopoly that Won't Divide' in A. Smith (ed.) *Television and Political Life: Studies in 6 European Countries*, London: Macmillan.

Tasca, C. (1990) 'Tasca: "peut-être ai-je manque de courage"' [interview by Phillipe Kieffer], *Libération*, 18 May: 8–9.

Tessier, M. (1990) 'Entretien avec Marc Tessier, Directeur-Général de Canal Plus International', *Médiaspouvoirs*, October–December: 76–81.

Thomas, P. (1980) *Karl Marx and the Anarchists*, London: Routledge & Kegan Paul.

Thomas, R. (1976) *Broadcasting and Democracy in France*, London: Bradford University Press/Crosby Lockwood Staples.

Thompson, J. (1943) *The French Revolution*, London: Basil Blackwell.

Toffler, A. (1971) *Future Shock*, London: Pan.

Touraine, A. (1974) *The Post-industrial Society, Tomorrow's Social History: Classes, Conflicts and Cultures*, London: Wildwood House.

Tunstall, J. (1977) *The Media are American: Anglo-American Media in the World*, London: Constable.

Tunstall, J. (1986) *Communications Deregulation: The Unleashing of America's Communications Industry*, Oxford: Basil Blackwell.

Vanegiem, R. (1981) 'Notes to the Civilised Concerning Generalised Self-Management' in K. Knabb (ed.) *Situationist International Anthology*, Berkeley, California: Bureau of Public Secrets.

Viénet, R. (1992) *The Enragés and the Situationists in the Occupation Movement – France, May–June 1968*, New York: Autonomedia.

Villepontoux, M.J. and Le Nuz, D. (1986) 'Révolution et dictature' in P. Vigier (ed.) *Blanqui et les blanquistes*, Paris: Sedes.

Voslensky, M. (1984) *Nomenklatura: Anatomy of the Soviet Ruling Class*, London: Bodley Head.

Wallerstein, I. (1984) *The Politics of the World-economy: The States, the Movements and the Civilisations*, Cambridge: Cambridge University Press.

Weber, E. (1977) *Peasants into Frenchmen: The Modernization of Rural France 1870–1914*, London: Chatto & Windus.

Wickham, A. and Coignard, S. (1988) *La Nomenklatura française: pouvoirs et privilèges des elites*, Paris: Pierre Belfond.

Y.M. and Y-M.L. (1992a) 'TF1, M6 et Canal Plus projettent un "CNN à la française pour remplacer La Cinq"', *Le Monde*, 22 January: 19.

Y.M. and Y-M.L. (1992b) 'M. Berlusconi veut placer La Cinq au centre d'un réseau Européen d'information', *Le Monde*, 5 February: 22.

Zeldin, T. (1979) *France 1848–1945: Ambition and Love*, Oxford: Oxford University Press.

Zeldin, T. (1980) *France 1848–1945: Taste and Corruption*, Oxford: Oxford University Press.

Zeman, Z. (1964) *Nazi Propaganda*, London: Oxford University Press.

Index

Published by Pluto Press

CLOSEDOWN?

THE BBC AND GOVERNMENT BROADCASTING POLICY, 1979–92

TOM O'MALLEY

'...[O'Malley] gathers together in one place so much
valuable and essential information that any student
of UK broadcasting policy needs.'
Professor Nicholas Garnham, Director,
Centre for Communication and Information Studies,
University of Westminster

Why did the BBC become the focus of so much intense activity
after the Conservative Party came to power in 1979? In this
illuminating and controversial study, Tom O'Malley focuses on
the impact of government policies towards the BBC between
1979 and 1992.

The book provides a thorough analysis of the origins, conduct
and significance of the 1986 Peacock Report on the BBC and
the development of public service broadcasting. An overview
of the relationship between broadcasting and the state and
shifts in the balance between commercial and public enterprise in the field of broadcasting concludes a revealing study
of how broadcasting relates to wider structures of power.

ISBN hardback: 0 7453 0570 9 softback: 0 7453 0571 7

Order from your local bookseller or contact the publisher on
0181 348 2724.

Pluto Press
345 Archway Road, London N6 5AA